GOD GAVE A GLASGOW GIRL

NINE LIVES

An autobiography

First Published in 2023

ISBN 978-1-7395379-0-6 (Paperback)
ISBN 978-1-7395379-2-0 (Hardback)
978-1-7395379-1-3 (Ebook)

Cover Design and Book Layout by:
SpiffingCovers.com

Published by: Great Expectations Publishing Press

GOD GAVE A GLASGOW GIRL
NINE LIVES

An autobiography

EUNICE IVY GRAHAM

CHAPTER 1 –
HOW I CAME TO BE

Typical! Bloody typical! The night before I'm due to go back to work after being off sick, I run out of sleeping tablets. At 5 a.m. I am watering the two dozen beautiful ivory roses that my daughter sent me for my anniversary and, to top it all off, I have a throat like sandpaper! (By the way, my name is Eunice but more about that later on!) The throat continues to get worse during the day and then I find myself staggering about like a drunk because I feel so light-headed. I stomp over to the chemist to get paracetamol, and I'm actually relieved when Helen the pharmaceutical assistant tells me I might have flu!

I'm due to be in work at 4 p.m. and decide that there is no way I'm capable of driving, so I phone a taxi at 3.30 p.m. to the Centre of Excellence (HMRC). With all the energy I can muster, I swipe my pass and take the lift to the second floor. The first person I meet is Ryan who is one of my much younger colleagues. I croak a request that he email Nazia (my higher officer) to let her know that I'm back. I then fetch a coffee from the machine, and Danny, who is my 26-year-old team leader, comes over to welcome me back. As I walk up the corridor to my desk, the coffee is spilling out of my shaky left hand and I'm holding onto Danny with my right hand to steady myself.

I sit down at my desk for all of five minutes and then Danny tells me that there is a meeting room free to do my back-to-work interview. Once again, I shakily stagger back up the corridor to the meeting room (thanking God I'm on phased return) and sit down with Danny to tell him what's been happening during my sick period.

Nazia walks into the room and tries to give me a hug. She physically jumps back when I tell her I think I have flu!

After a long conversation that involves laughter, Nazia says, "Eunice, you should write a book."

Now, over the years many people have said that, but this time something inside of me really connects and I seriously think about it overnight.

By the time I go back to work the following evening, feeling much better, I give Nazia a massive hug and tell her she has been my final inspiration! As you embrace this roller coaster of emotions, I hope the story of my life, full of laughter and tears, will show that whatever life throws at you, there is always *hope*.

I was born on 1 May 1954 at Duke Street Hospital in Glasgow, weighing a healthy 8 lb. My hair was red and, according to my mum, I had beautiful skin and lovely rosy cheeks. Obviously, that's not something I remember, but I have been blessed with a great memory and can account for my early childhood from the age of around two or three years onwards. My mum, Eunice, decided to call me Eunice Ivy, and to this day I still hate my middle name with a passion. I am from a staunch Catholic family and, because May is the month of Mary the Mother of God and I was also born on the feast of St Joseph (spouse of Mary), my relatives suggested that I be called either Mary or Josephine or both. My mother, who was also a redhead and a stubborn Taurean, decided that no one was going to dictate what my name would be and decided to call me after herself. The difference was, she had the name Eunice Margaret Patricia but stuck me with the middle name of Ivy – the name of my father's mother.

I don't remember my father at all and, to this day, I couldn't say if he is alive or dead, but I will be referring to him in the past tense because he has been dead to me all my life. Please don't think this is bitterness creeping in; I have seen photographs of my father, but my mother was responsible for shaping me into the adult I have become and I have never had any desire to seek the whereabouts of my father. I am presuming that since he was about six years older than my mother, he may no longer be alive.

At this point, I'm going to give you a little bit of background information about my mum and how she came to meet my father. My mother was born on 24 April 1927 and was one of a large family. None of my relatives seem to know just how many siblings she had because she was born in an era when infant mortality rates were high. My mother was the last child to be born to my grandmother Marjorie McAllister and my grandfather Owen Robinson who were both born and bred in Northern Ireland. The majority of their children were born in Northern Ireland including a little boy named Gerald. He had a fascination for lighting matches that caused him to burn to death at the age of five years. My mother had a slightly older sister, Geraldine, who died in early infancy, and she and my mum were the only two children to be born in Scotland. The reason for this was that my grandfather Owen was a gunner in the navy and when the work came to Scotland, the family were uprooted from Ireland and brought to Scotland. They initially stayed with relatives in the Gorbals area of Glasgow before finally settling into a house in Troon Street which is just off Springfield Road in Glasgow.

My mother was just one year and seven months old when my grandmother died on Boxing Day 1929 at the age of 42. She suffered from erysipelas which is nerve pain that can cause excruciating stabbing and burning around the jaw area. The particular bout of pain she had that day caused her to fall over, bang her head which caused a bleed on her brain. My grandfather could not cope with the death of his wife, became dependent on alcohol and, as a result, the youngest children, namely my mother, her sister Lena and my Aunt Irene, were taken into Nazareth House Care Home. Due to their age differences, the siblings were separated from each other. My mum's oldest sister, May, was 21 years old and went into housemaid service which allowed her to obtain board and lodgings in the various homes she served in. She was also courting her future husband, my Uncle Paddy. Her second oldest sister was my Aunt Vera. My Aunt Vera was 15 years old and managed to secure a trade in French polishing which was an art in itself when it came to restoring furniture. She went into a lodging house with a Mrs Bennett who had two offspring, namely Christopher and Lily. Lily married a man called John Broe, and my Aunt Vera eventually married Mrs Bennett's son Christie. I only knew Mrs Bennett as 'Granny Bennett'.

My mother's childhood memories of Nazareth House were ones of tenderness and kindness from the nuns and laypeople in charge. Up until the day she died, she maintained that the worst thing that happened to her was being taken away from Nazareth House.

Her sister Irene went straight back to Belfast as soon as she was of age and lived for a while with Aunt Sara who was Alice McMahon's mother. Now, although Alice was my mother's first cousin, she was affectionately known as Cissie and throughout my life I called her Aunt Cissie. (She had a profound effect on my own childhood which I will touch upon later.) Aunt Lena left Nazareth House at the age of 13. She was the victim of an unfortunate incident and, when that happened, my Aunt May immediately took my mother away from Nazareth House because she truly thought it was in her best interest. I think my Aunt May took my mother away on the pretext that they were just going out for the day, but unfortunately my mother lost the security of being brought up by the people she knew and loved from babyhood and, as a result, she resented it all her life.

The disruption it caused to her was really quite heartbreaking, as she was passed from pillar to post trying to hide from social service authorities and the Education Board. My Aunt Vera's in-laws (the Broes) played a major part in my mother's life and indeed my own. The Broes were like cousins to me, and I never remember their mother or father being called anything but Mammy and Daddy Broe. One of their daughters, Cathy, has always been a close friend of all the family, and she can recount the occasion when the social services and the Education Board came looking for my mother. As soon as Daddy Broe got wind of it, he hid my mum in a cubbyhole and put a wardrobe in front of it whilst warning her not to make a noise. Yes, the authorities did indeed demand access to the house and got it, but thankfully they didn't find my mother.

It was then that Aunt May decided to take my mum to Belfast to complete her schooling.

My mother told me that, on the day in question, she was walking up the gangplank of the Belfast-bound ship when the name 'Eunice McAllister' was called out. My mum tried to announce that she was Eunice Robinson, but my Aunt May shoved her forward before anyone realised that she was being smuggled out of the country under her own mother's maiden name.

My poor Aunt May must have been petrified, because I can honestly say that she was one of the most upright and moral people that graced this earth! My mum then lived with Aunt Sarah for a while and also with relatives who stayed in the Protestant part of Belfast. For those who are not aware of the Irish situation at that time, the tension between Catholics and Protestants was awful and, without a shadow of a doubt, a Catholic girl from Scotland living in the Protestant area of Belfast must have been a nightmare. King Billy of Orange was well and truly worshipped by Protestants but never more so than around the 12 July when effigies of the Pope were being burnt everywhere. My mum had to run the gauntlet every time she went outside. On one occasion, she was accosted by a gang of teenagers who decided that she should be the *live* effigy on top of the bonfire, and she believed that she would have been burnt to death if a boy had not said, "That's my cousin!"

I truly believe that my mum's education would have been much better if her sister Irene had offered to help, but my Aunt Irene and my mother detested each other! The strange thing to me was that both looked so alike with their red hair, nice skin and blue eyes.

My mother was forced to learn Irish Gaelic, which was a completely foreign language, and although she was really good at algebra, her geometry let her down. Whenever she asked Irene for help, she would tell her the answer but refused to show her how to work out the equation.

Sadly, my Aunt Irene always reminded her that she was the 'outsider' and continued to make horrible remarks at every opportunity, even when I was a little girl.

My mother was desperate to leave school and, when the time came, she worked until she was able to join one of the forces. She craved the stability that she had in her infancy and knew that she would get both if she joined the Wrens. Unfortunately, when she was 17 the Wrens were not recruiting, so my mum joined the British Army where most of her postings were in England and also where she eventually met my father, Stanley Graham.

My mum used to make me laugh my head off with some of her army adventures and the amazing people she met on her travels. She was always being put 'on a charge' (detention) for laughing during drill or staying out too late with her friends.

On one occasion, when she was confined to barracks with some of her peer rebels, she laughed so much that she knew she wouldn't be able to get to the toilet in time. Someone passed her a china mug to prevent the 'accident' and, after she had relieved her bladder, her friend immediately grabbed the mug and threw it out of the window! The sergeant major that had punished her recruits came along a few minutes later and immediately spotted the offending object. The four or more girls were mortified and, with listening ears at the window, they heard the sergeant saying to herself, "Oh what a lovely china mug. I'll take it home and make a cup of tea!" Needless to say, the girls knotted themselves so much after this comment that a mop and bucket were needed to clean up excess bladder loss!

My mother was always being asked to consider nursing but she point-blank refused! This was something she regretted and often referred to it during our many conversations. My mum was happy working in the NAAFI (Navy, Army and Air Force Institutes) where she learned bookkeeping, something she was extremely good at. She was always able to save money and had a great knack of dishing up inexpensive, wholesome meals where possible. This natural talent was to stand her in good stead later on in life! My mum freely admitted that she couldn't cook to save herself and that "Stan Graham was an excellent cook"! However, my mum always had good, wholesome meals on the table for me.

Mum and Dad (circa 1947)

Talking about my father, it was always strange to me as a child that my mum always referred to my dad as 'Stan Graham'. I don't know if it was a generational thing, just like the Broes saying 'Mammy or Daddy Broe', but to this day I still find it peculiar! Both my parents were posted to Germany through the NAAFI which is where they met. My father pestered her for a date, and I can understand why because, looking back at photographs of her as a teenager, she really was beautiful. Obviously those photographs were in black and white, but if you can imagine a young lady of 5' 2" with long, wavy auburn hair, bright blue eyes, beautiful skin and teeth and a gorgeous, wee figure, you are looking at my mum. She was as fashionable as she could afford to be, but her clothes always looked well on her and all of that, coupled with my mother's determination – not to mention the temper that went with her red hair – must have really attracted my father to her. My mum told me that at first she hated my dad. Well, we all know that there is a fine line between love and hate, and I think she secretly wanted to make him dance to her tune. Eventually, Private Robinson E (how she was addressed by the army) decided to go out with Corporal Graham S, and from that relationship I was conceived – but not born – in Germany. My mother used to be very proud of the fact that I could have been German and, as I got older, she made me learn German in school!

Apparently, when my mother found out she was pregnant, she left the army and came back to Scotland to stay between her sisters, my Aunt May and my Aunt Vera. By that time, my Aunt May had been married for a few years to my Uncle Paddy (O'Connor). He died very young, and my Aunt May had to solely raise three children with barely three years between them. As mentioned earlier, Aunt Vera was also married to my Uncle Christie (Bennett), and God knows how many children she had by then. (Suffice to say the family was large!) My own father was still in the army but came home prior to my birth.

I have to give a little bit of information about my father before I can continue this story. I don't know his exact date of birth but, if he was six or seven years older than my mum, he must have been born around 1920 in West Hartlepool, England, and he was of the Protestant faith. His mother's first name was Ivy, and I don't know if my dad had any other brothers or sisters. From pictures I have seen of him, he looked about 5' 8" in height, was of medium build, with dark hair and, from a genetics point of view and without seeing a coloured photograph, he must have had blue eyes. His skin and teeth looked really nice and, to me, he was a handsome, kind-looking man. I don't recall ever seeing a picture of my grandmother but, despite hating the name Ivy, I think I hated it even more when my mum told me she was a backstreet abortionist! That's a bit of a bombshell, but the next bombshell I'm about to drop is even bigger. My father was a *bigamist!* When he married my mother, he already had a wife and daughter of his own. Somewhere in this world, I have a half-sister.

My mum was a moral, innocent girl and to fall pregnant in those days, before marriage, was looked upon as something really bad. She must have been shocked to the core! The one thing she never wanted was to be a 'have-to' case. I am sure my mum really loved my dad and, eventually, they set a date for their wedding.

My parents got married in Martha Street Registry Office in Glasgow, just prior to my birth. Despite the bigamy bombshell, they tried to make their marriage work. They initially took lodgings with a lady in the Gorbals in Glasgow which, obviously, I don't remember anything about. As a little Catholic baby, I should have been christened within a week of being born – or even sooner – but my mum was having one of her many fall-outs with God and, although she may have doubted God at that particular time, I know in my heart that she always wanted me to be part of her own Catholic faith.

My mum bottle-fed me, nursed and sang to me and gave me the best possible nurturing. My father was still in the army during my infancy, and his sole earnings must have been enough to support my mother and me and to pay the digs money. I don't know if the army found out about his double life, but I suppose, in those days, numbers were more important than bureaucracy!

As far as baby presents go, the one thing my father bought for me was a Steiff German teddy which was given to me on the day I was born. Teddy was my constant companion as a child and, even to this day, whenever I feel down, I reach out for him to recreate and evoke some magical memories.

Whilst my mother was living in the Gorbals with her landlady, she was in constant touch with my Aunt May and Aunt Vera (the O'Connors and the Bennetts). My early childhood memories will mention more about the O'Connors than the Bennetts, but all my first cousins were more like brothers and sisters to me. My Aunt May's daughter Bernadette was 14 years old when I was born and decided that I was her baby. She honestly thought that babies could be bought from a shop and was always hoping my Aunt May would buy one! When I came along, her prayers were answered, and she was one of the most influential people in my life. As I said, Bernadette was 14 years, her sister Mary was 15 years and Roddy, the eldest of the O'Connors, was 16 years old when this 'little sister' popped out. The O'Connors lived in a tenement building in Bridgeton, Glasgow, and their house consisted of a living room, hall, bedroom and a large cupboard in the bedroom which was known as the 'cubbyhole'! Next door to my Aunt May was a very kind lady called Lily McCardle and apparently I shouted "Lily" at the age of seven months. My mum always went on about how I could talk before I could walk, and she definitely got that one right because anyone who knows me knows that I can talk for the United Kingdom.

According to my cousin Bernadette, I was eight months old when I shouted, "BERNADETTE!" I think the family got the shock of their lives, but an even bigger shock was to come! My Aunt May's in-laws cursed and swore like troopers and, naturally, I picked that up from them. One day, when Roddy was in the room washing himself, I was sitting in my high chair wondering where he was.

I shouted, "Roddy, Roddy, RODDY, WHERE ARE YOU, YA C***T YE!"

Even my Aunt May had a real smirk at that one and the rest of the family were in stitches. When they had stopped laughing, I was quietly spoken to and told NEVER to say that word again. I am shamefaced at admitting I used it even once.

Apparently, I began walking when I was about one year old and, by that time, my mother was under constant pressure to have me christened. The woman that we lodged with was a Salvationist, and both she and my father wanted me to be brought up in that religion.

My fiery, red-headed mother, with a temper to match, had a heated discussion about me one day with the landlady and my father.

She stamped her foot (a trait she had until a few weeks before she died) and shouted, "There is no way a child of mine is being christened under the Union Jack!"

She then packed her bags, bundled me in her arms and walked out on the landlady and my father without a backwards glance!

However, a difficult moment in early infancy arrived when my mum had to be taken to hospital for a blood transfusion. She had lost a lot of blood in labour and eventually needed a transfusion. She was told not to lift anything heavy and, as a result of her having to go into hospital, I was put into residential care for a short while. My mum's sisters had their own family problems and situations to take care of, hence the reason for residential care. I missed my mum so much that when she came to collect me and pick me up in her arms, I refused to be put back down. In the ensuing months, I never let my mother out of my sight in case she would disappear again.

CHAPTER 2 –
LIVING WITH MY AMAZING
GODMOTHER

My Aunt May, my beautiful godmother

In June 1955, along with my mother, my Aunt May and Bernadette, I walked into St Anne's Roman Catholic Church, Dennistoun, Glasgow and was baptised Eunice Ivy Graham. My Aunt May was my godmother and, if I had to choose a thousand times over, I could not have wished for anyone better! No doubt, there was a christening cake or dumpling or one of my Aunt May's many baking treats on hand afterwards, but from then, until I was almost five years old, my place of residence was at 82 Bernard Street, Glasgow with my mum, my godmother 'Mammy May', Roddy, Mary and Bernadette. It must have been really cramped, but my happiest formative memories lie in the tenements of Bridgeton.

My Aunt May's house was on the top of the three-storey tenement building. There were two flats on each landing and halfway down the landing was the shared toilet. It was the same the whole way down the tenement, and every tenant was given a key to their particular toilet, but I was always glad of an unlocked toilet when I was absolutely bursting for the toilet – an affliction that's been with me all my life! As I've mentioned, Lily McCardle lived opposite my Aunt May, and I used to pop in and out all the time. In fact, I used to pop in and out of most of the neighbours' flats and, although times were poor, I was always given a sweetie or a cake from those wonderful people who looked upon me as their own.

Inside my Aunt May's flat, the living room had a coal fire, a bed, a cooker, tables and chairs and 'easy' chairs and a long wooden sideboard. The sideboard (cabinet with drawers) always fascinated me, because all the family photographs, holy pictures, statues and endless reading material (including bills) were on view. I could really amuse myself by looking at the picture of the then Pope (Pope Pius XII), the large statue of the Sacred Heart, pictures of Our Lady (Mother of Jesus) and the drawings inside *The Sacred Heart Messenger* magazine.

Family photographs were of great interest to me. I loved looking at the old black-and-white wedding photograph of my Aunt May and my Uncle Paddy (whom I never met), and Holy Communion pictures of Roddy, Mary and Bernadette, army pictures of my mum and my baby photographs. I could amuse myself by chatting away to each photo which were precious icons related to my life.

Coal bunker and coalman

If you are not familiar with Glasgow at that time, the coal bunker and coalman played an essential role in our daily lives. A coal bunker was in the hall of the flat which was where the coal was stored and used for heat when bundles of sticks of wood would no longer suffice. These brave coalmen would walk down the streets of Glasgow for hours in some of the worst weather imaginable shouting "COELLLLLLLL AND COAL BRICKEEEEEETS". There was no need for a loudspeaker where a coalman was concerned, he knew he had a living to make and he successfully shouted at the top of his voice! The poor coalman had to carry enormous sacks of coal up and down flights of stairs (no lifts) just to keep fires burning. Many Glaswegians like me feel an enormous debt towards those who were covered from head to toe in black soot. I was completely banned from climbing my Aunt May's coal bunker, but I did take great delight in opening the lid and peeking in when no one was looking!

The Glasgow world at that time was totally unique and, even to this day, I recall the many stray cats, dogs, gamblers, drunks and women taking their clothes washing in prams to 'the steamie' (wash house). Some of you might not be familiar with 'the steamie'. It wasn't just a wash house, it was a place where mums could meet, swap stories and generally confide in people about what was happening in the family. The camaraderie was therapeutic, but the washing still got done. I was fascinated by the noise of the scrubbing boards, and every time someone hung their washing on the drying poles, I relished the warmth they exuded.

Some of my early memories are of climbing up onto everything and anything around me. Apparently, one day I climbed onto the bedroom windowsill and somehow managed to get the window open using all the force I could muster. I then stuck half my body out of it! Remember, the house was at the top of a very large tenement building. Fortunately for me, my Aunt May managed to put her hand across my mother's mouth before she screamed "Eunice!". She then crept up behind me and pulled me back into the safety of the room. My Aunt May knew that on hearing my mother scream, I would have fallen onto the street. However, being the obstinate person I am, my climbing escapades never stopped. I decided to climb to the top of the wardrobe and pulled the thing on top of me. Naturally, I was in trouble, but I escaped with a few minor injuries.

With my little, inquisitive mind, I found lots of things to keep me occupied. In the bedroom there was a high double bed and other places I've already mentioned, but the most fascinating thing for me was the amazing 'cubbyhole'. This large cupboard was a magical place for a child. It seemed endless with all its interesting items, and I thought about it as my own giant treasure chest.

In that cubbyhole, there was plenty for me to look at. The first thing that caught my eye was Roddy's bike followed by wooden toys and dolls belonging to Mary and Bernadette. There were also old-fashioned clothes which consisted of dresses, a fox fur and lots of hats! Apart from all the interesting stuff in that large cupboard, my Aunt May would store her own confidential information. I was too young to be bothered with that, but I was in my element as I tried on clothes, shoes, talked to the 'live' fox and climbed up onto Roddy's bike. I would open the lid of the treasure chest which had lots of photos and let my imagination run riot. I don't know how many hours I spent in there, but my Aunt May would let me have enough time before she would shout, "Eunice, stop plundering!" By that point, I was probably rummaging through all the boring stuff, so I willingly came back out and, although I would be told off for going in the cubbyhole, it never stopped me from going back time and time again! Sometimes, my mum and Aunt May would ask if I had been 'plundering' and I would vehemently deny it, following the same denial with the amount of things I discovered in the cubbyhole.

Every evening, my Aunt May set the table for tea. She always used nice china cups and plates and a special glass for my milk. This was a ritual where we all sat round the table, said grace and then tucked in. I was a very faddy eater and would only start scoffing when Roddy shouted "EAT!". I loved and still love Roddy to bits, and if anyone could make me eat, he would!

Perhaps he encouraged me a bit too much, because I distinctly remember one summer evening when my Aunt May was setting the table for a salad tea and she put a tomato on every plate before everyone sat down. She must have been trying to save a bit of time before the crowd descended, but when she left the room I picked up every single tomato and ate it without a trace of a seed! My poor Aunt May was demented looking for the tomatoes and, eventually, I had to own up. If that had been one of her offspring, she would have clouted them, but I got away with a small telling-off and a 'glad to see you're eating'!

Sadly, my Aunt May was always in poor health and was in hospital more often than I can remember but, despite that, she always looked the same to me since I was two years old until she died at the age of almost 70. She had snowy white hair, blue eyes, a lovely complexion and was very slim in stature. If the eyes are the windows of the soul, you could see that my Aunt May's soul was as pure as the driven snow. Her actions were, to me, always truly Christian, and I credit my Aunt May with the faith she instilled in me as a child and which has remained with me all my life. Whilst I was living in Bridgeton, she regularly took me to Mass. However, I truly loved going to devotions at the Sacred Heart Church in Bridgeton, where we sang hymns in Latin. I somehow knew the significance of the awe I felt when the Blessed Sacrament (the Host) would be exposed during Benediction. I so looked forward to these occasions when I would wear my best frock and happily skip alongside my Aunt May both to and from church.

I also liked the social aspect, because my Aunt May would talk to friends and neighbours and, with pride, would introduce me as her god-daughter. Before I forget to mention this, my Aunt May wasn't the only one to introduce me to my life of prayer. I constantly heard my mother say the Hail Mary out loud. Now for those of you who don't know this beautiful prayer to God's mother it goes:

Hail Mary full of grace, the Lord is with Thee.
Blessed Art Thou among women and blessed is the fruit of
Thy womb, Jesus.
Holy Mary Mother of God, pray for us sinners now and at
the hour of our death. Amen.

The difference between the Hail Mary and my mum's version was that when she said 'Holy Mary Mother of God' she would add 'send me down a couple of bob' (money) and was mortified when at one point during Mass I loudly said the Hail Mary, adding my version "send my mammy a couple of bob".

I'd like to tell you a little bit more about my cousins. Roddy was born Patrick Roderick Joseph O'Connor and always seemed really tall and handsome. He was like a big, older brother and has, until this day, an amazing way with children. As I said, Roddy was the one who got me to eat when I was being picky but always for my own good. He treated me just like a little sister. He was the eldest and, whenever he was out of the house, I couldn't wait for him to come home and light up the whole room with his laughter and his antics. He had the unique gift of being able to play with me at my level but also to teach and encourage me at the same time. Roddy played the bagpipes and, as such, had to warm up the chanter before getting the notes right. I would blow on that chanter until I was blue in the face and hardly got a squeak out of the thing, and then Roddy would play these massive-looking pipes with great melody! I could never figure it out, but Roddy was as patient as a saint with me, and I used to follow him everywhere when he was practising, hanging onto any attire he was wearing at the time. He must have been relieved when he secured himself a position in the merchant navy to get some peace from his bothersome little 'sister'.

Mary was born Mary Veronica and is a year younger than Roddy. In my early infancy, whilst staying with my Aunt May, I just remember that Mary was the quiet one. Again, to me, she looked tall, was slim, had a fair complexion and had medium-length, brown hair and blue eyes. She had lovely teeth, was quietly spoken and extremely gentle. She would always encourage me to sit on her knee for a *'wee nurse'* and I would chat away ten to the dozen! Mary was, and still is, the type of person who quietly gets on with things.

Bernadette (the youngest) was born Bernadette Catherine. She too was tall, slim, had blue eyes and long, brown hair. Bernadette was the feisty one of the O'Connors. She decided that I was her property and, by God, she would have taken on the devil himself if he tried to harm me!

My mother lost the rag with me one day and gave me a slap around the bottom which so enraged Bernadette that she had my mother by the throat against the wall for touching 'her baby'. Bernadette has always massively influenced my life, and I looked upon her as a second mother. I had to seek approval from two sources whenever I would make a decision and, even now, when I'm about to do something, I think, *Oh my God, what would Bernadette say?*

The O'Connor in-laws also stayed in Bernard Street. Agnes and Walter had seven children, all packed into their tenement flat. I looked upon them as my cousins and felt blessed that I had people of my own age group to play with, particularly Ellen O'Connor who was born the same year as me. Margaret, Ellen's sister, was the 'gobby' one and used to make me howl with laughter. She was a couple of years older than Ellen and, apparently, when she started school, the teacher commented on her dirty neck! Margaret fired back by saying, "Have you ever had a deck at yer ain!" (Have you ever had a look at your own neck!) I'm not going to go into detail on every single character, but Frankie (one of the brothers) really jolts my memory as his nose was constantly running. I used to watch him wipe his nose on his sleeve but, in those days, he certainly wasn't alone. We never had the luxury of paper tissues so the sleeve always came in handy.

He played at the back of his building in Bernard Street and was forever shouting up at his window, "Maw, wid ye throw me doon a piece n jam?" (Mum, would you make me a jam sandwich?)

Just around the corner from Bernard Street was a sweetie shop, and I just loved the women who owned it. Her name was Mrs Walker, and she was the epitome of the kindest old soul who loved to make children happy.

The children would come in with an old penny to spend on all the wonderful colourful sweets displayed there. She knew everyone by name and, when she handed you the sweets of your choice, she always made you feel that she had hand-picked them just for you! My happiest memories were staring into that shop and happier still when someone kindly gave me a penny to spend there.

It was the highlight of our young lives when a girl in Bernard Street was getting married, because the tradition was for the bride's father to throw money from the bridal car as soon as the car set off to take the bride to her spouse. You can imagine the scramble! Being under school age, I managed to get nearer the ground when the pennies fell, but the downside of that was putting up with the older children crushing me in the scramble! Nevertheless, I always managed to get a penny or two and went straight round to Mrs Walker's sweetie shop accompanied by one of the in-laws.

Whilst living in Bernard Street, I have told you more about my Aunt May and my cousins and not mentioned much about my mum. My mum was working as a bus conductress and other jobs in order to bring in money for our keep. She always had me beautifully dressed and would not allow me speak anything but proper English.

If I spoke any slang words, like 'gonnae' instead of 'going to', I was immediately reprimanded.

In Bridgeton, slang came naturally to the people living there, and please don't think I am condemning that because I truly love 'Glaswegian patter', but my mum was insistent on proper English and excellent table manners in my formative years to instil those values for future years. When mealtimes were over, I was not allowed to leave the table until I said, 'May I leave the table please?' Subsequently, my manners were always commented on wherever my mother took me, and I always spoke in a polite voice. As mentioned previously, the O'Connor in-laws were the salt of the earth but really coarse spoken and, although they never commented on how *I* spoke, other children would say I was a snob!

At this point in my life, I was approaching the age of four, and my mum was very much aware that if she remained in Bridgeton with my Aunt May, I would have to go to the local Catholic School in the catchment area which was the Sacred Heart Primary. I truly believe that there would have been excellent teachers in that school, but in terms of mixing with proper-spoken children, I would have been in the minority.

CHAPTER 3 –
MY TRANSFER FROM BRIDGETON
TO DENNISTOUN

When I was four, my mother announced that she was moving me from Bridgeton to Dennistoun in Glasgow. Naturally, I was heartbroken at leaving the wonderful stability I had living with my Aunt May and her family, but despite tears from both sides, it was agreed that my mum was doing the right thing.

Oddly enough, I can't remember the day I left Bridgeton, but my mum moved into 8 Whitehill Street, Dennistoun, Glasgow where she rented an attic room from Mrs Wishart, the landlady. She was always immaculately dressed, quite plump and wore lots of make-up. I never saw too much of her, as my mum just gave her rent money. Her house was at the top of the common close and was extremely spacious. In order to get to our room, we had to go in the front door and upstairs to the attic which housed three rooms and a communal toilet. There was a communal kitchen, and the lodgers in the other two rooms were men, one from London and the other from somewhere in the north. Our room had a big window, a bed, chest of drawers, a settee, some chairs and a small coffee table.

From the window, I had a clear view of Duke Street, which was the main road, and although we were surrounded by tenement buildings, they were far more upmarket than the ones in Bridgeton.

Dennistoun in Glasgow was considered a lovely area, and I was immediately at home in my new accommodation, although my mother would say to me over and over again, "Don't tell anyone you live in a room!" My mum was very self-conscious of the fact that we were poor, but the way she dressed me and the way I felt within myself, I considered myself one of the richest little girls in the world.

In geographical terms, I lived at the bottom end of Whitehill Street which was near all the shops. As you went further up Whitehill

Street, the left- and right-hand side of every street was called a 'drive' which were, in alphabetical order, such as Finlay, Garthland, Onslow, etc. until you got right to the top of the street which led onto Alexandra Parade, another busy road and another lovely area.

Many of you Glaswegians will remember Wills Cigarette Factory which was an extremely thriving industry, particularly before health warnings were put on cigarette packets! It closed down a number of years ago but, in doing so, seemed to rip the heart out of the place. How many lives? How many stories in that place?

Then, there was Robb's the newsagents just across from our flat and a grocery shop on Finlay Drive. Next to our building, there was Whitehill Parish Church which stood out not only as a place of worship, but also by its finely honed architecture and hallowed grounds. I immediately knew to keep quiet when I was creeping around the grounds (apart from weddings and scrambles). True to form, however, my favourite shop was the newsagents where the elderly owner, Mrs Robb, was the absolute epitome of Mrs Walker in Bridgeton. I was in heaven!

Once again, she treated me like a little princess and whenever I went to get messages for my mum, she would always give me free sweets or a wee bar of chocolate! My next favourite place was the downstairs chippie, and it was just the most amazing smell. Whenever I went in with my mum, I used to get excited just standing in the queue!

CHAPTER 4 –
NURSERY TIME

I don't remember exactly where my mum was employed when I was four years old, but she told me I would have to go to nursery and the nearest one was Onslow Drive Nursery in Dennistoun. I skipped alongside my mum as we walked up the hill, and was overwhelmed with excitement when I saw the massive old, detached house which had been converted into a nursery. There were colourful swings and see-saws outdoors, and all the windows had sun and rainbow silhouettes that looked so magical. I just couldn't wait to go inside! I remember walking in through the big entrance door and releasing my mum's hand, as I ran from one beautifully decorated room to another. There were numerous playrooms, and I had never seen so many toys in all my life! There was a massive staircase with a beautifully polished banister and, upstairs, there were little beds for children who needed a daily nap or to lie down during bouts of sickness. It was just so fresh, clean and bright that I could hardly contain myself with the thought of going there every day. I had no idea that it was not my right to be there and that I required to be assessed on whether or not I would 'fit in'. The nursery staff were simply wonderful and, just before I left, they showed me my peg for hanging up my coat and where to put my little duffel bag containing my tabard and gym shoes. When I was hopping and skipping back down the road, my mum told me I had been accepted and that's when it dawned on me that I had gone to be assessed by the staff! I would have been gutted if I had been refused acceptance.

Every day, Monday to Friday, I walked up Whitehill Street with gleeful anticipation of reaching the nursery where my mum left me at the door and went on about her business. I proudly put on my little apple-green tabard and slipped on my wee black gym shoes and then I was FREE. Free to be creative, explore all the little rooms, play with whatever toys I wanted to and, for one day, I was a family member of a massive, beautiful, old house in Dennistoun with back and front gardens. It was perfect bliss. I loved the staff, the structure, the routine mealtimes, the uniformity, discipline, children and all the lovely toys but most of all the feeling of being so proud to be part of that wonderful place. I can still taste the clean smell of every room but mostly the smell of the various flowers from all the lovely big trees (yes, I am a tree hugger!) surrounding the nursery. I hated it when time was over and I had to walk back down the road, but it was always a sunny day so halfway through the walk I'd hop and skip in anticipation of my tea for that night.

On reaching our close, I would ask if I could go outside to play, but my mum always insisted I change into something more appropriate for playing (at nursery she put my good dresses on knowing that the tabard would take the flack!). Before going out to play, I would slip into a T-shirt and shorts and run down all the stairs to the back garden which had a big wall I could slide along and pretend I was riding a horse. It had a big, old brick bin shelter where **all** the rubbish was tipped (no plastic bags) and a very large view of the tenement buildings themselves. You can imagine a four-year-old craning her neck to look to the top of the building to see the attic room she lived in. I did this so many times that you will now see a Eunice with a bit of a hump! (Come to think of it, it might be due to always leaning forward on that imaginary horse!)

I loved looking over the wall – I was the height of nonsense but a very determined climber – and when I got to the top of the high wall (and it was high), I sat with my legs dangling over the other side looking at other big houses and imagining children playing there. There were no other children in the immediate vicinity, so I had lots of imaginary playmates and the other side of the wall made for much more interesting ones. However, one day the unthinkable happened and a little girl from one of the houses caught my eye. She was about six or seven, and I waved to her. She waved back, and the next thing I knew, she had run out of her house and down the small field to the bottom of the wall. She was beautifully dressed and obviously well off (I could just tell), but she said, "What are you doing on the top of that wall?", and I promptly replied, "Riding my horse!" She said she wasn't allowed to climb, but she wished she could join me. I told her

I wasn't allowed to climb either but I could figure a way to help her up, so Anne (the name of my new playmate) carefully followed my daring instructions and ended up on the 'horse' with me. She told me she wasn't really allowed to mix with other children in case they were common, and she went to a private school in Glasgow. However, we had our own 'horses' and they were on fire that day, as we whipped and geed them up into moving faster. I think I told Anne she had won the race (I didn't want to lose my new-found friend). We played for too short a time on the top of that wall, getting more and more daring, and then I heard my mum shout, "Eunice, I hope you're not getting into any trouble – remember you are not allowed on that wall!" I shouted, "Just coming, Mammy." I quickly instructed Anne to get down off the wall on her side and I'd do the same. We said we would keep it our secret, and she told me whenever she saw me on the wall she would try to escape to join me.

That was a very special day for me – I had my own secret friend and I just hugged myself with delight. Of course, when I got a grilling from my mum about whether or not I'd climbed the wall, my face was so red that I had to admit it. I decided the shouting lecture on safety and watching my mother going crazy because I had been disobedient was well worth it. I took it on the chin, washed my small hands until they were squeaky clean and asked my mammy if I could help her with anything. She soon calmed down, and we would talk away naturally about the worries and woes of her economic situation (I listened with half an ear I must say but said, "That's terrible Mammy" in the appropriate places). I don't remember or care what I had for my tea that night, but my usual night-time routine was getting washed in a basin, put into my nightdress, brush my teeth, have my story read or read my own, bless myself, join my hands and pray to God to pardon my wrongdoings. Let's just say that night, my mother thought I had fallen asleep on my knees before getting into bed! My mother loved singing to me, so she was always anxious to finally tuck me down and then start singing the saddest songs ever. She did the same to Roddy, Mary and Bernadette and whilst they were crying their eyes out she would laugh her head off! However, even the sad song my mother sang to me that night could not stop me being so pleased with my day's events. I think my mum was a bit peeved and thought she had lost her touch, because she said, "Uch Eunice, just go to sleep." In a happy, wee voice I said, "Goodnight Mammy, sleep tight and don't let the bugs bite."

My time at nursery was really happy until one day I was taken away from the other children and put in the sickroom. I was too young to understand the meaning of the word quarantine, but I later found out that I had picked up a string of the scarlet fever virus and obviously had to be kept away from the other children until my mum collected me and took me to my own GP, Doctor Levy. I don't think I ever went back to nursery, but the illness happened during the summer of 1959 and I was due to start school in August that year. My illness altered my mum's work situation, because there was no one to look after me while she went to work, so she had to give up her job. This made the financial situation extremely difficult, and it's now I understand just how stressful it must have been for my mum with a sick child on her hands and little money to live on from the 'parish' (today's equivalent of Employment Seekers Allowance).

Before I begin to tell you all about my first day at school, I have to tell you about Doctor Levy whom I briefly alluded to in the last paragraph. He was Jewish and always extremely kind to me whenever I had to go for an examination. Now, I never really liked the name Eunice so I decided, in my infinite wisdom, that the name Maria was far more suited to me and one day, when I went to see Doctor Levy, I refused to answer to the name Eunice. I told the doctor that my name was Maria Graham and my mum went absolutely nuts with me, both in the surgery and when she got me outside. I got the biggest lecture on how stupid he must have thought I was, when at the age of five I didn't even know my own name. I was crying because my mum was angry but, although the tears were stinging me, I was so stubborn, I was glad I made a point about my name although I didn't try that one again!

CHAPTER 5 –
PROUD PRIMARY SCHOOL YEARS

My first day at school was approaching fast, and the day came for me to go for my school uniform. My mum had saved really hard to get me the best quality and took me to a place called Paisleys in Jamaica Street, Glasgow who specialised in school wear, particularly for private schools. I was enrolled at St Thomas' Primary School in Riddrie, and although it wasn't a private school, many of the children came from really lovely houses and the school itself was in a very affluent area. The colour of the school blazer was green, the tie was green and red, the skirt grey and the blouse white. But do you know what I loved most of all? My hat! It was that beautiful felt material with a green band round it. We were allowed to wear berets, but it was just so much more special to wear a hat. That day was absolutely brilliant. I got my school uniform, and my mum and I had a wee bite to eat in the centre of Glasgow. It was one occasion when, instead of walking, we took a bus and at the bus stop, I couldn't stop skipping about until the bus came. I had a beaming smile on my face all the way home and, although I was only five years old, I felt a great love for my mum because I knew she had sacrificed a lot for that very special uniform.

The night before the big day arrived, my mum put cloths in my hair. Nowadays, you can curl your hair with tongs or rollers, but we didn't have that luxury so my mum would cut up old rags, measure them so that they were the same length and I would hold each rag with my hand on my head while she twisted portions of my hair around them. They were then secured tightly and although they looked awful and hurt like hell, they were extremely effective in making great ringlets when the rags were taken out the next morning. Naturally, I was too excited to feel the pain; all I knew was that my ringlets were going to look great around the gorgeous hat that would be on my head.

St Thomas' Primary didn't have the mission statement that most schools have nowadays, but recently on reading online their current mission statement, I can honestly say that the values, goals and achievements are as relevant today as they were in 1959. My first day at school, in August 1959, couldn't come quick enough. I was so excited I could hardly eat my Weetabix breakfast, but the clocked ticked on and soon we were on our way to the bus stop. Years ago, in Glasgow there were trams that ran on lines like train tracks and trolleybuses that had cables attached above the top. My mum and I went on the trolleybus which stopped opposite the school. We crossed the two zebra crossings and, when we reached the school gates, I was so anxious to get through them I nearly forgot to kiss my mum goodbye! What I do remember is seeing a lot of children crying at leaving their parents and thinking that they were a bunch of 'safties'!

Sister John, a Notre Dame nun, was the headmistress of the school, and she rang the bell at 9 a.m. prompt to call us all into assembly where we said our prayers prior to forming lines for our Primary 1 class. Sister John commanded great respect and the buzzing conversation of the schoolchildren prior to the bell suddenly fell really silent. I think it was at that point I realised the significance of what was really happening

Our school lines were perfectly formed, with each person being exactly one arm's length behind the person in front, and one by one we walked into the classroom where we were shown to our seats and introduced to our teacher Mrs Brennan who was very soft-spoken and had that lovely quality of making us all feel very special and welcome. She took us along to the cloakroom, showed us our coat pegs with our names on them and told us that we would get our milk before the bell rang for playtime. To be honest, I think I was expecting to be doing some real schoolwork, but we were allowed to play with crayons, get to know our classmates and understand the rules of volunteering for little jobs such as milk monitor and collecting pencils, etc. I immediately made friends with a girl called Rosie Sewell because she made me laugh at every opportunity.

For the first few weeks, we were at school only until lunchtime. The morning flew by and in no time at all I was back outside the school gates eagerly trying to spot my mum amongst all the other anxious parents. I would run to her, give her a big cuddle and kiss and when she asked me how I got on at school, I gave the usual one syllable answer – 'fine'. The thing was, I wanted to keep my school uniform on all day, and I was delighted when my mum said we would be going to my Aunt May's for tea. I knew my mum was desperate to show me off and rightly so, she had worked so hard to get me into the education system that would then become life-changing for me.

When I got to Bridgeton, my Aunt May was waiting with open arms and, after all the compliments on my appearance, she put a pinny (apron) on me and gave me my tea. I felt a very special little girl, and I told her far more about my day at school than I had told my mum. When I mentioned Rosie, my mum said, "She better be good company and not a bad influence on you" (I think it was the other way around), but I managed to assure my mum that Rosie was from a good area and she too had got her uniform out of Paisleys! It was really quite a snobbish attitude, because there were children in that Primary 1 class – particularly the boys – whose parents could not afford the school uniform. These poor children came to school in worn-out shoes and trousers and stuck out like a sore thumb from the rest of the children. Years later, I realised just how socially disadvantaged they were and may God forgive my attitude towards them because, I know, I was one of the many children who treated them like lepers whilst my conscience was telling me otherwise.

You could say my mum was responsible for breeding the snob in me, but I will always stand by her for realising the importance of my education and having the correct clothes and social skills that go with that, particularly when we were living in a society where girls were expected to leave school at fifteen years old and bring factory work money to the table.

Getting back to that first day at school, once my tea was over, it was soon time to walk home with my mum with her voice ringing in my ear – "We need to get you home Eunice, you have school in the morning." As soon as I arrived home, my mum would wash me from head to toe using a basin – a ritual that went on until we had a proper bathroom which eventually came.

When I went into Primary 1, I was in room six, and for the life of me, I could never understand why we didn't go into room 1. I had a beautiful teacher called Mrs McLay. I loved going to school and, by the end of my first year, I was more than capable of going on the bus myself (supervised by my mum of course). Prior to the recess for the summer holidays, it was announced that me and a few of my other peers (including Rosie) would return after the summer holidays and go into room 9. When I told my mum, she was delighted. My report card showed I was doing well but, even better, I would jump ahead by two classes!

Because money was so tight, our treat of the week would be going to the chip shop to buy sixpence (2.5 pence) worth of chips. The chippie was right below our flat which made it all the more convenient.

My mum complained once that the chips were too greasy, and after that (usually a Friday night when there was a massive queue in the chip shop) my mum would insist on tasting the chips before she bought them, which was a constant source of embarrassment to me. However, it got worse! Eventually, my mum would send me for chips and insisted that I taste them before they were wrapped up in newspaper. I detested having to do this because I could hear people in the queue tut-tutting because they were made to wait a few minutes longer, but I didn't dare disobey my mum and the weekly ritual continued until we left Whitehill Street.

On Fridays, when I wasn't chip tasting, I would accompany my mum to my Aunt Vera's house in Brandon Street to visit my cousins. Aunt Vera was 13 years older than my mum and married to my Uncle Christie. Friday night was pay night, so inevitably my Uncle Christie would come home from work a little tipsy which meant my Aunt Vera didn't get much out of his pay packet. Unfortunately, this was indicative of the times we lived in, especially post-World War II in Glasgow.

My Uncle Christie (Bennett) was very jovial, particularly when he'd managed a win at the bookies. My Aunt Vera was a French polisher by trade and worked hard to feed her seven children. It's odd the things you remember about people, but I used to think my Aunt Vera didn't wash her hands properly because they were always stained. She did wash her hands, of course, but the French polishing stained her fingers and I guess it would have been too expensive for her to get stain remover.

The Bennetts lived at 22 Brandon Street, which is just off Abercromby Street near to the Gallowgate in Glasgow. Their house was diagonally opposite the Broes, which was mutually beneficial for my Aunt Vera and my mum to pop in and out. The Bennett's house consisted of two rooms and a living room/kitchen area. The eldest family member was my cousin Madge who was married and settled. Then there was Margaret, Tom, Robert, Christine, John and Maureen who is exactly six months older than me. I think Robert was dating his future wife Kathleen at the time, Margaret was married to George, and Christine was single but never short of a date. Tom was the black sheep of the family because he was always in trouble, John was a year or two older than me and the baby of the family was Maureen. It was natural therefore that Maureen and I hung out together.

Since we visited on a Friday, Maureen and I were sent to the chip shop in the Gallowgate where you could get four-penny portions of chips which meant if you asked for a couple of bags of sixpence worth of chips there was enough to feed an army! I don't know how my Aunt Vera managed with such a big family, but we would devour the chips with copious amounts of bread and butter.

Even a little doll can ballet dance

Because Maureen and I were close in age, and I think to get rid of us for a few hours, our mothers would pay a pittance for us to be taught how to dance. The highlight of my visit would be walking to Dennistoun for dance classes. These classes were busy and run by two sisters – named big Miss Hayes and wee Miss Hayes. No matter where I went, I always needed the toilet at some point and on one particular occasion, I put my hand up to ask if I could go to the 'lavvy' (lavatory). Everyone was gutting themselves laughing and, with a face as red as a beetroot, I went to the toilet wondering why asking to go to the 'lavvy' was so funny. That aside however, I really enjoyed my Friday nights at my Aunt Vera's, particularly when Robert would give my mum and I a lift home in his motorcycle and sidecar. The motorbike and sidecar rides never lasted for any length of time because, as I mentioned previously, Robert was going out with his girlfriend Kathleen and of course that took precedence. Later on, Robert married Kathleen and eventually they immigrated to Australia. Sadly, my cousins Robert Tom and Madge are now dead and very much missed.

An unexpected surprise

On Sunday afternoons, my mum would take me to see my Aunt May and family. These were always special occasions for me, but the highlights of my visits were when Roddy was home on leave from the navy. He always gave me a ten-shilling note (50p in today's money) which I would hand over to my mum on the road home. Even at that tender age, I was well aware that my mum needed the money more than me and the little windfall would earn me a bag of sweets.

However, on one occasion, Roddy told me to have a look in the box which was lying on top of the bed in the bedroom. I walked tentatively into the room and saw a big, long cardboard box with a lid on it. The box was at least three-feet long, and I remember thinking for some reason or other that there would be crayons and colouring books in it. When I took the lid off the box, I saw the most beautiful Spanish doll I had ever seen. She had long, dark hair, a gorgeous wee porcelain face, a dress with all the Spanish trimmings and white shoes. I noticed the name Diana at the end of the box and, when I took my new playmate out, I discovered that she could walk and talk, had big blue eyes and when I took her hand, the minute her left foot went forward, she turned her head to me and said 'Mama'. Diana became my favourite doll ever and even as I'm typing this, the most amazing memories come flooding back.

When I first took her for a walk in Duke Street with my mum, I let Diana walk for a little while and then I lifted her into my arms. A woman came running up to me shouting, "Put that wean doon – she's too heavy fur ye." My mum and I laughed and laughed and then the woman realised it was a doll I was carrying. If any of you out there are wondering if I still have Diana, I can tell you she is now in the safe hands of my daughter.

CHAPTER 6 –
HOLIDAY TIME AGAIN

I remember summer holidays with great fondness, as each year my mum took me to visit my Aunt Cissie in Belfast. My mum would stay for a few weeks and then left me for the remainder of the holidays split between Belfast and Glenarm in the beautiful Glens of Antrim.

I must tell you about my first ever trip on an aeroplane to Belfast which would have been when I was about eight years old. My mum could not accompany me that year, and I wanted to take Diana with me but she was too big. I was the only youngster on the plane, and the cabin crew were nothing short of amazing. They gave me lots of stickers and British European Airway badges. My mum put me on the plane, safe in the knowledge that my Aunt Cissie would be able to see me from the terminal building. What she did not expect to see was that I would come off the plane walking hand in hand with the pilot whom I had asked to carry my *small* favourite doll! Everyone was laughing their heads off including the air crew. Naturally, I was completely nonchalant about the whole thing and thought I was bestowing a great honour on the pilot, allowing him to carry 'Anne Knox' (the name of Roddy's ex-girlfriend).

Aunt Cissie had three sons called Seamus, Sean and Gerard. Seamus was the oldest, and I absolutely adored him. Sean was always out and about doing his own thing which nearly always involved some kind of practical joke, and Gerard, the youngest, who was only six years older than me, made my life a misery with his constant jibes. I would complain about him to my Aunt Cissie, and I watched smugly when he got a slap round his lugs! On the subject of Gerard, he asked my Aunt Cissie if he could take me to the local swimming baths. I have to say, I was quite surprised at his change in attitude and was delighted when she gave him permission. The only problem was that I could not swim! My mum had never been taught to swim and had a phobia about allowing me to learn, so apart from being delighted, I also felt quite defiant.

When we arrived at the swimming baths, Gerard met up with his mates and we went into our separate changing rooms. As soon as I came out, Gerard was waiting for me with an evil grin on his face and, before I could escape, he and his pals grabbed me and threw me in the deep end! I will never forget the feeling of panic I had and, in desperation, I grabbed onto the nearest legs I could find and held onto them like a terrier. The poor, unfortunate teenage girl tried to kick me off, but I refused to let go until I was able to hold onto the side bar of the pool and ease my way along to the steps where I could safely climb out. Gerard and his pals were laughing their heads off, but when I told my Aunt Cissie what had happened he was screaming like a stuck pig. The one thing that incident taught me was that NO ONE would ever dare do that to me again, and my determination to learn to swim as soon as possible certainly paid off in later years.

As I said, my holidays were split between Belfast and Glenarm and, unbelievably, I had another Aunt Cissie in Glenarm. She was one of the most gentle and beautifully dressed ladies I have ever met. When my wee Aunt Cissie collected me from Belfast, she took me to Glenarm and let me share her bedroom which was decorated in fluffy pink. The house was on Mark Street and was occupied by my Aunt Marie, who was a music teacher, Aunt Martha, who was elderly, small in stature and always wore her hair in pigtails, and Uncle Tommy, who was as deaf as a post! My Glenarm relatives were very good to me, especially my wee Aunt Cissie who used to send me parcels including a beautiful dress with matching stole.

Glenarm is by the sea, and I loved playing with my mum's friend's daughter Mona. Their house was directly opposite the beach, so we used to change into our costumes and run straight into the water. I had amazing fun and fondly look upon those days as the halcyon ones, particularly going to my first dance at the age of 14.

I loved my school holidays but was always desperate to get back to school and see my friends. As previously mentioned, I jumped two classes after my first year at primary and, before I knew it, I was in the Communion class. As well as adhering to the school curriculum, the teachers were tasked with preparing us for our First Confession prior to our Holy Communion. When it came to my turn for my First Confession, which took place at St Thomas' RC Church in Riddrie,

I was so nervous going into the confessional box that I had an attack of the drips (sweaty hands which are the bane of my life)! I can't remember anything except "Bless me Father for I have sinned and this is my first Confession". I could only think about negotiating the door of the confessional box with my sweaty hands to let the next child in. Somehow I managed it.

The first of my nine lives

Before I speak about my First Holy Communion in detail, I have to tell you about the **first of my nine lives**. In order to go to the dinner school, we had to cross a busy road. The lollipop man was called Jimmy, and he ensured that we hungry wee ones managed to safely cross the road. However, on one occasion after my lunch, I was standing at the kerb with my peers when Jimmy beckoned us over. I looked and saw a car driving at speed, and my first instinct was to stay on the kerb. I didn't want to disobey Jimmy and went against my gut. The next thing I knew, I was lying on the road because I had been hit by the car. I was in pain, but I think the embarrassment was worse than the physical suffering, so I got onto my feet and said I was okay. I bruise very easily, and I knew that when my mum was washing me before bed she would see the bruises. I was worried sick all afternoon and that night all the bruises in my body had surfaced. I had to tell my mum what had happened and, of course, I got the biggest lecture on road safety. At the time, I just wanted to forget what had happened and, after reassuring my mum that I wasn't in any pain, I climbed into bed. If the car had driven any faster, it would have been a fatal accident.

CHAPTER 7 –
MY FIRST HOLY COMMUNION
AND CONFIRMATION

A very proud little girl

The night before my First Holy Communion, my mum put so many rags in my hair I could hardly sleep, both with the mindset that 'pride suffers no pain' and a combination of excitement (not forgetting my empty stomach, because in those days we had to fast the night before going to Holy Communion).

When I got up the next morning, my hair was full of ringlets and I felt like the bee's knees wearing my beautiful white dress, veil and velvet blue cape. The sun was shining brightly, and there was great excitement when we all took our places in church. I was acutely aware of the special Sacrament of Holy Communion which is the reception of Jesus himself – which I was about to receive for the first time in my life.

I revelled in the atmosphere of awe, simplicity and purity, and when Father Morgan finished Mass, all the children and parents were invited to the church hall where we could have breakfast. We were all ravenous, but there was a terrific spread laid on and we filled ourselves to the gunnels! At the end, we were all presented with a medal. I must say, all the children were remarkably well behaved (including the boys who were so suited and booted that they were almost unrecognisable).

In June of the same year, I also made my Confirmation. This is a very special ceremony within the Catholic Church, because it was the final step to becoming a fully privileged member. Our Confirmation class were due to be confirmed by Bishop Ward of Glasgow, and we wore our Communion outfits whilst His Excellency bestowed this Holy Sacrament upon us.

The weeks leading up to our Confirmation were both exciting and frightening. We were excited because we were allowed to choose a Confirmation name but scared witless, because those who had already had the Sacrament conferred upon them took great pleasure in telling us that the traditional slap on the face by the Bishop was really painful and more like a punch!

I tried to keep my mind off this by convincing myself that I was a soldier of Christ, as this is what we learn prior to Confirmation. I was also concentrating on the Confirmation name that I had chosen – Maria. I chose this name because St Maria Goretti was a relatively new saint within the Catholic Church, and she died at the age of 11. This young girl was attacked and stabbed to death, as she tried to resist her attacker. It was a man called Alessandro, who worked on their family farm in Italy. As Alessandro forced himself on her, Maria cried that it was a mortal sin and that she would rather die than submit. Alessandro began to choke her and stabbed her 14 times.

Saint Maria Goretti was a holy, devout girl who forgave her attacker just before she died. I really looked upon her as a role model, but if I'm being perfectly honest with you, the fact that I now had 'Maria' as my name probably played a huge part in my choice!

When our Confirmation day arrived, all the children gathered outside St Thomas' RC Church prior to being ushered inside to the benches allocated for the Confirmation. Of course, everyone was talking about the name of the saint they had chosen and the forthcoming slap on the face! I couldn't believe the number of boys who were actually crying at their upcoming impending fate!

We walked into church with our partners. The girls were wearing their Communion dresses, and the boys were wearing suits with red sashes across their chests. The girls sat on the right-hand side of the church and the boys the left so that we could meet the Bishop in pairs. When it came to my turn, I was really surprised how softly spoken Bishop Ward was when he asked me my chosen saint's name. I was even more surprised that the 'slap on the face' was just a gentle touch on my left cheek! I don't remember much more about my Confirmation except that I felt immense pride at now being a fully fledged member of the Roman Catholic Church and personally meeting the Pope's vicar.

CHAPTER 8 –
THE THORLEY FAMILY

Before I continue talking about my primary school years, I cannot go ahead without including something about the Thorley family, as they were such a gift in my young life. Charles and Joan (Mr and Mrs) Thorley moved into the tenement building at 8 Whitehill Street Glasgow (a few floors down from where I stayed), along with their two children, Jane and Simon. When I first met them, I thought to myself, *this is fantastic as I now have playmates.* They moved close to us just after I made my Confirmation, and the family immediately took me under their wing.

Jane was a few years younger than me and was beautiful both inside and out. I could not help but notice she had a plaster cast on right up to her neck and suffered from extreme walking difficulties and, from a very young age, was always in pain, but she never seemed to complain. She wasn't allowed out to play but, fortunately, I could go to her house and play with her. Simon was a very contented, adorable, curly-haired little boy and the absolute image of his father. Mr Thorley worked for British Rail, and Mrs Thorley was a hairdresser. Since my mum and I lived in an attic, the Thorley family seemed well off because their house was so big and they had the luxury of a bathroom.

After a short time, my mum did various jobs for Mrs Thorley. I was allowed to look after Jane and Simon for some pocket money, which was great, but the biggest treat of all was having a bath with Jane and Simon on a Friday night. By this time, Jane had been getting her plaster casts gradually removed and, although she always walked with a limp, she was leading as normal a life as possible. It was such a wonderful time, as I was included in all their birthday gatherings, outings, funfairs but being invited to spend Christmas Day with them always exceeded my expectations.

Then there is another important person I need to mention – Mrs McCready who was the Thorleys' next-door neighbour. She made pancakes on Christmas Day. Looking back, it wasn't the Christmas dinner and all the trimmings I eagerly awaited – it was the pancakes! One Christmas, Jane and Simon got a Wendy house from Santa and Simon and I had stuffed ourselves so much with sweets and pancakes, we fell asleep together in the Wendy house – something I never lived down.

Whilst on the subject of Christmas, my mum scrimped and saved to make sure that I got everything on my Santa list and, unbeknown to me, as soon as I fell asleep, she would go to the Barras (then it was the biggest and best-known market in the east end of Glasgow) at midnight, when all the toys were being sold for next to nothing. This enabled my mum to get me all those little extras that I hadn't asked for, and I am truly grateful to her for doing this for me because it was quite a long walk from Whitehill Street to the Barras, particularly around midnight. Even when I asked for a bike and thought Santa had forgotten, my mum bought it and hid it in another lodger's room up in the attic just to see the look on my face. Needless to say, I was ecstatic and was dressed in no time just to take my bike out and about. It had stabilisers on it, but within months I had no need of them.

In those days, Christmas in Glasgow was more or less treated like another day and, although it was still a magical time and there was always the last-minute frenzy to buy gifts, most of the shops remained open. This worked to my advantage because, one year, instead of getting my usual *Bunty* annual for girls from the newsagents across the road, I was given a *Spaceship* annual. I didn't want my mum to make a fuss, but she went straight over to the shop to complain and came back with the pre-ordered *Bunty* annual which I devoured within an hour!

CHAPTER 9 –
MORE OF MY GREEN UNIFORM DAYS

Primary school class photo, I am third right, middle row

As I continued to blossom in primary school, I have to say that not all my teachers were as kind as my first one. I had my fair share of difficulties with some. In room 9, we had a very unkind teacher who ruled with a rod of iron. Talk about strict (by name and by nature) – that's what we all had to endure.

Moving up classes, we had a teacher called Mr Coyle and if anyone talked in class when he was out of the room and didn't own up to it, we all got the belt. The belt is a real thing of the past but was the method of punishment used in those days to keep unruly pupils under control. Thinking back, it was really unfair that we were all punished but, as a sweetener, Mr Coyle would offer us the thick end of the belt or the tong side which had about six mini belts at the opposite end of the thick side. This made your hands sting like crazy, so I very kindly got the thick side of the belt. I used to laugh at the boys who put their hands underneath each other and, just as they were about to get the strap, the first thing they did was pull their hands away to avoid it. Mr Coyle would then give a double punishment. I tell you now, the thought of the belt really worked because if Mr Coyle left the room, the class remained silent until he eventually returned.

However, there was a dark side to this man, and I thought I was the only pupil who got their knicker elastic twanged whilst he was marking my work, but it appears to have happened to other pupils. Just recently, I heard that Mr Coyle had been in prison (no surprises for guessing why) where he later died. I have no idea how he died, but I held no grudge against him when I heard that news. He was a great teacher but, unfortunately, had paedophile tendencies.

Summertime again

Soon the summer days came around again, and our class was looking forward to the school trip which was paid up for during the school year. Not everyone could go on the trip because their parents just couldn't afford it, but my mum never wanted me to miss out and made sure I went. It was the highlight of our school year, and I am eternally grateful for every little sacrifice my mum made for me.

Obviously, we had more than one school trip, but the one I remember most is when we went to Troon in Ayrshire. When the coach arrived just outside the school, we scrambled on as fast as we could in order to get the seat of our choice which was normally somewhere at the back. Rosie and I sat together with our summer dresses on and packed lunches at the ready. The teachers always seemed chilled out which surprises me, because if I had 30 plus children in my charge I think I would have been sick with worry. As soon as the coach drove away, our singing voices were in fine fettle and, to the tune of 'Here We Go Round the Mulberry Bush', we would loudly sing:

The front of the bus they cannae sing, cannae sing, cannae sing. The front of the bus they cannae sing they cannae sing for peanuts.

The roles were then reversed by the pupils at the front of the bus. That little ditty, as well as anything else we could berate the front of the bus with, went on until we arrived at our destination. Troon is in the south of Ayrshire and very famous for its golf courses. However, in the year of 1965, the only balls that were flying about were beach balls, and we were really fortunate that on the day of our school trip, the weather was absolutely scorching. I was so excited you would have thought I was in the Bahamas and, as Rosie and I scrambled off the bus as fast as we could (no attention was paid when asked to form an orderly queue), we checked our packed lunches to see what we could swap. It was still morning, so there was plenty of time to spend on the beach before we feasted on our packed lunches, after which we spent time at the mini fairground and had a look around the shops.

It was customary to bring a gift back to your parents; therefore spending money was limited to ice cream (even although I wasn't too fond of it) and the fairground. I can't remember what Rosie took back to her mum and dad, but my gift was a small, golden-coloured vase with a Japanese lady on it. I thought it was pretty, and my mum kept it for years before she gave it away, so I guess she liked it too. All too soon, it was time for us to get back on the coach and, with the sun still scorching through the windows, the pupils on board hardly noticed the time passing as we excitedly told each other what we had been up to. When we arrived back in Riddrie, most parents met their children getting off the bus. My mum was waiting for me, and I never stopped talking the whole way home. I remember lying in bed that night with a burning hot face, feeling the tiredness in my bones with all the exercise on the beach and the amount of walking we had done and visiting almost every shop in Troon to get the right school trip gift. The thing I remember most, though, was the feeling of blissful contentedness prior to drifting off to sleep without a single care in the world.

CHAPTER 10 –
MY COUSIN MAUREEN

Time flew by at school, and I always looked forward to the weekends when I would see Maureen on a Friday and my Aunt May on a Sunday. My mum and Aunt Vera could only be described as the best of friends as well as being the best of enemies particularly when they were always playing Maureen and me off each other. My Aunt Vera would always go on about Maureen's thick, long hair, and my mum would retort that I had nicer skin. Despite the rivalry between the two sisters, Maureen and I were very firm friends and remained so throughout our teenage years.

My cousins' family lived near the Bellgrove Street area of Glasgow where there are many tributes to Tommy Burns, the famous Celtic player, and also where members of the Orange Order (an anti-Catholic organisation) still take delight in banging their drums as they March past the famous St Mary's RC Church. This is an annual event around 9 July and, despite numerous petitions to have the march going another route, for as long as I remember, the walk still takes that route and the drummers bang as loud as they can when they pass the Catholic church. I never really minded the Orange walk. I took my teddy to see the marchers when I lived in Dennistoun and, I have to say, I love the songs they sing.

Maureen's friends and neighbours were my friends and neighbours too and whoever had the luxury of a television would find themselves invaded by two cousins eager to watch *Top of the Pops!* This was a real treat for us, and I particularly remember being really excited when Jim Reeves was at the top of the charts with his hit single 'Distant Drums'.

When it was time to walk home, my mum was stuck with me singing 'Distant Drums' at the top of my voice. Occasionally, we would walk past a bakery where the night-time workers sold off leftover chocolate éclairs from the previous day at next-to-nothing prices. My mum would go in and buy one for me and tell me it was a special treat, but I swear to God it was to get me to give my vocal chords a rest!

During these walks, my mum would tell me all sorts of stories which of course I believed. For some reason, swing parks in Glasgow forbade entry at night-time and the park-keepers would tie the chains of the swings together to prevent usage. My mum told me the swings had their 'tails' tied up (the metal ropes that held the swing together) because they told lies and the same fate would happen to me if I ever told a lie.

The mystery of the black suitcase

On Sundays, I would go with my mum to see my Aunt May and afterwards walk home. It was a fair distance but there was no other option as far as my mum was concerned, so I used to amuse myself by attracting stray cats behind my mum's back. My mother hated cats and, whilst we were walking, I would put my left hand behind my back and rub my thumb and fingers together to attract any cat I could see. It worked every time, and I was constantly in trouble as one of these poor unfortunate creatures would follow me all the way up the road until my mum shooed it away.

One night, just after visiting my Aunt May, my mum and I took the usual route home. Just as we were walking up Reidvale Street in Dennistoun, we saw a black briefcase lying on the pavement. My mum picked it up to see if it belonged to anyone. To my absolute astonishment, there were more banknotes in that briefcase than I had ever seen in my life!

My mum was distraught, because we couldn't see anyone looking for it, bearing in mind that it was very dark. Suddenly, a well-dressed gentleman came out of a close in a panic and was so relieved when my mum handed him the briefcase. Apparently, he was an insurance agent collecting weekly sums of money, and I can only thank God it was my mum who found it.

After my mum and I turned around to walk up the road, the man came running up to me to hand me a one-pound note which was a lot of money in those days. My mum hadn't seen him do this, but I knew our financial situation and immediately gave the pound note to my mum. You can imagine the hurt I felt when my mum said, "You didn't steal that Eunice, did you?" I became very indignant, and I think it was the first time in her life that my mum saw my feisty side and watched me stand up to her. I would not let the matter go until I got a complete apology, I was still raging mad when we got home and I wouldn't let my mum kiss me goodnight!

CHAPTER 11 –
MY NEW DWELLING PLACE

I thought a miracle had occurred when my mum was offered a private let house by a very good friend of my Aunt Vera's. This man was called Vincent, and he owned a house in Milnbank Street which is in a very desirable area just off Alexandra Parade in Glasgow. He reassured my mum, time and time again, that this was one property he would not be selling in a hurry. I was in heaven when I saw it. Although it was a tenement building, the neighbours were all really nice, polite and very well spoken.

Just around that time, I was really prone to tonsillitis and it was agreed that the only solution would be for my tonsils to come out. An appointment was made with Glasgow Royal Infirmary and my operation date duly arrived. Everyone who had already had this procedure performed told me that you had to blow up a gas balloon in order to be anaesthetised but, although your throat would feel like sandpaper afterwards, the great hospital treat was ice cream which was all very well for those who liked ice cream but, as previously mentioned, I didn't.

When the day arrived for me to leave hospital, my mum came to collect me and handed me a new pair of shoes. I will never forget these shoes because they were red (one of my favourite colours) but they were also a size 2 and, because I was getting close to an adult size in shoes, I paraded about in them like a grown-up. In addition, I was going home to our new house and this memory still evokes feelings of happiness.

Since it was almost the start of the summer holidays, I went out to play, but the local girls just would not accept me. My mum, jumping to my defence, immediately told them I was just out of hospital and that they should be ashamed of themselves, and from then on, I am glad to say, I was no longer the new girl on the block.

I had some amazing times with my new-found friends, but these were friendships that were doomed because, just after a few months living in my ideal home, Vincent informed my mother that he was selling the private let. What a blow for my mum and me. It was the worst thing imaginable and, although I was relatively young, I truly realised the seriousness of the situation. In a nutshell, we would be homeless in less than a month! What was even more embarrassing was that some of my teachers from my primary school came up to view the house and, when I met them on the stairwell, I pretended I lived elsewhere. My face was scarlet at telling a barefaced lie, but I was far too proud to say I was being made homeless. I suppose being young and selfish, I couldn't put myself in my mum's shoes, but she was the one who had to go to Glasgow Corporation, explain her plight and try and get a roof over our heads. My mother was told it would be a bad area, but the building was due to be demolished and eventually she would get a reasonable house offer.

CHAPTER 12 –
MY DAYS IN THE SLUMS
OF GLASGOW

The only place Glasgow Corporation could offer us was a house in Greenvale Street in the Carlton area of Glasgow which, at that time, was one of the worst areas possible. The building was shabby, the surroundings were terrible and every street you walked through just felt really unsafe. I very soon realised that I would not be making any new friends and going out to play would not be an option.

Not surprisingly, my mother's health broke down. We were not only living in a rotten area, but the house itself had a living room, a hole-in-the-wall bed, a terrible outside toilet and I honestly don't even remember a kitchen. But to me, the most worrying thing of all was the fact that I was now in the catchment area for St Mary's Primary School and compared to St Thomas' it was night and day. My mum told me she would go and speak to Sister John (headmistress of St Thomas') to see if I could remain at my primary school but advised me not to hold out much hope.

I clearly remember the day she went to see the headmistress. I was alone in Greenvale Street, just generally tidying up, and it seemed as though my mum was taking hours before I heard her put the key in the lock. Of course, the first thing I wanted to know was whether or not I had to change schools, and when my mum told me I would have to go to St Mary's I was absolutely inconsolable, only to be told by my mum that she was just joking and Sister John was delighted to keep me on as a pupil. I still couldn't stop crying, and my mum started getting annoyed because I couldn't take a joke. Some joke!

Things weren't all bad in Greenvale Street. At one point, my mum took in a stray dog – we called her Valley – which meant I could actually go out for walks. I came to love that little dog more and more, until one day after my mum took Valley out, she came back without her. By this point we had had her a good few weeks, but my mum told me that a man had said he was her owner and had been looking for her so my mum duly handed the dog over. I don't think I even cried – I just accepted that this was my lot in life.

To put things in context time wise, The Beatles got to number one in the charts with 'She Loves You' and, although Beatlemania was everywhere, the highlight of my life was when Mrs Thorley (Auntie Joan) brought my mum and me our first real Christmas tree. I was unbelievably excited, and Beatlemania had absolutely nothing on me that Christmas!

CHAPTER 13 –
A BETTER DWELLING PLACE

After staying approximately 14 months in Greenvale Street, my mum was offered a house in Appin Road which was in the Haghill area near Dennistoun, but I convinced myself that it really *was* Dennistoun and was excited about the move. It was a tenement building with two flats on each landing, and my mum and I were going to be living in the top floor of number 267. I don't know who helped my mum with the move, but I do know that when my mum tried stripping the wallpaper in the living room, there were layers and layers infested with bugs. Terrible!

I think the move, having a young daughter and solely having to tackle a place like that nearly killed my mum. Somehow she got through it, but later she always seemed to have severe migraines. Whenever I came home from school, my mum would be lying in bed with a scarf around her head. I used to dread coming home to find my mum like this. I was always full of beans and had lots of stories to tell, but the minute I walked into that house, I could feel the depressive atmosphere. I don't know if my mum was on medication for depression – I suppose she was because she seemed to be always at the doctor about her nerves – but I kept praying she'd get better and eventually she did. I realised that God was always there for me when I needed Him and would never let me down.

Living in Appin Road wasn't too bad. I managed to have a few friends there – a girl called Veronica McLaughlin who lived just across the road and another girl called Helen Sharkey. My mum became friends with both parents, and there was always a warm welcome when we went visiting. Helen's mum used to really amuse me with her singing and general patter and these relationships built trust. It was only natural that when Helen Sharkey's mum went into hospital for a couple of weeks that my mum would look after Helen at my house. She was a lovely girl and, for a few weeks (at least), it felt like I had a sister. I never remember a cross word being said between us.

CHAPTER 14 –
KEATIE BUGS

I was in Primary 6 at St Thomas' and had a teacher called Miss Keatings who was an absolute nightmare! I suppose it was hard on her trying to control a class of 45 children but, through certain things she did, I completely lost all respect for her.

At first, she seemed to quite like me, because I was a really bright wee girl, but that soon came to a halt when I came 13th in the class and my mother refused to sign my report card. The reason I was 13th was due to joint firsts and thirds which put pupils down the placing list and, because my report card had not been signed, Miss Keatings (or 'Keatie Bugs' as we called her) had to go to Sister John the headmistress. On her return, I was handed a note by Miss Keatings whose face was like thunder when she told me to pass it to my mum as soon as I got home. I duly did this and inside the note it read, "Please sign. Sister John."

My life with Miss Keatings became hell after that and she picked on me at every opportunity. She disdainfully referred to me as 'Miss Graham' and always made sure I got the hardest questions to answer. If I dared get one wrong, she would ridicule me in front of the whole class but, to be honest, if anything, it added to my popularity with my peers because no one liked Keatie Bugs at all. Dealing with the stress of that teacher made playtime all the more appealing to me, and it was great in the winter when we would make slides out of ice and slide down the highest parts of the schoolyard we could find. Summer playtimes were equally appealing because skipping ropes, ball and hopscotch were the order of the day. I never told my mum how rotten Miss Keatings treated me, and I doubt if I would have received any sympathy!

When I went into Primary 7, you can imagine my horror when I found out that Miss Keatings was going to be my teacher again. I knew I was in for another year of hell and, boy, did I get that right!

If it hadn't been for my remaining classmates I would have been one unhappy, little girl.

Before I go any further, I must tell you about Deirdre Reid. During the interval, she and some other friends managed to distract me from Miss Keatings when she had made an unkind remark about me whilst in class. Deirdre stayed in Dennistoun in a more salubrious area than me and, since she came from a financially sound family, Deirdre was sent to music lessons. Her music teacher stayed in the Carntyne area of Glasgow and was a really lovely old dear who had a very gentle and kind manner. I would go back and forth with Deirdre to her piano lessons on a weekly basis and listen whilst Deirdre had her practice. One day, however, Deirdre and I were absolutely bursting for the toilet after the music lesson finished. Suffice to say, there was an embarrassing incident and I never went with Deirdre to her music lessons again as I could not have faced the humiliation.

I got on well with Deirdre's mum and dad and, on one occasion, was introduced to her aunt who stayed in Onslow Drive, Dennistoun. All the drives were nice, but the further up you went the nicer they were, and the houses in Onslow Drive were really nice – even nicer than the nursery I had gone to.

Even though Deirdre's aunt was a bit stand-offish with me, I never really gave it a second thought so when Deirdre invited me a second time to go with her to her aunt's house, there was no hesitation on my part. I'll never forget standing in the large hallway whilst Deirdre went through to the living room to see her aunt. As I stood in that hallway, I could hear the conversation between Deirdre and her aunt.

Her aunt actually said, "If that's Eunice Graham, tell her she's not welcome here." I felt like someone had kicked me in the ribs, and my face was absolutely burning with embarrassment. I just knew I had to get out of that house. I was hesitant to do so in case Deirdre knew that I had heard what her aunt said. Instead, I waited until Deirdre came into the hall and, before she could say a word, I informed her that my mum had asked me to come home from school early because we were going out. I then quietly left that house with a face like a tomato and really had to compose myself before going home.

I never did tell my mum about that incident, but after that Deirdre and I were never close friends again. I don't want you to think that

I had ditched Rosie – I hadn't, but Rosie and a girl called Pauline Farrell seemed to gravitate towards each other and, as previously stated, I had another circle of friends (including a couple of boys!).

My mum would take me to the cinema as a treat if there was a good film on. This was normally at the Orient Cinema just off Gallowgate in Glasgow and, in those days, there would be a small picture prior to the main screening which ensured we got our money's worth. Obviously, films are personal choices, but if my mum enjoyed the films, I was equally happy. Just around Easter of 1965, one of the best musicals ever was made into a film, firstly in America and then around the globe. All my school friends were talking about this film and how great it was, so you can imagine my disappointment when my mum told me that she didn't think *The Sound of Music* would be up to much.

This was one occasion when I really dug my heels in until my mum was worn out with my nagging. She finally relented and took me to see it. My mother loved it, as did I, and I remember thinking that it would be a film I'd like my children to see if I ever had any. Many years later, I paid for my mum to go on holiday to Austria with a visit to Salzburg included. I don't think I need to tell any of you what the film was about. Suffice to say, it became more famous than *Gone with the Wind*.

CHAPTER 15 –
JOHN AND BERNADETTE

Bernadette and John

Before I say more about Primary 7, I have to tell you about Bernadette's wedding. Bernadette was dating a guy called John McDonald, and he would often come around to 82 Bernard Street to see his girlfriend. I can't remember them getting engaged, but the one thing I do remember is John saying he had given up smoking, but whenever I went to the outside toilet after him, I could always smell cigarette smoke. I never mentioned this to Bernadette (or anyone else for that matter) because I didn't want to cause trouble and it was really none of my business. Bernadette told me that she met John at a dance and he had a goatee beard when he asked her to dance, but I always saw John clean-shaven and to me he was the spitting image of a television presenter called Bamber Gascoigne who hosted *University Challenge*. John was always a great handyman and seemed to be able to fix just about anything.

John and Bernadette set a date for their wedding which was going to take place in August 1965 at the Sacred Heart Roman Catholic Church in Bridgeton. There was a real frenzy leading up to the wedding and since Bernadette was making all the outfits for the wedding party – including her own wedding dress – my Aunt May's living room floor was always covered in hemming pins which I would pick up and neatly stack on the table. Bernadette asked me to be her bridesmaid and I was thrilled to bits. I had never had the honour of being a bridesmaid before. Mary, her sister, was to be her matron of honour, and Roddy would be escorting her up the aisle and giving her away since her father was deceased. The upshot of that was that Roddy could not get leave from the navy in time for the wedding, and my cousin Seamus from Belfast filled the breach. In those days, it was customary for the bride, groom and bridesmaids to change into less formal clothes at night-time, and prior to the wedding I decided I wanted to wear a camel-coloured skirt and an orange jumper for my change of clothing. My mum and Bernadette totally disagreed with my choice of outfit and decided I would wear a gingham dress which was pretty enough but, to me, seemed a bit babyish. When the due day arrived, Bernadette looked completely stunning. Her wedding dress was gorgeous and she had let her hair grow long in order to wear it up. Obviously she wore a veil, but I could not stop staring at her headdress which was in the shape of a crown around her head and reminded me so much of the statues I had seen of Our Lady. I remember my Aunt May's outfit being a purple kind of colour but, for the life of me, I can't remember what colour Mary and I were wearing. I was quite in awe of Bernadette managing to make all those outfits, because I could hardly sew on a button!

The wedding reception was held in St Mary's Parish Hall in Abercromby Street and there was a free bar. Bernadette and John provided all the beer and John's parents provided spirits. There were about 80 people at that wedding and the entertainment came mainly from the guests. I had to do my party piece which was a song called 'You're My World' by Cilla Black, but I really did not feel comfortable singing it, mainly because it was a grown-up song being sung by an 11-year-old girl who had changed into a 'baby' dress. I think I still carry some resentment about not being allowed to wear my camel skirt and orange jumper, but I can see why the gingham dress was probably deemed more appropriate for the occasion. The free bar thing also puzzled me, because Bernadette and John were both Pioneers which meant that they had made a pledge at some point in their lives to abstain from alcohol. Obviously I was too young to imbibe, but my two young cousins, James and Gerard (Mary's sons), went around the tables and drank dregs of beer whilst people were up dancing. Much to my amusement, they got rather tipsy and danced round a pole in St Mary's Hall.

In those days, the bride and groom always left halfway through the wedding after having changed into the appropriate attire. I think the custom of the bride and groom keeping on their wedding garments for the duration of the wedding in these days makes much more sense than it did back then. The other custom at that time was to keep the honeymoon destination a secret. I thought Bernadette and John would go somewhere like the Bahamas or even Spain and would have an amazing tan when they returned home, so you can imagine my disappointment when I heard they had gone to Bundoran in Ireland. Absolutely nothing wrong with Bundoran but, being young and fanciful, I was dreaming of more exotic places.

John and Bernadette rented a flat in Duncruin Street which is the Maryhill area of Glasgow, and about 18 months later Sean was born. I knitted a pair of mittens, which I thought was a great achievement, but when I gave them to Bernadette she found a hole in the thumbs and burst out laughing. I was at an age when my face would go scarlet with embarrassment, and I think you could have fried chips on my face that night! I will tell you more about Bernadette and John and family a bit later on but, for now, I am taking you back to when I was in Primary 7 at St Thomas'.

CHAPTER 16 –
MY FINAL YEAR AT PRIMARY SCHOOL

My friend Cathy Brady arrived in Primary 7, having left Birmingham to relocate to Glasgow. All my classmates were totally fascinated by Cathy's accent and told me to ask her where she left her coat. When I did so, Cathy replied (in a thick Birmingham accent) "In the baby's cloakroom". I'll never forget those first words that Cathy spoke to me and, as a newcomer to our class, I felt it my duty to take her under my wing. At the weekends, Cathy and I would ride our bikes to Hogganfield Loch which was about two miles from St Thomas'. Once we got there, we would share our sandwiches and any other goodies we could find before cycling round the loch and heading home again. We had great fun together, and being Cathy's friend earned me the right to go to Cathy's house in Cumbernauld Road which was just about a ten-minute walk from where I lived.

Another girl who deserves a mention is Diana Cordonna. Diana was a member of the travelling family, so she would flit in and out of school depending on where her dad's fairground attraction was. Diana was a really popular girl and immaculately turned out. She wore a grey trench coat, instead of a green one, but that was the only difference compared to the rest of the girl pupils. When I say Diana was popular, a lot of the pupils became friends with her in order to get free rides at the carnival. I didn't speak much to her – not because I didn't like her but because I didn't want her to think I was 'on the take'. However, in Primary 7, I did become friends with Diana and, as such; she gave me free passes for the fairground at Glasgow Green. I was absolutely delighted and I think my mum was too, because it saved her money and allowed me to have an unexpected treat. I realised why it was always good to be true to your inner voice, even at that young age. The invaluable lesson learned was *never to use anyone.*

I remember that just around that time, there was a competition in one of the local tabloids. I can't remember the exact details, but I put in an entry to win a bike. I avidly checked the newspaper to see who had won the competition. I thought I had given a good enough account as to why I should win it, but on the day the results were announced I was really disappointed when I saw that Elizabeth McGuinness (one of my classmates) had been the lucky one. I liked Elizabeth but she was financially better off, and I remember feeling great resentment towards her. However, the very next day, Elizabeth brought a huge bag of sweets that her mum had made and she dished a couple out to every single person in our class. Naturally, I took my own fair share but, on the bus home, I kept thinking about that act of kindness; a beautiful gesture that caused all my resentment to disappear and recognise that Elizabeth was indeed the worthy winner of that bike. Anytime I become judgemental, I remind myself of Elizabeth's act of charity.

Well, I suppose I have to once again mention the formidable Miss Keatings. Keatie Bugs never gave the strap so, on the upside, it saved the skin on my hands and stopped me being punished for any little misdemeanour! However, I was now in the qualifying class to see whether I would pass for a senior or junior secondary school. In those days, there were no comprehensive schools and you were strongly judged by what secondary school you went to. It was expected that girls from a junior school would leave at the age of 15 to go and do factory work. A girl at a senior school had the opportunity to go to college or university or, at the very least, get a decent job.

Obviously, I was old enough to go back and forth to school myself, but I had an amazing dog called Roy and not a single day went by without him meeting me at the school gates when it was home time. I used to walk Roy home and he was just like a second guardian angel. In fact, he even walked into Mass when I went to church on a Sunday and sniffed me out during the service. I was absolutely mortified at the time but, over the years, I've discovered that a dog is really a man's best friend.

In those days, a rag-and-bone man would collect discarded items and come round various streets pedalling his wares. His signal was blowing a trumpet. Every time that trumpet blasted, Roy would start to howl at the top of his voice until the rag-and-bone man stopped. I used to just fall about laughing.

I settled into Primary 7 as best I could and had no problem keeping up with the work allocated to me. Our qualifying exam was in the summer of 1966 but, naturally, since Easter came prior to summer, we all did something for Lent (a 40-day period of fasting and abstaining). The natural thing was to give up sweets but, since I didn't get many sweets, I felt that my penance was too light so decided to do an additional one. St Thomas' RC Church is beautiful and, every lunchtime during Lent (and other occasions), I would pop into church and say the Rosary. It would just be Our Lady and me, and I knew she heard my prayers. Now when I look back at that little girl kneeling before a beautiful statue, I still feel the tremendous warmth and comfort I felt so long ago and, somehow, despite the obvious misgivings about my forthcoming exam, I knew God's Mother was definitely on my side.

I found my qualifying exam really quite easy and soon learned I had passed. Just around that time, those of us who had passed for Our Lady and St Francis Secondary were invited to sit the entrance exam for Notre Dame Private School in Glasgow. My cousin Bernadette took me to the school, and I honestly thought the exam was easier than my 'qualy', but there were only a couple of girls who were given a place, and I couldn't get my head round that one because I knew I had 'skated' the exam. It didn't make that much difference because both all-girls schools had excellent reputations. However, Notre Dame, I suppose, was very elite because it was a fee-paying school. I still wanted answers as to why I couldn't go to Notre Dame, and I wanted to find out if I had officially passed, so my mother went to see Sister John for the last time to find out.

When my mum went to see Sister John, she explained that I had indeed passed the Notre Dame exam with flying colours. In her gentle and kind way, Sister John also told my mother why I had not been chosen as a pupil. When I think back on the very wise words of that nun, I still get a lump in my throat. She told my mother I was a very clever little girl, but going to a private school, albeit where a bursary was included, she feared that I would be excluded from all the after-school activities that pupils were expected to partake in. Sister John knew that I came from a one-parent family where money was really tight, and my mother could never have afforded to allow me to be the same as my fellow peers. Most of the children's parents were wealthy, stayed in big houses in lovely areas and very quickly I would be aware that I was not of the same social standing as the majority of the pupils. Sister John, being a Notre Dame nun, knew exactly what she was talking about and how massive the undertaking would be for such an ordinary little girl like me. You may be asking yourselves why I was allowed to sit the exam in the first place but, as you are well aware, everything involves politics and, to the Exam Board, there would have to be enough pupils allowed to sit the exam. In no way did Sister John make my mum feel small, and I thank God for that. My mum was really feisty (remember the report card incident?), but somehow Sister John was able to convince my mum that by going to Our Lady and St Francis (affectionately known as Charlotte Street), I was still going to a girls' senior secondary school where the education system was just as good as Notre Dame. When my mum came back to give me the verdict, I wasn't in the least bit bothered because most of my friends were going to Charlotte Street and that suited me just fine! It is only as I reflect and write that I realise Notre Dame would have had a real knock-on effect on what I chose to do with my future.

Primary 7 is really etched in my memory. I suppose we were all getting older and slightly more mature and that year of 1965/66 was a memorable one, not just because our fate was being decided about junior or secondary schools, but in the August of that year, the Commonwealth Games were due to be held. This coincided with Father Morgan's (parish priest of St Thomas', Riddrie) special jubilee, and the Primary 7 pupils were asked to host a concert whereby a number of schools participated. The concert was to be held in June 1966, just prior to the summer holidays, and parents were invited along. The church hall was big enough to host participators and audience alike, and the best act was to be awarded a cup or a plaque which we were informed was really prestigious and an outstanding achievement.

I don't remember our song title, but I do remember having to sing solo in front of Sister John which enabled her to choose the best singers in the class. I was one of the chosen pupils, and we practised for weeks on end until the night arrived of the concert. Naturally, I was really biased and thought our school would be a worthy winner.

I can't remember how many schools participated, but our choir didn't get to see the other acts because we were behind the stage. Anyway, despite my wanting to believe that St Thomas' had won the prize, I kind of knew that St Mungo's Primary School had romped home with the Maori love song, 'Tamaki Village Rotorua'.

Not only were the pupils more entertaining than us, but they also wore the New Zealand national dress. I was so disappointed with my mum that night, because that is all she could talk about when we were heading home. Every time I asked my mum if our choir was good, my mum kept telling me, "Not as good as St Mungo's Primary."

Summertime came round again and walking to and from school was just the natural thing to do. There was a mini fairground on the route home and songs like 'Hold tight, count to three, gotta stay close by me' by Dave Dee were blaring out and constantly playing in my head, as well as 'Groovy Kind of Love' by The Mindbenders. I really loved that summer and also became friends with a boy (shockarooney)! John Quinn and I were great pals, and a small crowd of us put our bus fares together to buy one of the teachers a box of chocolates. We waited in anticipation for Mrs Cairns to come out of the schoolyard so that we could give her the gift. My peers thought I should be the one to do so but dared me to give her a kiss as well. I have never refused a dare and, although my face was as red as a beetroot and I had my usual 'attack of the drips', I gave the teacher a kiss – something that was totally unheard of in 1966. I was really surprised at the reaction of a massive hug in return. Mrs Cairns was well chuffed but certainly not as chuffed as I was. None of us thought about buying Keatie Bugs a gift – she just wasn't worth it.

During our last weeks at primary school, we were allowed non-uniform clothes, and my mum always dressed me immaculately. By this point, I had just turned 12 years of age. On the very last day ever at St Thomas', Miss Keatings called me out of the playground line, and my immediate thoughts were, *what have I done now?* You can imagine my shock when she turned round and said to me, "That's a nice frock you're wearing, Eunice." I don't know if she had an attack of conscience, but it took me a long time to believe she had actually paid me a compliment! I suppose it was a nice ending to what had been (in the main) a really happy life at primary school.

CHAPTER 17 –
NEW BEGINNINGS

The summer of 1966 was the beginning of a new chapter of my life. As usual, I spent my time between Glenarm and Belfast and, looking back, I can't really say which I preferred. I had friends in both places but I was also an avid reader and had read every Enid Blyton book I could get my hands on. I loved the Famous Five and Malory Towers, and I took as many Malory Towers books as possible to keep me occupied during my summer holidays. My Belfast friends were amazed at the speed I could read and often on a wet summer's day, they would gather round me whilst I regaled them with adventures of a book I had just read.

I also loved Belfast because I was so used to city life but particularly my Aunt Cissie's home-made chips. I used to see how many I could stuff onto my fork at one time and then be devastated when they were all finished!

Glenarm had a particularly different way of life. My mum's cousin Marie was a music teacher and, being a spinster, was very set in her ways. She looked after her cousin Martha, and also her Uncle Tommy who always had the radio up full blast because he was so deaf.

Glenarm is in the Glens of Antrim, near the Giant's Causeway, where the countryside is stunning. The village itself is small, but the coastline was particularly beautiful, and when I wasn't swimming in the water with my friend Mona, I just enjoyed watching the waves battering against the rocks.

That summer was one of anticipation, because all I could think about was starting my new secondary school and hoping that Rosie would still be friends with me. When I look back, I realise that I loved Rosie so much because she reminded me of Hayley Mills, the actress whose famous films were *Pollyanna* and *The Parent Trap*. There was a remake of *The Parent Trap* many years later but absolutely nothing like the original. I adored Hayley Mills, and my mum would save really hard to take me to all her films. I am digressing slightly, but I feel it important to tell you why Rosie was so special. She used to sneak me in to Dennistoun private swimming baths on a weekly basis, and that weekly treat was absolute bliss. It made me admire Rosie more because we did so many adventurous things together.

Leaving Ireland in the summer of 1966 didn't cause me to feel the usual wrench. By this point, I was travelling by ferry from Larne to Stranraer and then caught the train from Stranraer to Glasgow where my mum was ready to meet me coming off the train. I felt excited to see her and could hardly wait for the day when I would be shopping for my new school uniform. I knew my mum had saved really hard, and I accompanied her to Glasgow town to get my uniform. We were off to Paisleys again to find the uniform for Our Lady and St Francis. The difference between getting my uniform in Paisleys and some other city centre shop was that they welcomed cash buyers only, and the brown 'Charlotte Street' blazer's braiding only came halfway down the front of the blazer, whereas uniforms bought with Caledonian or Provident cheques (a form of loan) had the braiding all the way down and round the back of the blazer. I chose a pleated skirt and a brown felt hat with blue braiding instead of a flared skirt and a beret. Come to think of it, despite my mum not having two pennies to rub together, she bred a little snob. (Nowadays, I try to keep my snobbish side in check, but occasionally it rears its ugly head.)

CHAPTER 18 –
MY HIGH SCHOOL DAYS

In August 1966, the day came when it was time for me to go to school, and with a last look in the mirror, dinner money in pocket and a big, brown, leather briefcase at my side, I left the house about 8 a.m. I walked across the road and met my friend Veronica McLaughlin, and the first thing I noticed was that she didn't have a Paisleys blazer. (See what I mean about snobbery?) However, Veronica was a really lovely girl, looked great in her uniform and I was glad of her company, because we had a fair walk down Haghill Road to the main street where our bus stop was.

Our School Blazer

I had already done a dummy run with my mum, so I knew where to get off in the Saltmarket area of Glasgow city centre. At that time, it was a bit of a dump but is now part of the Merchant City area where accommodation costs a fortune and has an endless choice of bars and restaurants as well as street carnivals and outdoor markets. In fact, as I'm writing this, I can hardly believe how upmarket that area has become.

Our Lady & St Francis Senior Secondary School for Girls

After Veronica and I got off the bus, we had another long walk along London Road until we got to Charlotte Street by which time my heart was beating so hard, I thought it would burst out of my chest. Of course, we weren't the only ones making our way along London Road. There were so many brown uniforms that we looked like something out of a chocolate drop factory. As we approached our secondary school, the smell of Camp Coffee flooded our nostrils. The school was right next to a coffee factory and it completely permeated the air. However, the smell of coffee just added to the excitement of going to high school.

Once we were inside the confines of Charlotte Street, we were allocated our form rooms. I was in 1F2 and, reflecting on how clever I was in primary school, I think I should have been in a Latin class – even 1L2 would have done. Perhaps wee Keatie Bugs had something to do with that as well but perhaps not. I will never know. 1F2 had a great form teacher called Miss Fleming, and we all looked forward to her classes because she was easier going than most of the teachers.

Obviously, a timetable was part of the school curriculum, and nothing could have prepared me for the amount of jotters and books we were given to equip us for all the different classes. Because I was in a French class, I never learned Latin, but I did enjoy French and convinced myself that I was much better off than my Latin student peers.

My best subject was English, and my English teacher was a lady called Miss Fitzpatrick (RIP). I was delighted to know that 'Fitzie' would be teaching me English because she had taught my cousin Maureen in St Mary's Primary School and that gave me an opportunity to introduce myself. I was determined to be one of the best at English but did not devote my attention to many of the other subjects that were part of my curriculum. This is something I regret bitterly, because my mum had scrimped and scraped to get me well-educated and I suppose I didn't fully appreciate what she had foregone as a result. In fact, my mother was eligible to apply for me to get free dinners but she wouldn't hear of it, and every Monday she gave me the appropriate dinner money for parents who only had one child (the more children in a family, the cheaper school dinners were). That must have been a great sacrifice for her because she didn't get benefits until a Monday, and I think she would have been tempted on many an occasion to dip into the money at weekends.

I am second from the right and my friend, Josephine O'Donnell, back second left

The class of 1F2 comprised of a lot of nice girls, and I was really friendly with a girl called Josephine O'Donnell who had been at St Thomas' Primary. Rosie was in 1F4 and, although we were still friends, we naturally sought friendship with our class peers. Josephine always had an amazing packed lunch with home-made cakes and she very generously shared them with me. There was another girl in my class (again from St Thomas') called Ellen Beaton, and there are two outstanding moments in my memory about this petite girl. The first is, during one interval, she came up to Josephine and said, "You have one blue eye and one brown eye, Josephine, and that just tickles me pink." I found this really amusing. The other moment was when we were in religious education discussing Catholics and Protestants. Our class discussion came heavily down on the side of Catholicism. Ellen was in the row in front of me and immediately shot her hand up. When the teacher asked her what she wanted, Ellen said, "I don't care what anyone says. My best friend is a Protestant and that's my daddy." I admired Ellen so much for her courage and that admiration was tinged with envy because, although my dad was also a Protestant, I couldn't exactly say he was *my* best friend.

Mary Murray was another girl I was friendly with in first year and sometimes, at the weekends and school nights, Mary would invite me to her house in Edinburgh Road in Glasgow. Edinburgh Road is in the east end, with mainly four-in-a-block-type houses and was classed as a really nice area. Again, Mary was an ex-St Thomas' Primary School pupil, so I had known her prior to going to Charlotte Street. There are a few things I remember about Mary. Her mum was a lovely person and always greeted me warmly. One instance was on 5 November 1966, which as you know is Bonfire Night. My own mother would never allow me anywhere near a firework because of the danger involved, but Mary's mum gave me a sparkler to hold and then lit it. I was absolutely delighted and couldn't wait to tell my mum, but her reaction to that was literally a damp squib.

Christmas was approaching. Mary told me that her mum was going to give her a watch, and when I asked her how she knew, I was rather shocked to hear that she had found it hidden somewhere. I suppose I have no right to say that considering the amount of plundering I did as a toddler. Anyway, Mary duly got her watch and she also got a pair of tights. In those days, tights were a precious commodity and, compared to my long socks at school, Mary's tights looked really glamorous. Mary promised to give me them as soon as she got a new pair and she kept her word.

Tragically, Mary's mum died in the new year of 1967. Naturally, Mary was off school to attend her mum's funeral and, whilst she was off, Miss Fleming tasked me with telling the rest of the pupils and arranging a collection for a small sympathy present for Mary. I was to do this in class and when I made the announcement, I shouted it out like everyone in the class was deaf, which caused the 40-odd pupils to gut themselves laughing including the teacher. It seemed to have the desired effect, however, because we managed to collect enough money to get some really nice toiletries.

Sweets and treats

Part of the delights of attending Charlotte Street was the fact that there was a sweetie factory close by where we 'chocolate drops' could get a bag of sweets for next to nothing. The staff who worked in the sweetie factory were never all that nice to us, and my theory (for what it is worth) is that the employees were not much older than us but, through lack of education, left school at 15 to help support their siblings and resented it.

Sweets and treats galore

Charlotte Street was also in close proximity to the famous Glickman's which is the oldest sweet shop in Glasgow, founded in 1903. What an amazing family business, originally founded by Mr Glickman who died in 2020. You could have your choice of any types of sweets from cola cubes to pineapple chunks, cherry lips to aniseed balls not forgetting bonbons and toffees. The sweets are all home-made and, whatever their recipe, the fact that Glickman's has stood the test of time is testimony to the founder whose quality and delightful array of confectionery made it difficult for us Charlotte Street pupils to choose from.

Our Lady and St Francis was very near the Glasgow Barras and Glasgow city centre. We pupils were forbidden by our headmistress, Sister Felicitas, to go the short walk into Glasgow town centre. This was something which always puzzled me but, in hindsight, I can understand now that any pupil caught shoplifting or guilty of any other misdemeanour would have disgraced the reputation of the school.

The beautiful St Alphonsus Roman Catholic Church on London Road (again within walking distance of the school) was founded in 1846 by a Conforti Xaverian priest. This priest was canonised in 2011, but this is a fact I was not aware of when every year, during Lent, the church was filled to capacity by teachers and pupils from Our Lady and St Francis. As young girls and subsequent teenagers, we never thought twice about missing Mass. Obviously, some girls who lived near the school went home at lunchtime and others elsewhere, but I just remember running out of school to the 1 p.m. Mass which normally lasted 30 minutes and then running back to school to eat my lunch with my school friends. Obviously, Glickman's and the sweetie factory became a no-go area during the six weeks of Lent because our penance allowed us to have healthier teeth and gums!

CHAPTER 19 –
THE LEGENDARY SISTER FELICITAS

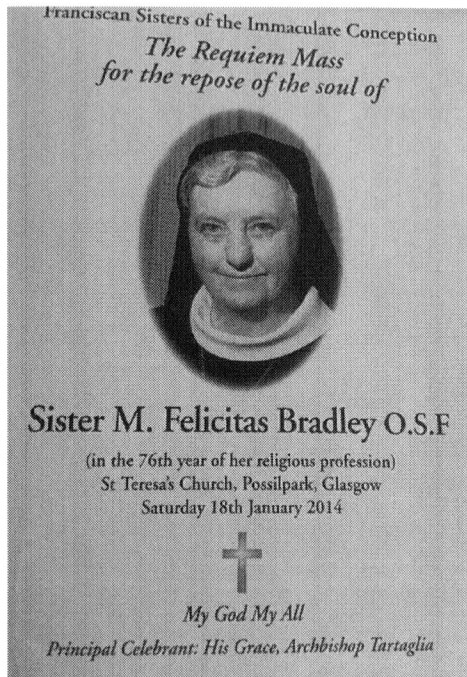

Franciscan Sisters of the Immaculate Conception
The Requiem Mass
for the repose of the soul of

Sister M. Felicitas Bradley O.S.F

(in the 76th year of her religious profession)
St Teresa's Church, Possilpark, Glasgow
Saturday 18th January 2014

✝

My God My All
Principal Celebrant: His Grace, Archbishop Tartaglia

One amazing lady

I have mentioned Sister Mary Felicitas, our headmistress, who was a formidable force and whose presence demanded instant silence. I can still hear her shouting, "Silence in the corridor there." If you were sent to Sister's office by a teacher for a misdemeanour, you would get a good tongue-wagging. What head teacher, come rain, hail or shine, could command every single girl in the school to give up 15 minutes of her lunch break to say the Rosary during the month of October? (*The Rosary* is an important devotion that honours Mary while focusing on the events of the life of Jesus Christ.) It amazes me to this day that one woman could have such a presence and influence on our lives. I am therefore so glad to share some of the following obituary which appeared in the *Glasgow Herald* in 2014:

Sister Mary Felicitas Bradley
Educator and Superior General of the Franciscan Sisters of the Immaculate Conception.
Born: July 12, 1918; Died: January 11, 2014

SISTER Mary Felicitas Bradley, who has died aged 95, was for almost a quarter of a century the inspirational head teacher at Our Lady and St Francis Secondary School in Glasgow. She later went on to become the leader of the Franciscan Sisters of the Immaculate Conception, the only Catholic religious order to be founded in Scotland.

She died less than a week after celebrating a remarkable 75 years as a nun. Although formally retired, she had continued to work tirelessly within her local community on the South Side of Glasgow, tending to the poor and the sick.

However, she will be remembered best for the many years she spent at the all-girl Our Lady and St Francis Secondary, better known as Charlotte Street School. As first an English teacher and then its head teacher, she helped create a truly outstanding school which provided exceptional educational opportunities to generations of young women many of whom came from poor and disadvantaged families.

Situated in the East End of the city, close to Glasgow Green, the school taught as many as 1,000 girls at any given time. Sister Felicitas knew every one of them by name.

A talented teacher and perceptive leader, she successfully managed the school's seamless transition to co-educational status. Charlotte Street closed its doors in 1989 following its merger with St Mungo's Academy, an all-boys secondary situated nearby.

Margaret McGowan Bradley was born in Hamilton, Lanarkshire. Her mother was a teacher and her father a local journalist. She was taught at St Mary's Primary, Hamilton, and then Elmwood Secondary in Bothwell, both schools run by the Franciscan order she was destined to join.

She entered the convent in 1936 straight from school and made her first confession in 1939. Now Sister Felicitas, she studied English and history at Glasgow University, graduating in 1943. After a year's teacher-training at Notre Dame, she became an English teacher at Our Lady and St Francis.

Apart from a brief period at the end of the Second World War (when she had to move temporarily to St Mungo's Primary to make way for male teachers who had been demobbed and returned to their jobs at Charlotte Street) she spent the next 35 years there.

She was 38 when she was appointed head teacher in 1956, replacing the formidable Mother Philippa who had taken over as Mother Abbess of the Glasgow-based religious order.

Under her leadership, the school acquired a reputation for academic achievement. Sister Felicitas demanded the very best from her girls. She knew every one of them, knew what each of them was capable of achieving, and helped them reach their goals and realise their ambitions.

Though a disciplinarian, she was also compassionate. If anyone – whether it be a teacher or a pupil – found themselves in trouble or difficulty, she would go to great lengths to help them.

When she resigned her post in 1980, she was one of the most respected and influential educators in Glasgow and was awarded the OBE for services to education and the Pro Ecclesia et Pontifice, the Catholic Church's Cross of Honour.

Now in her sixties, Sister Felicitas was ready to follow in her predecessor's footsteps and become head of the Franciscan Sisters of the Immaculate Conception. She was elected Superior General (the new title for Mother Abbess), serving two six-year terms in the post.

She took up the job at a time when the religious order was expanding. It had taken its mission well beyond Scotland with projects and houses in England, Ireland, the US and Nigeria. As Superior General, she established the order's first mission in Kenya, starting a major project to combat AIDS and HIV. One of the saddest moments of her life was when two Scots-born Franciscan sisters were killed in a road accident in Kenya. The tragedy prompted the order to re-think its plans and, had it not been for the insistence of a third sister who had survived the accident, the mission would have been abandoned.

The overseas missions meant a lot to Sister Felicitas and, after her retirement in 1992, she went out to Nigeria to work alongside her fellow sisters.

Back in Glasgow, she settled in a house which the Order ran in Dixon Avenue. She fashioned the property into a house of prayer. Every day, whatever the weather, she walked the streets of Govanhill and Crosshill, visiting the sick and giving them Communion. She often said this was one of the most fulfilling periods of her life.

I am so very proud to say that I had the privilege to know Sister Felicitas both within and outwith the school confines, but I'll tell you more about that later.

CHAPTER 20 –
JUST ANOTHER 'BROWN GIRL IN THE RING' (SONG BY BONEY M)

I'll now take you back to the first year at school. I was really only interested in English, French and religious education classes – the latter because it was, to me, an hour of not really having to work. I guess I was quite lazy when it came to it and working towards exams meant a quick look at my books the night before. In the sewing class, I was so bad that the teacher ended up finishing my apron in order that she could give me a pass mark. Obviously, I excelled at English and came second in the class next to Josephine O'Donnell who was first in the class with one higher mark. Josephine had the right idea, however, because not only did she excel at English, she excelled in most of her subjects and it was that diligence that separated us in the second year when she was moved to a Latin class whilst I was stuck in a lower French class. Most of our teachers seemed absolutely ancient. My geography teacher, Miss Rafferty, looked old and frail, but she was amicable and very gentle. I was terrible at geography and that was no reflection on Miss Rafferty's teaching – I just did not pay attention.

There was a teacher called Miss Quail who was in charge of the library. Miss Quail had two grey plaits wrapped around each ear, and we pupils were under the impression it was because she only had one ear! Every time I went to the library, which was just across the hanging corridor overlooking the assembly hall, I occupied my time looking at Miss Quail's ears from every angle I could in order to confirm or dispel the myth about the one-ear theory. I never found out and Miss Quail, for the remainder of my school life, always wore the two grey plaits around her ears.

After our exams were finished and results given, obviously we all breathed a sigh of relief. I passed some subjects and was absolute rubbish at others, but I don't recall my mum being mad at me so I must have done okay. I guess the real time for knuckling down was from third year upwards – oh boy, I got that one wrong!

School broke up for the summer holidays in June 1967, and I was really envious of the school pupils who were Italian because they went back to see their relatives and, to me, Italy just sounded so sunny and amazing. However, I had Belfast and I think it was that year my mum decided she was coming on holiday with me. My Aunt Vera had asked if Maureen could go as well which meant I had a companion.

The due day arrived, and we all went to Central Station in Glasgow to board the train bound for Stranraer which was timed for us to meet the Stranraer-to-Belfast ferry line. Maureen and I chatted non-stop with excitement but, after a while, decided that the fairly long (well it seemed like that) train journey merited a sleep. We arrived at our destination and already, Glasgow was an all-too-distant memory for me as we waited our turn to walk up the plank to the boat. The sea from Stranraer to Larne is a choppy one. In fact, it is very prone to snap gales, huge waves and if you are susceptible to seasickness, you can bet your life that it will happen whilst crossing the Irish Sea.

My mum told Maureen and me that if any of us felt sick, we should go up on deck and watch the waves. Probably an old wives' tale but none of us were sick on that crossing, unlike other times when I have done nothing but wretch.

When we finally arrived in Belfast, my Aunt Cissie was waiting for us and, after a short bus ride, we arrived at 27 Cawnpore Street which was going to be home to us for the next four weeks. Aunt Cissie was always busying herself in the kitchen which let the three of us unpack our suitcases in time for tea. My Aunt Cissie's house was quite big, but my recollection of sleeping arrangements is very vague.

The infamous Falls Road is the main road through Belfast and predominantly Catholic. Conversely, the Shankill Road – one of the other main roads in Belfast – is predominantly Unionist and Protestant. Visions of the 'Red Hand of Ulster' and 'King Billy riding on his horse' were painted all over the walls.

The Shankill Road left you in no doubt what territory you were in, and many fights broke out between the youths of the Shankill

Road and those of the Falls Road. There was always a feeling that a bubble was about to burst, and that bubble certainly burst in 1969. I'll tell you a little bit about that later but, in the meantime, I will concentrate on the Falls Road which runs from Divis Street to the city centre of Belfast.

On a lovely, sunny day, my mum, Maureen and I decided to walk up to the Black Mountain which meant walking from the Falls Road through to Divis Street until we reached the mountain. It has always astounded me how you could be at the heart of Belfast city one minute and climbing a mountain the next. The 'three musketeers' set out that afternoon to climb up the mountain which is 1,568 ft high. We did not reach the top but, at the halfway mark, we decided to rest and take in the spectacular scenery over the Mountains of Mourne, Donegal and even Scotland. Normally, if you were going on such an adventure, you would have prepared a packed lunch, but we forgot.

When the three of us eventually sat down to rest, my mum produced a bar of chocolate which we split amongst the three of us, and I swear to God that chocolate never tasted so good. We were all really hungry and could have wolfed half a dozen bars of chocolate, but that memory of sharing exactly what we had will live with me forever. When one is young, you don't really appreciate the value of money and, as I ponder over those summer days in Belfast, I realise that it must have been a daunting experience for my Aunt Cissie having an extra three hungry mouths to feed.

Interestingly enough, she worked as a wardrobe mistress in the theatre in Belfast and got to meet many famous people including the English comic, actor and film-maker Charlie Chaplin. My Aunt Cissie's husband worked in Wolverhampton, because it was too difficult at that time for an Irish Catholic man to be gainfully employed. It makes no sense to me now, but bigotry was rife back then and being of the Catholic faith didn't help when applying or going for a job interview.

I've digressed a little bit but felt I had to give you that information prior to coming back from the Black Mountain and being more than ready for teatime, by which time my Aunt Cissie was home from work. On this occasion, there were no home-made chips, but my disappointment was abated when Maureen and I were asked to go to the chip shop instead. Maureen would probably be able to tell you more about this experience than me, because she reminded me of it a few years ago. We duly went to a chip shop and when it came time for us to be served, the proprietor asked us where we were staying. When we told her that it was Cawnpore Street, we were ordered out of the shop and told to go to the *other* chip shop. It seems that even the chips were either Catholic or Protestant!

At this juncture, I'm going to tell you a little bit more about Maureen. We were both the same height, but she inherited her dark brown eyes from her father whilst my eyes are blue just like my mum's. I have previously alluded to Maureen's hair. The length and thickness of it wasn't just Maureen's pride and joy (and rightly so), but also my Aunt Vera's. My Aunt Vera would always refer to her youngest as 'Ma Maureen' and she treated her like a princess. No matter what crisis befell, Maureen always came first.

Maureen was a good dancer and, eventually, we both went to Jean McLelland's School of Dancing where we were taught ballet, tap and Highland dancing. My Aunt Vera worked her socks off to ensure that money was available for Maureen's dance lessons but, although I too loved dancing, my mum just could not keep up with the fees required and therefore I had to quit. It's a bit ironic really, because although my Aunt Vera was holding down a job, she would borrow my mum's social security money on a regular basis because money was so tight. In fairness, although my Uncle Christie worked as well, it was not uncommon in those days for men to dip into their weekly pay packets to prioritise alcohol and gambling before giving the remaining money (if any) to put food on the table for the family. I don't remember my Uncle Christie without a wee drink in him on a Friday night (pay day), and I guess he deserved it after labouring all week, but Maureen and I benefitted from his benevolent nature when he was a bit tipsy because he would produce chocolate bars and crisps for us which we eagerly devoured. In fact, it was my Uncle Christie who introduced me to cheese and onion crisps when they were first marketed, which is a bit hard to believe nowadays when we have so many different flavours. I can still savour the taste of the cheese and onion crisps as opposed to eating plain ones.

After we all came home from Belfast, it wasn't long before school beckoned again and, of course, I was no longer 'a wee first year' but a second-year pupil. In my six years at Our Lady and St Francis (yes, I did stay six years), second year was the only year I did not have Miss Fitzpatrick for English. Shakespeare was always the order of the day in an English class and, having read *A Midsummer Night's Dream*, it was now time to concentrate on *The Merchant of Venice*. We had a lovely young English teacher, Miss Gallagher, who was the opposite of 'Fitzie'. She was much more relaxed and carefree and, when it came to essays and exams, her marking was way higher than Miss Fitzpatrick.

One day, Miss Gallagher decided that she would select some pupils to do some public speaking and the topic was 'pet hates'. My desk was at the front of the class and I kept my head down in the hope that I wouldn't be picked. Yes, you guessed it, I was first up and I was desperately thinking what pets I hated because I had taken my teacher literally. It was only when she said, "Is school one of them?" that I realised I could forget about animals and come up with a sensible answer. I remember saying that I hated being forced to go to my aunt's when I really didn't feel like it, a statement which was met with approval from the class, thank God. I said that was my only pet hate and, with a scarlet face, I went back to my seat. I couldn't concentrate on anything else but my lucky escape from thinking literally. It reminded me of the time I was at the Brownies and Brown Owl asked me to do a 'P' on the floor, something which I took literally until the Brown Owl used her finger to draw the outline of the letter 'P'.

Second year at school meant quite a lot of new friends. Rosie was now in a Latin class as was Josephine O'Donnell and many others who actually decided to study in first year. I loved school but sometimes I think I treated it as one big joke. I didn't really like PE because we had a teacher called Miss Kelly (RIP). She hated the smell of body odour and made sure we knew about it. She was also very strict when it came to having our gym kit with us, and if anyone had forgotten theirs, they knew all about it. I guess in hindsight she just tried to keep things orderly, but no one ever wanted to incur her wrath.

When the weather was half decent, we would play netball in the schoolyard and, because I was taller than most of my peers, I was goal shooter. I used to pray like mad that I would score a goal in case Miss Kelly went nuts at me. In second year, we were entitled to our BCG vaccine and had to form an orderly line prior to being inoculated. Miss Kelly oversaw the line and scrutinised each and every pupil to regulate not only good behaviour but to ensure we looked smart in our uniforms. As always, I was immaculately turned out, so you can imagine the feeling of dread I had when Miss Kelly asked me to step out of the line to have a word with me. I was quaking and shaking in my shoes, at the same time wondering what on earth I had done wrong. My hair was short in first year but by second year it was long enough for a high ponytail. However, because I was showing too much of my neck, Miss Kelly kindly asked me to tie my hair back at the nape of my neck instead. Lots of my peers were whispering, "Don't do it Eunice, your hair looks fine as it is", but there was no way on God's earth I was going to defy Miss Kelly, so I quickly pulled out my elastic band and tied my hair back at the nape of my neck which earned me a "good girl" from Miss Kelly and a "teacher's pet" from my peers. Sometimes you just can't win.

CHAPTER 21 –
LIVING IN HAGHILL (OR HATCHET HILL AS SOME MAY SAY)

I want to tell you a little of the council house we stayed at in Appin Road, Glasgow. At the Alexandra Parade entrance, Appin Road was classed as Dennistoun, but further along, where I lived, it was called Haghill. At first the area wasn't too bad, but eventually it was known as Hatchet Hill due to the amount of thugs that took up residence there. When anyone asked me where I lived, I would always say Dennistoun and not Haghill. Even to this day, the inherent snob in me will not admit to being brought up anywhere but the Dennistoun area of Glasgow. You can imagine just how tough it was for me having to navigate Haghill Road going forwards and backwards to school every day, particularly when I chose to wear a hat instead of a beret. It wasn't so bad in the morning, because Veronica McLaughlin and I would set out around 8.30 a.m. to catch the bus to school. However, Veronica wasn't always around on the way home from school and I was forced to run the gauntlet to escape catty remarks and jeers from teenagers who resided at the left-hand side of Haghill Road. I am deliberately saying the left-hand side because at the right there was a cleansing department where mice and rats were the order of the day. The place was infested with them and, because I was trying to escape the jeers, taunts and downright bullying from the teenagers who lived opposite, I had to cross the pavement just outside the cleansing department. One day, when my opponents were not around, I decided to leisurely walk up the right-hand side of the road (I was too scared to go up the left side in case some of the usual bully culprits would be hiding in their common close). Anyway, just when I thought all was well with the world and I was getting some verbal respite, a bloody big rat ran over my foot!

However, I am definitely not a coward and the following week I decided that I would have to tackle the bullying head-on. After alighting the bus and a backwards glance at the nearby bridge which had 'tongs ya bass' graffiti everywhere, I decided that I would walk up Haghill Road on the left-hand side. I was, of course, in full uniform, hat on the head and a heart that was thumping out of my chest. It was a sunny day and the gang were out in full force. I heard the usual jeers and comments, but I decided to stop and introduce myself to everyone, ask them a bit about themselves and, after a brief conversation, I waved a friendly goodbye just in time to hear someone say, "She's okay. She's no really a snob"! This tactic really worked, because after that my shoes were rat- and mice-free due to being able to walk on the left side of Haghill Road. Never again did I get any grief from those teenage girls and boys, and the valuable lesson for me was that if you treated people the same way as you expected to be treated yourself, you couldn't go far wrong. (Well, that and a cheeky wee decade of the Rosary just in case.)

Mother's Day

At the bottom of Haghill Road there was the less busy end of Duke Street in Dennistoun. It may have changed now because it's years since I've been there. Anyway, there were a few small shops, one of which was an Asian shop with a plastic parrot in the window. The shop opened from Monday through to Sunday, and there is a reason for my telling you this which I will get to in a minute.

Every time I was out with my mum and we passed the Asian shop, my mum would pass remarks about the colourful parrot. It was the month of March and really cold, but I decided that if I walked to and from school – a good five miles round trip – I could save my bus fare and have the right amount to buy the parrot for Mother's Day. The parrot cost two shillings in old money which would be 12 pence now. I carefully counted out the money and had an extra six pence to buy my mum a card. On the Saturday prior to Mother's Day, I carefully wrapped up the parrot and wrote a nice message on my mum's card. I really felt I had accomplished something because my mum was none the wiser to my leaving early to go to school and getting back home a bit later after school. I went to Mass early on the Sunday but couldn't concentrate for any length of time due to anticipating my mum's face when she saw the parrot. As soon as I got back from Mass, I gave my mum her card, which she was delighted with, and eagerly waited for her reaction when she saw the parrot. You can imagine my dismay when she opened the brown paper packaging, looked at the parrot and said, "Why did you buy me that Eunice, I hate it!" I was absolutely devastated. I couldn't believe my mum didn't want it, because she always commented on the parrot when we went by the Asian shop. What I perhaps should have realised was that the comments were derogatory and I should have listened properly. I picked up the parrot (which I actually quite liked) and, with tears streaming down my face, I went back to the Asian shop to see if I could change the parrot for something else. The shopkeeper must have seen my tear-stained cheeks and felt sorry for me, because he gave me a little cream lamp with a bulb which cost more than the parrot. The parrot then took its rightful perch back in the shop window.

CHAPTER 22 –
MY SATURDAY JOB

In 1967, I decided it was time I got a Saturday job. The first one was in a busy fish and chip shop, and you were given your dinner free of charge. When it came to my break, I ordered steak because I hadn't had that in a long time. I didn't really like working there and decided, after a few weeks, that I would not be returning. It was back to the drawing board for me because I really needed some pocket money. I decided, one day after school, that I would walk the whole length of Duke Street in Glasgow, go into every shop available and ask for a Saturday job. For those of you who are familiar with Glasgow, you will know that Duke Street is very long and stretches almost as far as the city centre. Despite various knock-backs, I undauntedly continued on my quest until I came across a hairdressing shop called Peter's. It was only a ten-minute walk away from where I lived, and I was overjoyed when Peter offered me a job. He told me that my salary would be £1 per week and that I would get 15 minutes for my lunch. I had to start at 9 a.m. the following Saturday and finish at 6 p.m. The pay on offer was completely incomparable with the hours I had to work, not forgetting the short lunch break, but I was absolutely desperate to earn some money and was just glad that I could now rest my weary legs and break the good news to my mum. I had some great fun at that hairdressing shop, but I'll tell you more about that later.

I have to say that 1967 was a really good year for me and not just because I now had a wee job and was doing really well at school (apart from chemistry and geography which I hated), but because my mum decided that she would also go back to her previous employment as a bus conductress. Years ago, all corporation buses had a driver and a bus conductress – affectionately known as a 'clippie' because they punched bus tickets with a machine. After school, I sometimes went swimming and then jumped on a number six bus knowing that my mum was the conductress. My mum always paid for my ticket because she was naturally honest and also because an inspector could embark the bus en route. I always went upstairs on the bus and settled into a window seat near the front, but inevitably I would fall sound asleep only to be awakened by some kind soul tapping me on the shoulder in case I had missed my stop for getting off. I was full of pride when I said it was my mum's bus and I was just having a nap.

My mum was quite well paid as a bus conductress but obviously had to be disciplined with her break time in order to stick to the bus timetable. My mum would come home for her break, and she would tell me exactly what had to be cooked for dinner in order for her to eat a hot meal and then go back to work. I always complied with her wishes and things ran smoothly for a while, but one day I had brought a friend home from school and didn't cook the dinner early enough. When my mum appeared, the potatoes were only parboiled and she went mental at me in front of my friend. I will never forget the humiliation and embarrassment of trying to hide the tears in my eyes. My friend asked me if I was crying, but I managed to mumble some excuse about having watery eyes due to the steam coming from the potato pot. I think by this point my mum was 'bad with her nerves' (as she would say), because approximately six or seven months after that my mum stopped working. Obviously, this meant that we were almost back to square one, as far as our financial situation was concerned, which meant that my £1.50 from my hairdressing job was stretched to capacity. If you have been reading my book carefully – and I truly hope that you are interested in the content – you will have noticed that I said £1.50 instead of £1. That's because Peter asked me to work at the hairdresser's after school on a Friday for another 50 pence which kind of made up for all those hours on a Saturday.

In second year at school, I became friendly with a girl called Rosemary who was kind and generous, particularly when it came to handing out sweets. We had a classroom friendship but rarely outside of school. Rosemary told me that Miss Fitzpatrick was her cousin which was music to my ears because not only did I find out that Fitzie's first name was Jean but that she stayed in Onslow Drive in Dennistoun. I remember thinking that anyone related to Miss Fitzpatrick had to be a really nice person and Rosemary certainly was. She stayed in the Tollcross area of Glasgow and, because my mum would be working on Christmas Day, I was invited to spend Christmas with Rosemary and her family. My mum was getting paid double time for her shift, and I could hardly contain my excitement about going to my friend's house. My mum didn't tell me what time her shift finished and I never thought to ask.

Prior to leaving the house, I gave my mum and Roy a kiss and set off to catch one of the few buses in service to Tollcross Road. When I arrived at Rosemary's house, her whole family made me feel really welcome. The house was decorated for the festive season, and I hadn't felt that warm, fuzzy feeling since Auntie Joan had bought my mum a Christmas tree when we were living in Greenvale Street. I had a blast of a day and got home around 8 p.m. with Christmas music having a field day inside my head. I lived on the top floor of Appin Road and just down below was a lady called May Dollan, a spinster and a real dog lover. I liked May and found her quite modern particularly when it came to current pop albums. She was always kind to me but, on that Christmas Day in 1967, I had hardly gone past her door when she came out and read me the riot act about leaving Roy for so long. I was scarlet with embarrassment and mumbled an apology, but it wasn't good enough until she saw me five minutes later with Roy on a lead. Despite that incident, May and I have kept in touch over the years via Christmas cards and, although she was probably right about Roy being left too long, I felt Christmas Day wasn't really the time for bad-temperedness.

That Christmas, my mum was able to afford more presents than usual because of the extra money, but one of the best presents I have ever received came in the shape and form of Elizabeth Ann Thorley who was born on 6 December 1967. She was the youngest child of Joan and Charles Thorley. This new, little baby girl with blonde, curly hair and brown eyes was to be the sister I never had, and I have to say that the bond Elizabeth and I have has never been broken. I'll tell you more about Elizabeth as this book unfolds, because she has remained the one constant in my life and will always have a very special place in my heart.

A Christmas miracle

Shampoo and set

I'm going to take you back to Peter's the hairdressing shop. Although I walked the whole of Duke Street to find a Saturday job, the one job I always wanted was to work in a hairdresser's, and I think this was influenced by Auntie Joan who (as mentioned previously) was a qualified hairdresser. (In fact, at the age of ten, Auntie Joan gave me my first perm, and I really thought I was the bee's knees with my curly hair.)

Peter's shop was quite small, but there was a great atmosphere in the place and certainly plenty of customers who came in all shapes and sizes. My job was to shampoo, clean the shop and go get the lunches. I remember this vividly because the lunches always consisted of rolls with cheese and crisps. I liked the staff because they were cool and not that much older than me. However, when anyone asked me if I was going to be a hairdresser when I left school, I used to feel quite offended. The snobbish side of me always rose to the surface and I suppose I was too immature to look upon hairdressing as a work of art. In those days, when you were shampooing a client's hair, they would sit with their faces to the sink, which was all very well until the regular, well-endowed ladies came in with heads that looked like peas on top of a mountain. These heavily endowed ladies were the bane of my life because, inevitably, I would completely soak them when trying to shampoo their hair. This led to me being reprimanded by Peter, and the only way I could avoid drowning them was to use as little water as possible. At first, I didn't get the right mix of water and shampoo, which led to vigorous towel drying prior to one of the girls taking over, but eventually I worked it out and there were no more complaints. I did feel a bit guilty when these ladies gave me a tip but certainly not guilty enough to refuse.

Third year at Charlotte Street

Third year at Charlotte Street

Third year at school was fast approaching, and my mum greatly influenced my choice of subjects. English was, of course, compulsory as was arithmetic, French and religious education, but apart from that we were free to choose our other main subjects. I wanted to choose domestic science, but my mum nearly had a fit. She told me, in no uncertain terms, that I would not be leaving school at 15 years of age and therefore should be choosing subjects in keeping with my level of intelligence. In order to appease my mum, I chose German and my mum compromised by allowing me to choose art. I thought art would be easy although I couldn't paint or draw to save myself. I couldn't have been more wrong. The excitement of being a third-year pupil soon waned. It was brilliant that I had Fitzie again for English, and I just managed to get by in French, but for German I had a teacher called Mrs Alexander. She was a nice lady but my German grammar was rubbish. I hated German and would have done anything to get out of that class.

The art class wasn't much better. I had a teacher called Miss Fynn who tried her best with me to no avail. No matter how hard I tried, my art was never good enough. I remember, on one occasion, having to draw a building as my art homework to be done over the weekend. That particular weekend, Maureen and I went to stay with Robert (who was now married to Kathleen) and on the Sunday I chose to draw a building overlooking their front window. I was pleased with myself because it was the best artwork I had done, and I thought it truly reflected the architecture of the building. As far as I was concerned, Rennie Mackintosh didn't have a look-in!

My English homework was an essay and, once again, I secretly complimented myself on my outstanding work so, instead of dreading another week at school (despite the German), I was actually looking forward to it. I handed in my English essay and could hardly wait for it to be marked. On the Wednesday of that week, my essay was handed back to me with the following comments: "Your story is good and your writing is very good but your grammar lets you down badly." I failed my English essay for the first time ever.

On reflection, I probably got too carried away with the story, but I will never forget those comments. Just when I thought things would not get any worse, Miss Fynn took one look at my artwork and told me that I should not have picked art as a subject. She advised me to choose something else because I was only good at drawing head shapes. I was absolutely gutted.

The art class merited a double period, and I thought I would have a go at Russian. What a terrible mistake that was. The class consisted of very studious pupils who were already familiar with the Russian alphabet. I just couldn't catch up and, once again, I found myself getting as much opposition for Russian as I had for German. I was desperate to get out of both German and Russian classes when I suddenly had this amazing brainwave that if I dropped German and Russian, which equated to two periods, I could do the double period of domestic science. I duly did this with an overwhelming feeling of relief. At last, I was free from German and being the bane of Mrs Alexander's life. I knew I would have to tell my mum but, considering I was thrown out of art, I figured she would be okay about my choices. Oh my God, my mother went ballistic. The following week, she marched up to the school, told Mrs Alexander that I would be going back to the German class and, after speaking to Sister Felicitas, it was agreed that my spare, single period of approximately 30 minutes would be a free one which I would spend in the Assembly Hall. I was the only pupil in third year with a spare period in my timetable, and I was utterly ashamed.

I think all of this had a knock-on effect on my health, because I caught one virus after the other and spent half of third year at Elizabeth's house. My mum was asked to babysit Elizabeth to allow Auntie Joan to get back to work. This was a great arrangement, as far as I was concerned, because it meant I got more time to spend with Elizabeth and, due to my poor health, I was avoiding German. My mum was never as strict with me when she was looking after Elizabeth, and Auntie Joan's shopping was more exciting than my mum's which meant that mealtimes always consisted of a dessert to follow, normally Angel Delight.

CHAPTER 23 –
SUMMERTIME AND THE LIVING
WAS CERTAINLY NOT EASY

The summer rolled round once again. I couldn't wait to go on my summer holiday in Belfast, because my Aunt Cissie's youngest son Gerard was getting married, and I was really looking forward to the wedding. Although my mum was invited, she couldn't really afford for us both to have a holiday, so she bought me a new dress and hat and told me to get the heels of my dress shoes repaired at the cobblers. I will never forget that year of 1969, not just because of the wedding, but it was the year of trouble between Catholics and Protestants and many lives were lost in the conflict. At first, I didn't pay too much attention because I was now 15 years old and into fashion and make-up, but my Aunt Cissie's eyes were glued to the television at every opportunity and I knew then that things were serious.

Aunt Cissie's son Gerry was due to get married on 15 August. Obviously, the church ceremony at St Patrick's had already been booked, as was the Reception Hall, but we all found ourselves just living from one day to the next. Riots were breaking out everywhere between the Irish Republican Army and the Ulster Volunteer Force, and what seemed to be a clash between the two organisations led to almost 30 years of hatred and bigotry which claimed the lives of 3,600 people.

Gerard's older brother Seamus was a member of the Irish Republican Army and ended up serving time in Long Kesh Prison, more commonly known as the Maze. However, this happened many years later. Belfast 1969 had a real ugly feel to it. My awareness of the Catholic/Protestant division of the Falls Road and the Shankill Road was certainly heightened during that summer. I think I've previously mentioned that my Aunt Cissie stayed in Cawnpore Street in Belfast and just round the corner there was a cobblers' shop where I left my dress shoes to be heeled. Just prior to the wedding, anyone living in Cawnpore Street was evacuated to the nearest Catholic school where we were given mats to sleep on and blankets to cover us. The school hall was packed with people, and I admit to being quite excited about my new adventure. My poor Aunt Cissie was really worried that she wouldn't have a house to go back to because bombs were going off everywhere and it was pot luck if you managed to escape them.

The following morning, we were told that it was safe to return to our homes, but you can imagine my dismay when I found out that the cobblers' shop in Bombay Street had been bombed. All I could think of was that I needed shoes for the forthcoming wedding, and I nipped the ears of my Aunt Cissie until she took me into Belfast town to get me a new pair. In the grand scheme of things, I only lost my shoes whilst so many people were losing their lives. I don't think I truly understood the severity of the situation and thought it would just blow over. St Patrick's Church remained standing, but the hall where Gerry and Mairead were going to have their reception was a pile of rubble which meant they had to find another venue with hardly a moment's notice. Although things were really grim, Mairead's family gathered in her house for a party prior to the wedding. I was invited and had a brilliant time. I had a bit of a crush on one of Mairead's brothers, but he was studying for the priesthood at the time so I knew it could only be a crush. It didn't stop me dancing with him to a song called 'Little Arrows' which had been released in 1968 by an artist called Leapy Lee.

The week before the wedding, my cousin Madge came over from Scotland with her daughter Allison who was to be a flower girl. Allison was an adorable child, and I was delighted to see both her and Madge. The wedding itself I don't remember too much about, apart from us all saying 'cheese' for a family photograph. I think the events leading up to the wedding had been far more eventful for me, but I was glad that the actual wedding went without a hitch and that I was going to have the company of my relatives on my return journey to Scotland.

Madge and I always got on really well and, whenever the opportunity arose, Maureen and I would go visit her in the Maryhill area of Glasgow. Her husband Andy was great fun and would turn up the radio volume as soon as a favourite pop song was playing. I enjoyed those times and didn't mind helping with the housework, particularly when Madge had a rotten pregnancy with her son Allan.

Before I knew it, fourth year was looming and so were my O levels. With my appalling attendance in third year, I found myself playing catch-up all the time and had little interest in any of my subjects apart from English. The fourth, fifth and sixth year pupils could now attend homework classes from 4.20 p.m. until 6.20 p.m. This allowed for study time as well as homework, and I have to applaud the dedicated teachers who facilitated this but it was lost on me. Hindsight is a wonderful thing, and I should have been in really good shape for my O levels with all the extra schooling, but the simple truth is that I just did not apply myself. I put in these extra hours at school and probably gave my mum false hope (something I am not proud of), but as soon as I finished my homework, I would ask the presiding teacher if I could go to the library where I would meet up with my friends and then go wandering about until it was nearly 6.20 p.m. I usually got home about 7 p.m., had my tea, read a book and went to bed.

CHAPTER 24 –
MY ATTEMPTS AT PLAYING PIANO

Whilst I was in fourth year, I decided that I should have piano lessons because my mum was earning a bit of extra money looking after Elizabeth and I thought she could afford it. There was a lady downstairs from me who had a piano going spare which, in theory, I could practise on.

Anyway, the teacher I chose was a lady called Monica Stephenson, and she lived downstairs from Miss Fitzpatrick which, of course, was a literal case of 'music to my ears'.

As it so happened, I was going upstairs to Mrs Stephenson's house in Onslow Drive, and by sheer coincidence, Miss Fitzpatrick was coming downstairs. I couldn't believe my eyes when I saw her wearing trousers. At school, she was always formally dressed. I could hardly mutter a 'hello', I was so dumbfounded, after which I carried on with my music lesson. Most of the time was spent talking to my music teacher instead of learning piano. My mum kept asking me when my music exam would be, and when I mentioned this to Mrs Stephenson, I couldn't understand why she became so angry. The atmosphere was extremely tense in her living room because she kept ranting and raving at me to such an extent that I felt humiliated, embarrassed and, for the first time, wished that my lesson was over.

When I went home, my mum asked me how I got on and I honestly couldn't explain it. The simple truth of the matter was that I didn't practise enough and I would have been set up for failure if I had taken a music exam. Just shortly after, my mum said she could no longer afford my piano lessons and I was to tell Mrs Stephenson which I duly did. She seemed quite pleased about my news and I think it was then I realised that I was wasting her time and my mum's money. To compensate for this, I remember my mum buying me a beautiful lace, turquoise dress which had long sleeves and gathered in at the waist. My mum also bought me new shoes to complete the outfit.

Although at that time my mum wasn't going to church (one of her many fallouts with God), she insisted that my dress should have its first 'baptism' on a Sunday. I normally went to the 12 noon Mass in St Anne's but, on this occasion, I left the house early and took the long route to show off my dress. As I was walking down Whitehill Street, I became aware of familiar voices and, lo and behold, Fitzie and Mrs Stephenson were walking behind me. I was so full of myself and my new attire that I thought they would be staring at my dress because it was so beautiful, but when I turned round to have a peek it was obvious to me that they were just engaging in normal conversation and my dress didn't have a look-in. What a lesson in humility!

CHAPTER 25 –
HAIRDRESSING HIGHLIGHTS

I loved my job at the hairdressing salon and was delighted when a girl called Eileen became a member of staff. On her first day, Eileen was allowed to accompany me for the lunchtime shop, and we certainly took advantage of it because we walked to the opposite end of Duke Street from Peter's shop, which caused us to be really late back. The other members of staff were annoyed because they were so hungry and we had encroached on their break time which resulted in me having to go solo for the lunchtime filled rolls, the following Saturday. Eileen was very bohemian in her dress style and, come rain, hail or shine, she wore a sleeveless, maxi, brown fur coat, dubbed 'flea coat' by my downstairs neighbour whenever she came to visit me.

We would go out on the town on a Saturday night and, because I looked older than my 16 plus years, Eileen and I would get into the pubs no problem. Eileen was a few year older than me and loved to sing (as did I), so we would head for pubs that had entertainment. We went one time to a pub in Sauchiehall Street with a toy tambourine, and after a few drinks, we decided to make a show of ourselves by singing 'Bye Bye Love' by the Everly Brothers. Eileen played the toy tambourine so hard that the metal jingles came apart and were flying all over the tables of the poor unsuspecting punters. We laughed non-stop and, because we had been the 'comedy show' for the night, the clap from the audience was thunderous.

The following week at my Saturday job, Maureen, who was one of the senior stylists, asked me if I would be her model for her final exam at the Hairdressing College. I was delighted to accept. I duly accompanied her to the college and Maureen did an up-do on my long, dark hair which earned her a marking of 100%. That night, I never moved a muscle because I wanted to show off my hairstyle the next morning at school. I will never forget my German lesson that day because Mrs Alexander said, "If you had as much inside your head as you have on top, you would do." Another humiliation!

O Levels

My school life in fourth year had suffered immensely, and I am not one bit proud of the fact that I passed only one O level – no prizes for guessing which one that was. In those days, you either passed or failed an O level so you had no inkling if you had scraped by or had managed a 70+ mark. I tried to persuade my mum that O level English was better than none and in fact was a necessary subject, but I knew she was really disappointed despite my rattling off the names of people who had not achieved an academic award. In response to this, my mum would say, "They should just have left school at 15."

I was still working away at my job in the hairdresser's and, from my meagre £1.50 per week plus tips, I had to buy tights, make-up and other bits and bobs that I needed as well as giving my mum some of the money that was left over on Sunday to tide us over until she got her social security money on a Monday. On Sundays, sometimes my mum and I would spend the afternoon in bed to pass the time until dinner which was usually around 6 p.m.

Roy was still alive at the time, and we had a female, tortoiseshell cat called Topsy who would swing on Roy's tail at every opportunity. Roy was so placid he didn't mind in the least, and he and Topsy got on great. My mum hated cats and the only reason we had Topsy was to prevent mice being in the house. Topsy loved jumping onto the bed and my mum would chase her off. She also jumped on my mum's knee more often than mine which would make me quite jealous. I loved the cat and wanted all her affection. On one of our Sunday afternoon naps, Topsy came into the bed whilst I was waiting for my mum to come through. I decided to let Topsy go under the covers and the cat and I feel asleep. I didn't hear my mum coming into bed, but I sure heard her scream when Topsy decided to go walkabout. I think the poor cat got the biggest fright and, believe me, I got a roasting from my mum which became more like merry hell when I could not stop laughing!

The beautiful Antrim coast

It was summer holiday time again and I went over to Ireland, only this time I spent most of them in Glenarm. It was that summer that a distant cousin called Sadie taught me to crochet and, as ponchos were all the rage at the time, I was able to churn them out at a rate of knots. This became quite lucrative for me because, when I eventually returned home, quite a few people that my mum knew would request a crocheted poncho. Of course the extra money I earned was an added bonus. That aside, that summer in Glenarm was brilliant. Mona and I went dancing together in one of the nearby villages and going dancing in Ireland was amazing. I loved the music, the bands, the dances themselves and indeed some of the boys.

During that holiday, my Aunt Marie's cousin Kathleen Robinson married a widower called Alec Stewart. Alec had a son who was a couple of years older than me and was really quite handsome. I think Marie and Kathleen were plotting for Michael and me to get together because, in their minds, we were the perfect match. Kathleen and her new husband took us out for a meal and thereafter took some photographs which were duly sent to me. I got the impression that Michael was really uncomfortable around me which made me feel a bit sad. I wasn't too bad looking and had a reasonably good figure, but Michael simply showed no interest in me. I thought it was because I was Scottish and he would have preferred an Irish girl, but at least I would have the photos to show off 'my boyfriend' to my friends when I went back to school. Years later, I found out that Michael had no interest in girls of any kind, Scottish or otherwise.

Fifth year at Our Lady and St Francis

When I finally went back to school, I had quite a lot of friends in fifth year because class numbers were greatly reduced. In actual fact, I think there were only two fifth-year classes, and I did knuckle down a bit with my schoolwork. On Fridays, a large group of my friends and I would spend our time in St Alphonsus Primary School hall which was just across the road from Our Lady and St Francis.

Father Joe was an absolutely amazing priest who oversaw the entertainment which was usually in the form of a disco. We also used the teachers' staff room to make tea or coffee for ourselves.

Parties were held in the main hall and every other week I seemed to be invited to a party. Of course alcohol was smuggled in – we were 16-year-old teenagers going on 22, but I cannot recall a single one of my friends ever getting really drunk. There was an incident, however, that year when I noticed a young girl being really sick down the toilet of the staff room. She was very intoxicated and only 14 years of age. Her friends had deserted her because they didn't know how to deal with her, and I found myself holding back her hair while she puked. Afterwards, I made the girl coffee to sober her up and then phoned her mum to pick her up. When her mother arrived she thanked me profusely but asked me not to tell anyone that her daughter was so drunk. The woman was the mother of a famous singer and the girl was the singer's younger sister. I never did tell anyone about that incident and it is only now, when I look back on that Friday evening, I can understand why the woman was so concerned. The newspapers would have had a field day with information on the sister of an up-and-coming star.

In January the following year, Father Joe took a group of us skiing in Glenshee which is in the north of Scotland. We left on the Friday and came back on the Sunday. It was my first time skiing and I felt completely exhilarated. The group was about six in total – all girls – and by the time our skiing was finished for the day it was a fight to get to the toilet. I'll never forget how cold I was with falling so much in the snow, but communication from one toilet to another left me in no doubt that the rest of the party felt exactly the same. Father Joe organised meals for us all and said Mass every day in a small room of the hostel we were staying at. I was really sad when that trip came to an end and vowed I would take up skiing as a hobby, but it is an expensive hobby and not one that my mum would have been able to afford. Photographs were taken by Father Joe and we each received one in a cardboard frame.

I am last on the right. My friend, Josephine Boyle, last on the left beside the priest

Break a leg

The Bundy Club

On Saturday nights, some of my school peers went to the Bundoran Club which was situated in the centre of Glasgow, namely Sauchiehall Street. I was desperate to become a member and arranged to meet a girl called Eileen F. at around 7.30 p.m. I waited and waited for Eileen to show up but, after 30 minutes or so, Eileen never appeared. In those days, mobile phones were never heard of so I had absolutely no way of getting in contact with her. Since I was all dolled up, I decided to go into the Bundy Club myself. I knew there would be other girls there from school and, because it was predominantly Catholic, some of the St Mungo's boys would be there too. I remember being stopped at the door and being asked if I was a member. I just blagged it and said that I had forgotten my membership card but I had the entry fee. The man took pity on me and let me in, but you can imagine my dismay when I saw Eileen on the dance floor.

After the dance, Eileen came up to me to find out how I managed to get into the club, but I simply questioned her as to why she didn't meet me. Eileen said she forgot that she was meeting me, but I knew it was a blatant lie because being a member of the Bundoran Club was quite elite and outsiders were never welcome. I had a great time that night and went to see the doorman about getting a 'replacement' membership card. I got one without any problem and subsequently my own group of friends also became members.

The Bundy Club hired live bands and the last dance was always a slow one. As 'Knights in White Satin' was playing, romance was definitely in the air. Whilst I'm on the subject of the Bundy Club, there was one Saturday night when I decided to take my purse with me. You may find this a bit odd, but I normally took whatever money I needed from my Friday and Saturday job and left the rest of my money at home. My mum didn't receive any money until the Monday of the following week and she depended on what money I had left to help with food for the Sunday. This arrangement was fine until, one

Saturday night, I decided to rebel and carry all my money in my purse which was inside my handbag. Everything was fine until the end of the night. When I looked in my handbag, my purse had been stolen. Oh my God. Can you imagine what it was like for me to go home and face my mother? One of my friends gave me my bus fare, which was fine, but my stomach was churning at the thought of my mum's reaction, and yes, just as expected, she totally lost it with me. The upshot was that she had to borrow money from May our downstairs neighbour (previously mentioned) to see us through Sunday. I'll tell you something, I never again put all my eggs in one basket when I went dancing in the future.

At the age of 17, quite a lot happened in my life. (At this juncture, please don't worry about my regaling you with every single year I have been on this earth because *War and Peace* would not have a look-in.) The first thing I remember was that my Aunt May and my mum thought it was time I had a party which was to take place in the hall at St Alphonsus School. I clearly remember that my Aunt May baked me a 'clootie' dumpling. For those of you that don't know what that is, the ingredients are breadcrumbs, suet, flour, treacle with lots of currants and sultanas thrown in. Those are not all the ingredients but everything that goes into a dumpling is stirred together and wrapped in a cloth ('clootie') before boiling. My Aunt May made many clootie dumplings over the years, and the surprise in the middle was normally a three-penny bit or a sixpence. I was really excited about having a party and it was a roaring success. Nowadays, 18th and 21st birthdays are celebrated, but I am so glad of that party on my 17th birthday because, unbeknown to me, it was going to be my last for a very long time.

The Boyle family

I had an amazing circle of friends throughout my school life, but this book would not be complete without the Boyle family getting a mention. I was friendly with a girl called Josephine Boyle. Her parents and her sister Patricia welcomed me as one of their own. They stayed in Ingleby Drive in Dennistoun, and I just loved going there for a visit. Their extended family became my family and, in the summer of 1971, I was invited to go to Ireland for my summer holidays. This enabled Josephine and her sister to see their aunts and grandmother who lived in an area of Northern Ireland called Crossmaglen.

I'll tell you a little bit more about Crossmaglen later on but, since the holiday was going to be for the whole six weeks of our school holidays, I had to let Peter know what was happening with regard to my Saturday job. When I told Peter that I wouldn't be available, he advised me that he would have to let me go. I couldn't believe my ears, and I honestly thought he would have got someone temporarily to stand in for me. I remember saying that it was okay but felt shaken up by this decision. I had worked for three years for Peter and quite often opened up the hairdressing shop at 8.30 a.m. with my shift finishing at 6 p.m., all for a 15-minute break and £1. I must be a good actress, because Peter said I didn't seem too bothered. I was devastated to say the least, but I wasn't going to pass up on the chance of spending six weeks with Josephine and family.

I don't remember much about the journey to Crossmaglen, but I do remember being in the annex of the big house that Josephine's granny lived in. Crossmaglen is a village in County Armagh and, although it is deceptively peaceful and remote looking, the Troubles were still very prevalent. On the border with Crossmaglen is the Irish Free State town of Dundalk where most people went shopping because it was cheaper than the village. To get to Josephine's granny's house we had to walk along a country road full of trees and bends, and to me it was the epitome of quiet countryside. One of Josephine's aunts lived in Newry, 27 miles away from Crossmaglen and, although I never really felt threatened by the Troubles in that small village I stayed in, I was certainly aware of trouble brewing between Catholics and Protestants in Newry which was gripped with riots between the British Army and the local Catholic population.

Whenever Josephine, Patricia and I stayed in Newry, we frequented pubs and clubs that were predominantly Catholic. Entertainment consisted of contemporary Irish rebel songs such as 'Men behind the Wire' by The Wolfe Tones. I want to quote a couple of verses just to give you a flavour of how bitter things were between the Catholic/Protestant divide:

Armoured cars and tanks and guns
Came to take away our sons
But every man will stand behind
The Men Behind the Wire.

Heedless of the crying children
Dragging fathers from their beds
Beating sons while helpless mothers
Watched the blood flow from their heads.

Although the Troubles were quite horrific, I don't think I truly appreciated how scared people really were. There was a massive drinking culture and, of course, the more drunk people became, the more the rebel songs would surface. I imbibed and enjoyed all the entertainment on offer. I remember going into Dundalk in a lorry with Josephine's uncle who went into the local pub while we wandered about. I can't remember the uncle's name, but he was a little bit tipsy and I asked if I could drive us back to Crossmaglen. He let me take over the wheel of the lorry. I had never driven before but that gave me a real taste for driving, and I vowed to myself that I would learn to drive as soon as I possibly could.

I loved going to and from Dundalk and sometimes Josephine, Patricia and I would hitch-hike there and back. There was always a Good Samaritan willing to give us a ride and none of us felt in any way endangered.

Finally, our six-week holiday came to an end and when back home to my mum I sang nothing but Irish songs. I can still hear her saying, "I sent a daughter on holiday and I got back a rebel."

Blackpool Illuminations
In September of that same year, Josephine invited me to go and visit her aunt in Leyland. We travelled by coach to Leyland on a Friday and our plan was to stay the weekend and come home on the Sunday. Josephine's aunt and her husband took us to Blackpool to see the illuminations, and I was completely mesmerised. I have been to Blackpool many times since then but never recaptured the feeling of awe and excitement I experienced that particular weekend. It was the

custom then to bring a present back if you were on holiday and, thanks to the generosity of Josephine's aunt and uncle, I was able to buy my mum a candlewick bedspread with my pocket money. Most people settled for a stick of rock, but I wanted to get my mum something really nice and, although the September weekend was truly magical, I looked forward to giving my mum her gift on the Sunday night when I arrived home. My mother wasn't one to beat about the bush and when I gave her the bedspread, she told me that I had won it in a raffle. I don't think my mum ever believed that I had purchased the item with my pocket money, but I was bitterly disappointed with her reaction.

It was now time for me to go into the sixth year at school, and instead of having blue ribbon round my blazer I had the yellow braid of a prefect. A prefect was allowed to dish out lines to erring younger pupils but, having been a recipient in my early years at Our Lady and St Francis, I was in no rush to mete out the same punishment.

I had a tiny guitar which I used to practise basic chords and songs that would accompany it. At first my mum would go ballistic every time I practised, because the noise I made gave her a headache. However, when I finally managed to hammer out a tune, my mum would ask me to play and 'Ten Guitars' was her favourite. At this point in my life, I wasn't sure where my vocation would lie (certainly not as a musician), but I loved sixth year in school and was enjoying life to the full. During homework classes, I still made the excuse to my supervising teacher that I wished to go the library when in reality I would head for the basement cloakroom to meet up with my friends and practise guitar playing.

Those were my halcyon days despite the fact that I didn't have a Saturday job and my trips to the Bundy where somewhat curtailed.

However, in the run-up to Christmas of 1971, for some reason I had a look at the *Glasgow Herald* – a good journalistic newspaper. It wasn't a paper that my mum bought, because it was more factual than entertaining, so I must have glanced through it at a newspaper stand. Anyway, there was an advert for Saturday staff in a music shop situated in Sauchiehall Street called Biggars.

Biggars was famous for selling all types of quality musical instruments as well as sheet music and entertainment systems. I applied for the Saturday position and managed to get an interview. At the interview, I was asked where I had heard about the position, and I was ever so thankful for being able to say that I had read the *Glasgow Herald* and decided to apply for the job. I was quite optimistic about my interview performance, and I was hired for the few months leading up to Christmas. The pay was much better than Peter's, and I thoroughly enjoyed working there. It's strange how things stick in your mind, but I remember going out for lunch with a girl similar in age to myself and treating myself to fish and chips, only instead of putting salt on my dinner I used the sugar container instead. I was quite bloody-minded and decided that I would eat the dinner rather than waste the money it cost. I certainly don't recommend trying sugar instead of salt for a fish supper because it was vile. Another thing I remember was that a slightly older, permanent member of staff kept boasting about buying her parents a record player for Christmas, but after a bit of prodding in the right direction, I found out that the same young lady really wanted that sound system for herself. I couldn't believe her selfishness.

Getting my mum a job

Whilst at school, a Russian teacher called Mrs McKee happened to be supervising my class. The McKee family were really well known for writing articles in the *Scottish Catholic Observer* (sold every Friday in school without fail), and they lived in a detached house situated in either the Newton Mearns or Clarkston area of Glasgow. People with money owned these houses and it was really a 'them' and 'us' class difference. Mrs McKee was quite a formidable-looking woman and I would never have dared approach her but, on the day she was supervising my class, she asked if any of our mothers would be looking for a cleaning job.

Two of us put our hands up and Mrs McKee said she would speak to us at the end of the class period. When the bell rang, another girl and I went to speak to Mrs McKee and, awkward as it is to write this, I truly believe she chose my mum because I was wearing a school uniform from Paisleys and not one where the braiding went all the way round the blazer. I feel snobby about saying that but appearances went a long way and, thanks to my mum, I was more smartly turned out. It was a Friday afternoon and no homework classes, so I couldn't wait to go home and give my mum the good news! My usual travelling companion on the bus home was a girl called Marion who was always willing to share her latest boyfriend news with me. Anyway, when I got home, I told my mum she had a new job as a cleaner for the McKee family and handed her a note giving Mrs McKee's contact details. It never crossed my mind that my mum wouldn't take the job, I knew she needed it and would be glad of the extra money which came in handy for the up-and-coming pilgrimage to Lourdes organised by Sister Felicitas in the early summer of 1972.

Sixth year at school was one of my most enjoyable. For a start, there were fewer pupils and I seemed to knuckle down to my schoolwork. I guess it was a case of last chance saloon where I was concerned. The only downside for me was Higher French. I had a compensatory O level in French, which basically means you have just missed getting the Higher, therefore I had to repeat Higher French. Our teacher was a nun called Sister Josepha and all her pupils were visibly shaking every time she walked into the class. It was horrific and, during that class, I prayed constantly that I would get a question right rather than incur Sister Josepha's wrath. Every time I told my mum what was happening, she told me that she was glad I had a nun teaching me French. No sympathy there!

I forgot to tell you that I had my German O level under my belt. It took me two attempts but on the second attempt I knew I had passed with flying colours. Mrs Alexander even asked me if I was going to do the Higher. I politely replied in the negative but in my head I was thinking, *No chance, absolutely no chance.*

CHAPTER 26 –
ALMOST RAPED AND
POSSIBLY STRANGLED

Terrible things can happen to us in our life, and I believe God protected me in the terrible attack that I was soon to endure.

As my sixth year progressed and I was finally taking my studies seriously, I decided one Friday night to go to Dennistoun Library. I still had my school uniform on, as it was cold and frosty and I was going to be walking there and back, so I wrapped my school scarf around my neck. I went after I'd had my tea, so it must have been about 6.30 p.m.

The second of my nine lives

The library closed around 9 p.m. and, in those days, libraries were places that exuded peace and quiet. Talking even in a whisper was frowned upon, and if you dared disobey the rules, you risked the wrath of the librarian. I had a big brown, leather briefcase and took all the books I needed with me to study. After a few hours, I felt quite satisfied with what I had achieved and started to head home. For some reason, my mum didn't really want me to go to the library, but since I was about seven or eight months shy of my 18th birthday, I thought I knew best. However, as I was walking along Appin Road, which is a very long road, I became aware of someone following me. My instinct has never failed me, but I shook off the feeling and carried on walking. I can't believe how stupid I was because, even as I reached the stairs going up to the common close at No 267 Appin Road, I still had the feeling someone was following me. I felt like turning around but I did not. I took the short walk up the common close and, as I put my foot on the first step up to the first landing, I felt one hand going round my mouth and another hand going up my skirt. I cannot fully describe the terror I felt in that moment, but I knew I was in serious danger. I bit full force into a finger of the hand round my mouth which temporarily paralysed the perpetrator – a man – and I screamed with all the lung power I could muster. The man then clapped his hand around my mouth and dragged me three steps down to the back of the close. I was no match for my attacker, but there was a family called the Hewitts who occupied a house on the right-hand side of the close. On hearing my screams, they immediately opened their front door, the attacker let go of me and fled. To say I was a complete shaking wreck was an understatement. It was the most horrific moment a young girl can go through.

Thank God for that family who took me in and went up three flights of stairs to fetch my mother. I still had some of the man's finger in my mouth and was spitting out blood. My underwear had a massive handprint where my attacker had put his hand up my skirt.

My mother repeatedly scolded me for going to the library in the first place when I could have studied at home. I should have listened to her. It also made me realise that God had spared me from my assailant and that my **second life** had just been used up.

The Hewitt family offered me a cigarette but, although my mother was a smoker and addicted her whole life, she did not want me having the same dependency. The police were called but I could not describe my attacker, and in 1971 there was no such thing as DNA evidence. My attacker managed to flee, but there is no doubt in my mind that he would have raped and strangled me with my own scarf. For many weeks after that attack I was a complete wreck. I was frightened to go anywhere on my own and kept clinging to my mum like a child. Obviously, my mum spoke to my headmistress about the incident, and I thought I would never be able to shake off the fear of going out, especially in the dark. In a way, Sister Felicitas came to my rescue, because she invited some of the sixth-year pupils to spend a weekend at Merrylee Convent where she was based. I think there were about six of us who thought we would give it a go and, to be honest, I think my mum was just glad of the distraction the up-and-coming weekend would cause.

CHAPTER 27 –
FIRST INTRODUCTION TO
MERRYLEE CONVENT

I duly went to Merrylee, with my little overnight bag, and was introduced to Sister Mary Francis who was going to be in charge of our little group. Sister Mary Francis was quite elderly but she chuckled constantly, and her lovely face reminded me of a Halloween cake where the icing on the front is puffed up full of cream. At that time, she was the headmistress of St Mary's Convent School in Dennistoun where my gorgeous little Elizabeth would eventually be a pupil. I cannot remember how many nuns we sixth-year pupils met, but I was struck by the fact that most of them were teachers. The younger nuns were really entertaining and very musical – something which I could relate to.

Merrylee Convent was big, but there was a small wing at the west of the convent that was kept for retreat purposes. The main part of the convent housed St Gabriel's Church which was absolutely stunning. The nuns would kneel at their prie-dieu on the right- and left-hand side of the body of the church and the congregation would be seated at the rear.

Although I never missed Mass on a Sunday and went to Mass every day during Lent, I never experienced what I felt whilst at Merrylee. It was the most wonderful, overwhelming feeling of peace and contentment and, although I had thought about teaching as a career, I just knew that God had other plans for me. I felt an indescribable joy within me which still fills me full of awe. I decided there and then to give my life to God and become a nun. The girl who was afraid of her own shadow when she went away for that weekend retreat was replaced by a girl full of confidence, peace and joy.

I could not wait to tell my mum and I knew that the following week I would tell Sister Felicitas. I was buzzing with enthusiasm when

I got home and told my mum every single detail about the amazing weekend I'd had but, when I got to the part where I had decided to give my life to God, my mum's reaction was quite lukewarm. Now, with hindsight, I can understand why, but at the time I was puzzled and truly believed that my decision would make my mum really proud of me. Nevertheless, I went straight to Sister Felicitas' office on the Monday and told her of my intentions. To say she was delighted would be an understatement. Just prior to leaving her office, Sister Felicitas handed me a beautiful badge with Our Blessed Lady on it and that badge meant more to me than *anything* I had ever received.

My friends told me that I looked like I was over the moon (the first time I had ever heard that expression). There was absolutely no doubt in my mind about my decision and, just like someone who is in love for the first time and constantly mentioning their relationship, I could not stop talking about my vocation. Wild horses could not have stopped me from the path I was about to embark on. I knew then, and I know now, that it was absolutely the right thing to do.

Of course, my teachers soon got to know about my vocation and I think, at that point, I was one of the most popular girls in sixth year. Teachers that I had never spoken to in my life came up to ask me if I was *really* going to become a nun. To be honest, I never knew what all the fuss was about, but I suppose people are naturally curious when someone is going to take vows of poverty, chastity and obedience.

Naturally, I went to Merrylee Convent at every opportunity I could get. I wanted to get to know the nuns, particularly the younger ones who were still in the novitiate prior to making their final vows. I always wore my best outfits but, on one occasion, when Sunday Mass was on, I walked up to Communion whilst wearing a small pair of furry slippers.

The sisters were stifling their giggles and the congregation at the back just openly burst out laughing. It was a really long time before I lived that one down! I liked most of the nuns but became friendly with a nun called Sister Ninian whose aunt lived just around the corner from me. That lady was a seamstress and she made me two dresses suitable for a postulant to wear. For those of you unfamiliar with this terminology, I should explain a little bit about the hierarchy of nuns. Firstly, you become a postulant, then a Novice and after a couple of years you take your first set of vows (poverty, chastity and obedience), you then take another set of vows a few years later and then final vows after a seven-year period. It might be different now but that's how it was in 1972.

CHAPTER 28 –
SCHOOL TRIP TO LOURDES

However, let me tell you about my school trip to the shrine at Lourdes in France.

For those of you who may be unfamiliar with the grotto and shrines, I think I should give you a little bit of background information.

Lourdes is a town in south-western France and is situated at the foot of the Pyrenees Mountains. It is a major Catholic pilgrimage site and each year millions visit the Grotto of Massabielle (Grotto of the Apparitions) where, in 1858, the Virgin Mary appeared to Bernadette Soubirous. In the grotto, pilgrims can bathe in water flowing from a spring. I noticed how many sick people were there – people in wheelchairs, people on crutches and people suffering from many other different ailments but full of faith. Lourdes is famous for miraculous healings that have taken place over the years, but I don't think I'm generalising too much when I say that those who go to Lourdes via an organised pilgrimage don't really expect a miracle but, through the power of prayer, come home refreshed – perhaps not in body but certainly in mind.

Lourdes was the obvious choice for our pilgrimage given that Our Lady and St Francis was very proud of its reputation for teaching French. I was excited about my week-long trip and, if my memory serves me correctly, I think my mum was able to pay for my trip in instalments otherwise there would have been no way she could have afforded it. My mum bought me a new, nylon-strung guitar when she found out I could actually bang out a few tuneful chords and that instrument went everywhere with me, including the Lourdes trip which took place at Easter time.

The due day arrived. I don't remember too much about the journey there except that I was with Veronica and some other school friends. Sister Felicitas and a handful of teachers accompanied us pupils on what seemed like the longest train ride ever. The seats were rock solid and uncomfortable, but that did not deter our high spirits and the number of times we swapped places for a window seat.

Eventually, we arrived at our hotel, where there were four pupils to each room, and it didn't take long for any of us to go to sleep. We were exhausted and knew that we would have a hectic but exciting week ahead. That week was amazing and, surprisingly enough, it didn't go too quickly. When we pupils were attending services, we always wore a white mantilla (lace covering) over our heads. We had great fun singing and playing instruments on the coach trips that were included, and one of the highlights of that trip was being allowed to play my guitar to accompany the hymns being sung at the Basilica.

Moreover, it never ceased to amaze me that you could bathe in (the miraculous) ice-cold water – affectionately known as the Bernadette Bath and come out bone dry. That was a miracle in itself.

Whilst in Lourdes, I became friendly with a nun from Walthamstow and when I told her about my own vocation, she said she would come and visit me in Merrylee Convent.

Finally, the day arrived for us all to go home but not without a group photograph being taken with us all wearing our white mantillas. We then embarked on the plane with bags that smuggled cigarettes and booze for the teachers. I don't think I brought my mum any cigarettes back, thinking that a small bottle of Lourdes water would suffice. I'll leave you to guess what she would have preferred!

Towards the summer of 1972, about six of us went to a convent in Saltcoats for a weekend and God love Sister Felicitas for doing all the cooking. We also had a priest to say Mass for us, but the highlight of the weekend was when we all piled into a single bed, hands and feet everywhere, because we had been telling so many ghost stories and were terrified of our own shadows.

Millport

Next came the school trip to Millport, and we had the run of the ferry crossing from Largs over to Millport on the island of Great Cumbrae. Ask anyone what Millport is famous for and you'll be sure to hear about the bikes for hire to cycle round the island. The bike shop was always the first place we went to and, after a refreshing but tiring bicycle ride on that lovely summer's day, the next stop was the Ritz café, famous for its knickerbocker glories.

The end of the school term was fast approaching and, quite frankly, I was dreading it. Our Lady and St Francis had been in my life for six years and my memories of my time there were fond. Even Miss Kelly and Mrs Alexander had gone up a notch in my estimation. By this time, I had been to a hairdresser to get my long hair cut prior to settling in with the Franciscan Sisters of the Immaculate Conception, but I must have been reasonably attractive because at our school leavers' dance, I was not in short supply of suitors.

There was always sports day in the month of June which the sixth-year pupils were responsible for organising. We had all the usual type of stalls but, until the day I die, I will never forget the wheelbarrow race. Rosie and I had won the three-legged race but instead, the wheelbarrow race was really tough going. My partner and I were mismatched and between us we just couldn't make it to the finishing line. I had a massive fit of the giggles, so much so that the tears were running down my legs as well as my eyes, and when I turned round to see if anyone noticed my wet legs, Fitzie and a crowd of other teachers were behind me in hysterics at the puddle I had made on the ground. Even to this day, I can feel my face lighting up like a belisha beacon when I recall that memory.

Unlike my peers, I was not thrilled with the thought of school holidays and that summer I did not go to Ireland. That did not bother me because I had already been to France, Saltcoats and Millport.

My friend, Sister Ninian, lived in Saltcoats prior to becoming a nun, and she invited me to meet her mum, dad and family. We were both quite excited about my up-and-coming vocation and, just as I was getting comfortable in the knowledge that I would soon be joining my friend, Sister Ninian announced that she was being sent to one of the Franciscan Convents in America. She had taken her vow of obedience and therefore had no choice in the matter.

I think her calm acceptance made me realise that my own will was not conducive to convent life, but it did not deter me from the mission I was about to embark on. I even knitted myself a long, black cardigan just in case the postulant dresses weren't warm enough.

I should have realised that my mum was unhappy about my decision, but I was so wrapped up in my thoughts and feelings, I simply could not see her point of view. My mother encouraged me to apply for jobs during the few short months prior to entering Merrylee, even to the point of going for an interview with Glasgow City Council. It seemed to me that the only person really supporting my decision was my Aunt May and, of course, the lovely Franciscan Sisters who were happy to get a new recruit. I have always been obstinate, stubborn and determined whenever I've had a goal in mind and becoming a nun was no exception.

I stayed at school until the very last day and, with heartfelt sadness, I heard the school bell ring one last time. I reflected on the many wonderful teachers and pupils who attended Our Lady and St Francis, but the uppermost thought in my mind was a poem about courtesy by Hilaire Belloc placed on a wall opposite the door of Sister Felicitas' office. I will give you a small excerpt of it because the words have stood me in good stead throughout my life:

Of Courtesy, it is much less
Than Courage of Heart or Holiness,
Yet in my Walks it seems to me
That the Grace of God is in Courtesy.

A stopgap after leaving school

I was excited about my future and there wasn't a single doubt in my mind about my religious vocation, but until my entry date at Merrylee on 19 September 1972, I had to give my mum 'keep money'.

My mum, therefore, accompanied me to the local DWP office, otherwise known as 'the broo'. The young guy who processed my application asked me what my career choice was and, with a great feeling of pride, I told him I was going to become a nun. He immediately replied, "A nun? A currant bun?" I didn't know whether to laugh or be insulted, but I decided not to say anything in case my mum did not get my money.

During that summer, my friends arranged a party for me at the Bier Keller in Glasgow city centre and, as we slugged back schooners of beer, we ended up dancing on the table. It was an amazing atmosphere and everyone came up with the most stupid religious name possible for me. I don't remember paying for a single drink, but I do remember shouting and singing in Appin Road much to the embarrassment of my mum. I was as drunk as a skunk!

I also spent quite a bit of time at Merrylee Convent and got to know the nuns in the novitiate. Most of these ladies were well on their way to making final vows, but they were great fun and welcomed me warmly every time I saw them. There was also the added 'bonus' (and I put 'bonus' in inverted commas for a reason which you will understand as this story progresses) of another young lady by the name of Anne who was entering Merrylee Convent as a postulant on the same day as me. All the nuns I spoke to told me that the night before they themselves were about to enter religious life, they didn't sleep a wink. I can truly vouch for that.

CHAPTER 29 –
ENTERING MERRYLEE CONVENT

On the morning of 19 September 1972, armed with my guitar, suitcase containing postulant clothes and a black cardigan which I had proudly knitted, my mum accompanied me by bus to Merrylee – a very upmarket area of Glasgow. I was welcomed by Mother Paul, my Novice Mistress, who gave my mum the assurance that I would be well looked after.

My mum was offered tea (in a china cup) and biscuits prior to her departure, and I honestly don't remember feeling all that sad when I said goodbye to my mum – I knew she would visit me a month later and, besides, I was feeling far too excited about my new life.

I was now about to see parts of the convent that were forbidden to visitors, and my new living quarters were on the east wing whereas I'd only seen around the west wing during my schooldays. Merrylee Convent was massive and the upkeep must have been astronomical. I was struck by the smell of polish inside and how clean and shiny everything was. That suited me just fine because I'm a bit of a neat freak and, compared to my previous humble origins, Merrylee Convent was palatial. It was not just that the convent seemed massive, but there were various buildings around the grounds with lots of different entrances. I felt like a child again when I used to go plundering in my Aunt May's house. I had already seen the gardens, which were beautifully kept, and of course there were many religious icons as well as greenhouses for growing flowers and vegetables. Not being much of a gardener, I tended to ignore the greenhouses, but my ignorance of pot plants, fruit and vegetable plants would come back to bite me a good few months down the line. Ignorance is bliss, of course, and it's just as well because I would have had a major attack of the drips if I'd known then what I know now. In fact, even as I type, my fingers are slipping off my keyboard at the memories!

Mother Paul was an older sister with white hair sticking out from her veil. She had obviously been a tall lady but was a bit stooped with age. Mother Paul had an amazing dedication to religious life and was a very holy woman. In those days, the nuns' habits (dress code) consisted of a black dress with white collar, black tights and shoes and a black veil with white around the edge at the front. Compared to my oversized postulant dresses and cardigan, the habit was très chic indeed! But for now I will take you back to that very first day of religious life.

The first thing that happened, after my mum said goodbye, was for me to be taken to my cell (room) where I was able to unpack my things. The cell consisted of a single bed with an iron headboard, a cupboard and drawers for my clothes, a toilet and a little bedside cabinet with a Bible on it. Above the iron headboard was a crucifix. The floor was wooden and immaculately polished. In fact, I considered my cell quite luxurious considering I had never had a bedroom of my own and there was plenty of room for my worldly belongings. There was also a writing desk with stationery thereon and I remember feeling quite chuffed, albeit a bit nervous, about my new life.

Anne, my fellow postulant

Just prior to teatime, Anne, the other postulant, arrived with her parents. She was about 28 years of age and we had written to each other a couple of times prior to entering. One of my many faults and failings is that I can be quite pass-remarkable and Anne did not strike me as someone I would normally be friends with, but the inner voice in my head kept telling me to be charitable and I greeted Anne with as much enthusiasm as I could muster.

We were both shown around the convent after Anne's parents had left and, by the time the tour was finished, I was absolutely convinced I would get lost every time I ventured out of my cell. We were taken to the refectory (dining area) where we were both shown to different tables in order to get to know some of the older sisters. That was really quite daunting and, for once in my life, I didn't have much to contribute in the way of conversation. I was quite astonished at the amount of food on the table and, after saying grace, we ate the three courses which were delicious.

The next morning, I was awakened to the sound of a knock on my door with a sister's voice saying, "Let us bless the Lord." It was about

6 a.m. and Mass was around 6.30 a.m. I hurriedly got myself washed and dressed and, thankfully, I was able to follow some of the other nuns in the direction of the chapel. Although it was St Gabriel's RC Church and used by fellow worshipers mainly for Sunday Masses, I always felt it solely belonged to the Franciscans because of the separation I mentioned earlier.

I was shown to my prie-dieu, which was about fourth down on the left-hand side of the church, and the Divine Office/breviary was said prior to the commencement of Mass. The Mother Abbess was a nun called Sister Mary Gabriel and she led the Divine Office whilst the rest of us made our responses. I felt really proud and just loved singing hymns during Mass. After Mass, we had a hearty breakfast and then Jimmy the caretaker took the nuns who were qualified teachers, to their respective schools. The Franciscan Sisters of the Immaculate Conception was mainly a teaching order, and whilst I had been in sixth year a nun called Sister Kevin had repeated sixth year in order to obtain the qualifications required for teacher training. I had got to know Kevin quite well and, although she didn't have the voice of an angel, she was amazing on the clarinet. By the time I was in Merrylee, Sister Kevin was attending Teacher Training College (I think the Catholic college was Craiglockhart and the non-Catholic college at the time was Jordanhill).

When all the young sisters were out during the day, either teaching, nursing, or attending college, the retired sisters remained in the convent. Some of these sisters were very old and, in some cases, had dementia.

Since this was an illness I never knew about (God forgive me), I sometimes laughed inappropriately at some of the odd things they would do such as wearing a slipper and a shoe together or putting shoes on the wrong feet. I suppose in my defence, I was young and didn't fully understand how cruel an illness dementia is. Thankfully, there were only a few sisters who suffered this illness, and the majority of the elderly sisters were just simply affectionate and very kind. Sometimes a kind word or a cuddle would be all it took to make their day, and I got to know and love these sisters dearly. In addition, whilst the younger sisters were out, Mother Paul would take the opportunity to educate Anne and I about what was expected of us in religious life.

We were encouraged to use the library as often as possible, spend time with Our Lord in the chapel and complete biblical exercises. We also had free time to walk around the grounds, admire the scenery and sometimes sit in one of the classes at St Gabriel's Primary private school which the convent grounds encompassed.

Quite often as Anne and I were wandering about, we would see Mother Gabriel (the Abbess) pottering about in the greenhouses. She was precious about her plants and was green-fingered – something I certainly was not. I remember thinking, *I hope to God the Abbess never asks me to look after her plants if she's away anywhere, because they'll be dead by the time she comes back.*

Although Anne and I got along reasonably well (or so I thought), I couldn't wait for the younger sisters to come home from work. We all socialised together in the juniorate, a terminology used for nuns who were a few years away from making final vows.

The Franciscans had convents in America and, as stated previously, my friend Sister Ninian had been asked to go there after she had made her final profession. There were also convents in Ireland, England and Nigeria and probably a few others that escape my mind at present. In the juniorate, the sisters in that particular part of Merrylee were Adelaide, Louise, Maria Goretti, Bernadette and Kevin. The parlour in the juniorate was very tastefully decorated and not in the least bit austere like I had imagined prior to entering Merrylee.

I just loved it when we played our guitars and sang and listened to records. The two main albums that we played over and over again were ones that had been made by the Medical Missionary Sisters of Mary entitled, *I Know the Secret* and *Joy is like the Rain*. These are albums I listened to on YouTube recently and the memories of these beautiful songs, which fed my soul, came flooding back. There was also a television in the parlour and never a night went by without there being a box of chocolates.

Initiation ceremony

A short time after Anne and I had entered Merrylee, we unwittingly became victims of an initiation ceremony in the juniorate. One night, Anne and I were told to kneel down with our hands in the air and thereafter to bow down saying, "Oh wa, tana siam." As we did so, we were told to repeat this action faster each time. It suddenly dawned on me, when everyone was creasing themselves laughing, that in actual fact we were saying, "Oh what an ass I am!" Poor Anne couldn't figure it out (she wasn't the shiniest button on the jacket) and kept swaying backwards and forwards until we told her that this was an initiation prank.

I loved our time in church when we were saying our daily Office of Matins prior to Mass and vespers as our night-time prayers. The most uplifting thing for me was the music, but poor Anne was tone deaf and put me off-kilter on numerous occasions because her prie-dieu was right behind mine.

Cleanliness (being next to godliness) was paramount, and there was never a shortage of toiletries liberally given every night prior to showering. I have mentioned previously that there was always a rich smell of polish aided and abetted by a polishing machine called Joseph.

Oddly enough, Sister Mary Joseph, a young professed nun, had the duty of operating Joseph as well as being the sacristan. Sister Joseph was a really quiet, kind, gentle soul and I liked her as soon as I saw her. I have to be honest and say that I liked most of the sisters. What struck me about Sister Felicitas, when I saw her in the convent, was her sense of humour and her warm personality. I saw her very differently when she was our headmistress which I guess makes sense.

I was settling well into convent life and, about a month after I had entered it, my mum was allowed to visit me. I was looking forward to seeing her but, from the minute she saw me, she criticised my appearance.

By this time, my hair had been cut short by Sister Mary Adelaide, and my mum said to me that I wasn't washing my hair properly. I could not understand her attitude because I had been doing my own hair for years. My Novice Mistress, Mother Paul, brought us tea and cakes during my mum's visit but, for once in my life, I just had no appetite. You could have cut the atmosphere with a knife and, when my mum's visit ended, I remember feeling really sad – not because I was missing her but because I just couldn't figure out what I was doing wrong. Little did I know that things were going to get much worse before they got better.

Blue murder

After a couple of months in Merrylee, Anne and I were looking out of the window in the juniorate parlour. The grounds in Merrylee were massive and it was a lot for the naked eye to take in, but Anne kept saying to me, "Do you see that nun over there?" I knew I had good eyesight but I simply could not see any nun. She was very insistent about it and I kept peering to find out what she was referring to. The next thing she said to me was, "You know, Eunice, I feel like killing you but I haven't decided when your murder will take place." I burst out laughing until I realised that Anne was deadly serious.

After she had repeated this a few times and was pointing to other 'imaginary' nuns, I knew I was dealing with a 'fruitcake' and decided to get away from Anne immediately by going to pray in the chapel, but Anne followed me. I don't know where Mother Paul was – she must have gone out – and I did not feel confident enough to approach the Mother Abbess, so I just went along with the nonsense Anne was spouting out and tried to appease her as best I could until the younger nuns came back from their respective teaching jobs.

However, as soon as Sister Mary Adelaide appeared, I told her that I needed to confide in her, but when I tried to explain the situation, I couldn't do it because of my nervous laughter.

Eventually, I calmed down enough to let her know what had happened during the course of the afternoon, and she immediately went to Sister Gabriel (Mother Abbess). Anne was sent to her cell and told to get into her bed just after tea, but obviously her behaviour was giving cause for concern and I was questioned about what had taken place.

Later on, all the juniorate nuns, the Mother Abbess, Mother Paul and I were standing around Anne's bed. In hindsight, I think the sisters were hoping this was a one-off incident but, after handing Anne a cup of tea, she was offered the sugar bowl to sweeten her tea and she threw it on the floor shouting, "Louis must pick up the sugar." She was referring to Sister Louise and, in some perverted way, I remember thinking that Anne's action completely verified what had taken place earlier that day. It was really frightening to watch Anne getting steadily worse and having a complete nervous breakdown before my very eyes.

The next morning, Anne's parents were summoned, told about the incident and asked to take their daughter away. I don't remember saying goodbye, and I never heard about Anne again. However, after Anne left, Mother Paul asked me if I still wanted to stay since I was now the only postulant, and I told her that it never crossed my mind to leave.

I loved Mother Paul but Sister Kevin was her real prodigy, and I was sick to death of Mother Paul singing her praises. Please don't get me wrong, I wasn't in anyway jealous, but I felt that a precedent had been set and at every opportunity a comparison was made between Kevin and me.

Sister Paul liked to see her postulants spending a lot of time in the chapel and, may God forgive me, I used to spend my time in the chapel catching up on sleep. I justified this by telling myself I had run out of prayers. I even managed to kneel and sleep at the same time. No one ever told me that I snored, so I suppose that was a positive.

Saint Thérèse of Lisieux

I have always had a great devotion to St Thérèse of Lisieux who entered the Carmelite Convent (enclosed Order) at the age of 15 years and died in her early twenties. She was a very devout nun and, prior to her death, decided that she would spend her Heaven doing good upon earth. St Thérèse always practised 'her little way' which meant that she strived to do at least one act of charity every day no matter how hard. This is an amazing mantra and, although I don't always manage, I try to imitate this as much as possible. With old age comes wisdom, but when I was in the convent there was no comparison between the beautiful St Thérèse and me. I was absolutely full of mischief!

If you want to learn more about my favourite little saint you can read her autobiography, *The Story of a Soul*.

An enclosed Order of nuns like St Thérèse's is purely contemplative and they devote their life to prayer. This is not an easy choice for anyone to make, because basically you are shutting yourself off from the outside world and in order to survive their harsh but fulfilling way of life you have to have a very strong vocation. I am writing this because I wanted to make a comparison to my life with the Franciscan Sisters of the Immaculate Conception and that of an enclosed Order.

Equality

When I entered Merrylee Convent, we were all treated as equals, but that was not always the case. Years ago, there was a distinction between choir nuns (those who were fortunate enough to bring with them a dowry) and those amazing girls who gave their lives to God despite coming from an underprivileged background knowing full well that there would be a place for them in the kitchen or in the laundry. Unfortunately, there was an element of snobbery amongst the choir sisters, and I am not saying that everyone was like that but it is something that I noticed for myself amongst the older nuns and it really riled me.

One evening, I was sitting at the same table as the Mother Abbess and instead of having a dessert we had cakes on the table. I think it is fair to say that everyone had their eye on the big cream meringue that seemed to be winking up at all of us. Before the cakes were passed round the table, Sister Mary C. (ex-choir nun) said in a very childish voice, "Mother, Mother, can I please have that cake?" I was mentally daring the Abbess to refuse the request but Sister Gabriel granted it. This might sound petty, but I couldn't help making the comparison between Sister C.'s selfishness and the selfless acts of Sister Vincent who cooked our meals as well as doing the laundry. Perhaps I am still a bit miffed about not getting a sniff at that meringue, but I could never feel charitable towards Sister C. because that and her many other actions led me to believe that she must have been a very spoiled child.

I liked helping Sister Vincent in the kitchen, and she would regale me with stories that made me laugh. One such story was about a tramp that came to the kitchen door saying, "Sister, do you believe in the hereafter?" Sister Vincent immediately retorted, "Of course I believe in the hereafter", to which the tramp said, "Well, I'm here after a meal!" The tramp was given some leftovers and sent on his way.

I also heard a story from one of the younger nuns in the juniorate about Sister Vincent. The young nun told me that, at one time, Sister Vincent didn't have a lot to work with in the way of food and kept serving sausages for dinner night after night. The poor nun was mortified when the novices made up a song to the tune of 'All kinds of everything' (Eurovision Song Contest winning song for Dana) and started singing:

Last night at supper time
Guess what we had,
French fried potatoes
Nothing so grand.
Was it eggs?
Was it cheese?
Anything fried?
Oh no t'was none of these
T'was sausages disguised.

I am so grateful I never needed a dowry when I entered Merrylee Convent, because my background would have had me working in the kitchen and if that had been the case there would have been a mass exodus!

I adapted to my new life relatively quickly and soon I was tasked with doing readings during Mass and other little duties such as awakening the nuns for morning Office. That involved knocking on the cell doors with "Let us bless the Lord", the response to which was, "Thanks be to God."

On one occasion, I had to ring the Angelus bell (known as the prayer of the devotee). The Angelus bell rang at 6 a.m.,12 noon and 6 p.m. I was slotted in for ringing the bell at midday, and I knew that this would prove to be quite a hard task because I had never rung the bell before.

The bell was on the roof and a big, heavy rope was attached to it to facilitate the ring tone. For those of you unfamiliar with the bells of the Angelus, you ring it three times, say prayers to Our Lady, ring it three more times and then more prayers, with the final bell ringing three times and then nine in quick succession.

When I rang the bell the first and second time, I was quite pleased with myself because it went without a hitch. However, when it came to the last three rings and the nine rings that were supposed to follow it, I found the rope too heavy to pull. I had this crazy idea that if I swung on it like a monkey swings from tree to tree, it would make the bell easier to ring. I was not prepared for the consequences, because I pulled the rope so hard that it came apart from the bell and the bell went completely out of control.

The nuns saying the Angelus must have wondered what on earth was going on when the bell rang like the clappers. To make matters worse, it wasn't just the nuns that could hear it. The nearby Catholic residents heard the Angelus. I was totally mortified. My face was as red as a beetroot and my hands were sweating like crazy but, the odd thing is, only one sister asked me what had happened. The Mother Superior and my Novice Mistress never said a word about it, but guess what? I was never asked to ring the Angelus bell again!

The arrival of the three sisters from Nigeria

There was great excitement in the convent when the Mother Abbess announced that three sisters were coming over to Glasgow from Nigeria. The day duly arrived and we were introduced to Sisters Monica, Cecilia and Kozito. Monica wanted to become a doctor, Cecilia was a nurse and Kozito was to become a teacher. Obviously, the Nigerian sisters came from a very hot climate and had very dark skin, and I realised just how dark their skin was when one night, after lights out, I got up to go to the toilet. As I was returning to my cell, I got the fright of my life when all I could see was white teeth coming towards me. I practically jumped out of my skin and Kozito, the culprit in question, could not stop laughing at me. We became firm friends really quickly partly because we were of a similar age and because Kozito was full of mischief. Monica was serious and never faltered in her goal of wanting to become a doctor. Cecilia was great fun and a very spiritual nun whom I loved to talk to, but Kozito remained my firm favourite. I couldn't help but admire how quickly those three nuns adapted, not only to our climate but their swift command of the English language.

On the Feast of the Immaculate Conception, which takes place on 8 December every year, we had a celebration. We had already celebrated the Feast of St Francis of Assisi but, being the Franciscan Sisters of the Immaculate Conception, it would not have been fitting not to celebrate. Fortunately, the feast day fell on a Friday and a wee party was held that night. Sister Adelaide had taught us some country dancing, and we put on a show and a skit for the other nuns. Everything was quite simplistic, but it's the little things in life that we take for granted, despite the lingering memories.

For once, we were allowed in the parlour where the finally professed nuns had their recreation time. Many songs were sung, plenty of food was eaten and we all had a few sherries. Towards the end of the night, Sister Kozito and I hid in a cupboard, with the door slightly ajar, in order to get a good view of one of the sisters who had a face as red as a beetroot due to her sherry consumption. She was less than steady on her feet in her efforts to go back to her cell and bed down for the night. Kozito and I were trying to smother our laughter in case we got caught.

Christmas in the convent

I had the choice of going home for Christmas or New Year and decided that I wanted to spend Christmas in the convent. My mum was invited to the Thorley family for Christmas but, prior to that, she wrote me a stinker of a letter stating that she had no money and if I had been employed things would have been a lot different. I remember crying when I read it, and Mother Paul picked up on the fact that I wasn't my usual bouncy self. She asked me what had upset me and, when I told her, she said my mother should not have been burdening me with her financial problems. This did little to ease the anxiety I was feeling – and to be perfectly honest, I was not looking forward to New Year.

When it was time for the Christmas Midnight Mass, I was so excited that I was shaking. We had already said Compline which we prayed using our evening Office book. Because it was a relatively new Office, we had been instructed on how to pray it with the Mother Abbess. Due to the Abbess being present whilst we were getting familiar with it, each and every time we practised, my hands were soaking wet with nerves which meant the pages of my book were so sodden they came away from the binder. I am fortunate enough to have a good memory and was able to chant away quite confidently without anyone finding out but, on the evening prior to Midnight Mass, I was dumbstruck. I am trying to work out how I felt so nervous that year and can only put it down to it being such a special time that I just didn't want to get anything wrong. The Mass itself was beautiful, as was the singing, and the following day we were allowed a bit of a lie-in to compensate for being up so late the night before.

New Year with the Boyle family
It was soon time for me to go home for New Year accompanied by my guitar which I had been playing on a regular basis. I can't really remember how I travelled back to Appin Road but I am assuming I took a bus. Of course I was looking forward to seeing my mum.

By the time Hogmanay came, I was glad that my mum and I had been invited to the Boyles' house. I took my guitar with me and played it whenever I was inevitably asked to sing a song or two. It was the custom then to do a turn and normally that would be singing. The usual rebel songs were sung as well as the laments that came out of my mouth. My friend Josephine thought I was unhappy in the convent because the songs I sang were sad, but nothing could have been further from the truth. I just happen to like sad songs.

A night out in Glasgow with Sister Kozito
I think it was in the January of 1973 that the Abbess was given a couple of tickets for 'The Three Priests' concert. She very kindly passed them to Mother Paul to give to the younger sisters. I must have been in favour that day because Paul gave me the tickets and said I could bring one of our Nigerian sisters. I chose Kozito, and we duly made our way to the city centre of Glasgow for the concert. Not only was the singing brilliant but the jokes were really funny. I don't know if Kozito understood them or saw how much I was enjoying myself, but she laughed at all the appropriate places. We stayed until the end of the concert and duly boarded the number 38 bus back to Merrylee.

However, when I looked at my watch I couldn't believe that it was almost 11 p.m. In the convent, lights were normally out at 10 p.m. but since Mother Paul had not told us to come back early, I was not too bothered. Kozito and I discussed the concert the whole road home, and we finally got off the bus at the correct stop. You can imagine our horror when not a single light was on in the entire building. I just kept thinking, *How on earth are we going to get in?*

Merrylee Convent was spacious and had many doors but every door we tried (to our great dismay) was locked. I kept wondering why all the doors were locked since we were expected to return, but rather than stay out in the cold we managed to open a window and climb through it. My heart was sinking at this point, but we metaphorically gave ourselves a pat on the back as we crept along the corridor to our cells. Mother Paul's door was diagonally opposite mine, so she must have heard me close my cell door despite the fact that I was as quiet as a mouse. The next morning, I alone got merry hell for being out so late. When I tried to reason with Mother Paul about the concert not finishing until nearly 11 p.m., she nearly blew a gasket. She told me that I should have known better than to stay until the end of the concert. I had to suck that one up and apologise, but the mischievous part of me was not the least bit sorry because we had such a good time.

CHAPTER 30 –
BECOMING A WHITE VEIL

Around the beginning of February of 1973, the Mother Abbess decided to make me a novice or 'white veil' as it was commonly referred to. This was rather unusual, because normally a postulant would wait six months prior to becoming a novice. In those days, a novice was given a saint's name rather than retain their Christian name which seems to be more fashionable nowadays. It was also compulsory to wear a veil, and for a novice that meant a white veil whilst inside the convent but a black veil like the professed nuns outwith the convent. Obviously, I was pleased about this and was teased unmercifully by the rest of the sisters about my forthcoming name. I really wanted the name Maria Goretti (my Confirmation name), but we already had a sister called Maria Goretti and I knew there wouldn't be another one.

All the nuns were referred to as Sister Mary followed by the name conferred on them as a novice. In addition, when you became a novice you were endlessly scrutinised in order to obey God's will rather than your own. Although a nun didn't take the vows of poverty, chastity and obedience until their first profession (a more public ceremony), a novice was expected to follow the vows she would take at some future date.

Any nun would tell you that obedience is the hardest vow to keep. The day duly dawned when I would learn what my new name would be, and I was hoping to God that I wasn't called something too way out there because some of the younger nuns had confessed to me that they hated their religious name.

The Mother Abbess summoned us all to the parlour in the juniorate and told me that I would now be known as Sister Mary Margaret after St Margaret of Scotland. The devil in me wanted a really funny name, but when I saw Sister Mary Louise shed a tear or two because her own name was Margaret, I decided that I liked the name after all. Sister Gabriel (the Abbess) was Scottish through and through, and I guess it was only fitting that she should give me the name of a Scottish saint. When I put my white veil on for the first time, Sister Adelaide told me that I was acting as if I had a stiff neck! I suppose, I just wasn't used to turning my head backwards and forwards with a veil on it, but I became more relaxed wearing it as time went on.

A new novice is under scrutiny and since I was the *only* novice, every little fault was picked up. Sometimes I would deliberately say or do something knowing full well I would be in trouble. I remember shouting "Goretti" from the top of a stairway in front of my Novice Mistress and being chastised for not applying the suffix 'Sister'. I was chastised for eating my soup with the spoon towards me instead of away from me and putting my knife in the butter at the same time as one of the finally professed sisters.

One of the things that impressed Mother Paul was spending a lot of time in the chapel so I duly complied, but once I'd said initial prayers, I would sit on the chapel seat and sleep. We were up so early in the morning that I used to look forward to my chapel nap and just hope that any other nuns who were there didn't see me slump over.

One day my duty was to clean the juniorate parlour and I spent a good while polishing and hoovering the room. Anyone who knows me would say I'm a neat freak, therefore I knew that by the time I'd finished cleaning, the parlour was spotless. Anyway, Mother Paul came in to inspect my work and told me that I hadn't dusted the room properly. My temper broke and, instead of being obedient and asking where the dust was, I fired the duster at her and told her to do it herself! I don't know who was more shocked by my actions, Mother Paul or me, and my immediate thought was that I would be thrown out that very night, but my Novice Mistress just stared at me and nothing more was said about the matter. I don't think she mentioned it to the Abbess because I'm sure I would have known but, needless to say, my cleaning skills were not called into question again.

My mum came to visit me in the March of that year and told me that an elderly man by the name of Michael Donnelly had moved into the house where the Hewitts used to live. I really wasn't prepared for the next words she was about to utter, and I still shake my head in disbelief at the suddenness of it all, but my mum said that Michael had asked her to marry him. I remember feeling quite stunned and tried to figure out how things could have happened so quickly. When my mum said to me, "Eunice, do I have your blessing?" I was so shocked I could hardly speak and just nodded my head. My mum duly thanked me and her parting shot was, "I'll let you know when the wedding is."

I returned to my cell, trying to figure out what had just happened, but thought I should let Mother Paul know. I can't really remember what I said to her, but she did advise me to accept this and it could actually be a good thing for my mum.

Obviously, I couldn't answer any questions about Michael and my mum's relationship because I had been too gobsmacked to probe my mum at the visit, but Mother Paul said I could go to my mum's wedding. Even as I write this all these years later, I am still mystified about how speedily the marriage took place. My mum wrote me a letter after the visit and told me that she had been doing household chores and shopping for Michael and he wanted a more permanent arrangement.

My mum's wedding

My mum also informed me that she was getting married within six weeks of her visit to me and that the marriage ceremony would take place at St Thomas' RC Church in Riddrie. Who would have thought that after all the times I had prayed in that church during my primary school years, my mum would end up getting married there.

The first time I met my new stepfather was when I arrived at St Thomas' Church for the wedding. It was a very simple ceremony, and Michael's son John and my mother's friend Mrs McLaughlin were witnesses. I knew Mrs McLaughlin because, as mentioned previously, her daughter Veronica and I went to secondary school together and subsequently on the trip to Lourdes.

I was glad that my mum had chosen Mrs McLaughlin as her witness because she was a comfortable person to be with, particularly when I was still trying to get my head round my mum getting married. After the church service, I hopped on a bus back to Merrylee Convent. During the journey, my thoughts were on the wedding ceremony and, although I hadn't had a decent conversation with Michael, I was glad, albeit a bit reluctant, that my mum had someone she could depend on.

Nun and Mum

A special day for my mum

I know that sounds really selfish because I had left my mum in the lurch when I entered the convent, but my mum's marriage had been really unexpected and I suppose I felt a bit miffed that my mum now belonged to someone else rather than me. Having said all that, my mother was entitled to some happiness and she was a lot better off financially than before.

Convent life continued to be steady and happy. I got to do more readings in church and I would look for the most obscure bidding prayers (prayers that you say for the intentions of the church and others). I would search in the convent library in order to find something unique to pray for and duly deliver them during Mass. I remember one of the nuns saying to me that she had never heard bidding prayers like those in her life. I don't know if I was being criticised or complimented, but I let the nun see the book I'd extracted them from and that seemed to satisfy her.

Because I was a good reader, Sister Mary Adelaide asked me to do a reading at her final profession of vows which took place after seven years of Convent life. I'm not sure if that's the case now, but I do know that after making final vows, a sister has to get a dispensation from the Pope if she chooses to leave. At that time, I thought seven years was a long time to wait, but I totally understand that it was a major commitment.

In the interim, a nun would take her first vows after two years and then two years later her second vows, but a final profession was a public ceremony and a declaration of choosing God above all else. Adelaide was a lovely nun and very charismatic. I had never witnessed anything close to her being annoyed until the day she asked Mother Paul if I could do a reading at her final profession and was refused. However, to Adelaide's credit, she accepted Mother Paul's decision.

I was bothered by the fact that I could not wear my black veil at the Mass but my white veil. In my opinion, I was going to stick out like a sore thumb being the only white veil in the congregation, but the sweetener for me was that Mother Paul and the Abbess had made that decision because they were proud they had a postulant. When I thought about it, I accepted the obedience that was expected of me and I never gave it another thought.

Primarily, the Franciscan Sisters of the Immaculate Conception was a teaching Order who did various works of charity throughout the word.

I loved going around the different convents in Scotland with the Franciscan Sisters. Merrylee was of course the 'Mother House', but there were convents in Bothwell, Dennistoun, Kilsyth and Greenock. I was always made to feel welcome, and I suppose that meeting the new novice was a novelty.

Touring around the different convents

One time, I went to the Bothwell Convent attached to what used to be Elmwood Private School. I accompanied Sister Imelda to the local psychiatric hospital, namely Kirklands Hospital, which I now know to have been established in 1879 as a private asylum following an amendment clause to the Prisons (Scotland) Act 1877. Under these auspices, the Glasgow District Board of Lunacy in 1888 was formed.

I thank God mental health issues no longer carry the same stigma as they did all those years ago. However, in 1973 on my visit with Sister Imelda, my first impressions were negative. There was absolutely no doubt that the patients were very troubled. We were shown into a secure women's room and I was so struck with terror, I could not even speak. I felt the panic rising in me as I listened to the wailing and screaming from these poor souls, and I was desperate to get back outside.

Sister Imelda remained very calm throughout the visit, but I was visibly shaking. This got worse when one of the patients, a young girl about my own age, suddenly began staring at me and then, from being huddled up in a corner, she stood up and started walking towards me. As she was coming at me, I kept going backwards until I was against a wall. I think Sister Imelda must have pressed a panic button, because a nurse appeared and took the girl to her room. Relief came flooding through me when it was time to go back to the convent. That was my first and last time at the Bothwell Convent in Glasgow, and I kept thanking God that my novitiate was in Merrylee.

Just after Easter in 1973, Mother Paul told me that I was to go to Cinderford for a couple of months. I think after the duster incident, she was probably glad to get shot of the feisty Sister Mary Margaret. I had never heard of Cinderford before but was informed that it was near Gloucester and that Sister Pius would be driving me down. Sister Pius was teaching Year 7 in St Anthony's Primary School – a fee-paying school which adjoined the Cinderford Convent – so she was more than familiar with the route. I didn't have a clue that her nickname was Stirling Moss, but I soon found out for myself when Pius was driving on the motorway. I was quite shocked when she took off her veil and threw it in the back of the car in the middle of the journey. She told me that her veil was in the way and felt more comfortable driving without it. I am not a nervous passenger, but what a roller coaster of a ride that was! What they said about her driving was true. She may have been a fast driver but she was a very confident one.

CHAPTER 31 –
MY CINDERFORD DAYS

We duly arrived (safely) at Cinderford, and I was introduced to the nuns who lived at 93 Belle Vue Road. The Mother Superior was Sister Chrysostom and I immediately liked her. Whenever she said something funny she would chortle to herself and that amused me no end. The other nuns who lived there were Sister Cassimer, who I nicknamed Casper, Sister Brigid and last, but not least, Sister Celestine. Celestine was the youngest of them all and was always smiling. I immediately liked her and I think that, because she was only 13 years older than me and had a real talent for music, I had more in common with her than the other nuns. I was shown to my room which was prettier than the cell I occupied at Merrylee, and I knew that I would happily settle into my temporary accommodation. Once I had unpacked my bits and bobs, including my guitar, I was called down to the kitchen to have dinner. You can imagine my surprise when on finishing the first course of soup the same plate was used for the main course. I began to wonder if the same plate would be used for the dessert as well and what if I didn't like the soup or the main course, but my fears were unfounded because after dinner was served, dessert was brought out in a different plate. Once dinner was finished, Celestine showed me around the primary school where she taught Year 1. I was impressed with the layout of the building and the classrooms were warm and inviting.

Celestine was really chatty and I felt that I had known her for years, instead of just a day, by the time the tour of the school was over. We returned to the convent house, where tea and biscuits were in abundance. I went to bed tired and happy and, better still, I had plenty of food in my tummy.

Regarding the habit of the Franciscan, most had a black dress or pinafore with a black veil with a white border that allowed some of their hair to be shown. The exceptions to the rule were the Nigerian sisters who wore a white habit due to the hot climate. I think I've mentioned previously that I can be quite pass-remarkable and of course the Cinderford nuns were no exception when it came to my scrutiny of them. When you see a picture of me, I know you'll be thinking, *She has quite the cheek to talk*, but it is my nature and I cannot help being observant.

When I first met Sister Celestine, I was struck by her fringe which looked like a curly, black ball of wool but that 'ball of wool' never seemed to move. No matter what time of the day or night, it remained the same, until eventually I asked Celestine if she wore hair lacquer. She said she did and then asked me whether or not I approved. I didn't want to say that I thought it was rather vain and just mumbled, "Oh, I just wondered." Celestine and I became firm friends. She played the organ at mass and sang at every opportunity. I taught her what little I knew of guitar playing and, in the weeks and months that followed, we played the guitar for the sisters and sang lots of different songs. I have the ability to immediately hear a harmony in a song and we didn't sound too bad.

At one point, Celestine made a tape of the two of us singing and I was pleasantly surprised. I was in Cinderford for my 19th birthday, and I remember, prior to morning Mass commencing, Celestine whispered over to me, "Happy birthday Margaret." I was chuffed that someone knew it was my birthday and I was spoiled rotten on that day.

I was so glad that I was able to attend some of the classes in St Anthony's Private School, Cinderford, and I was completely unfazed by this because I knew (or thought I did) that someday I would be a qualified teacher. I had been allowed to take some classes in St Gabriel's Private School at Merrylee, so I had a little bit of experience under my belt.

I enjoyed this part of my convent life, but I think I was a bit too strict because there was a little girl in my class in Cinderford whose mother came to see me to tell me that her daughter was quite sensitive and to tread warily with her. It was an excellent lesson in humility because I realised that with children, and indeed adults, you cannot have a one-size-fits-all attitude. This helped me change my methods.

As Confirmation time was approaching in Cinderford, Celestine and myself were asked to provide the music. Folk music seemed to be quite common in many churches, and I felt quite proud that I had managed to teach Celestine basic guitar chords.

At Merrylee, the younger sisters would play the guitar every night as part of recreation and sometimes during Mass. We were also invited to partake in concerts, and I truly thought playing at a Confirmation Mass would be a breeze. I was quite confident and for once my hands weren't wringing in sweat.

Sister Celestine and I chose the appropriate hymns for the Confirmation Mass. As is the norm, the Bishop was the main Celebrant and, unlike Scotland, the Mass was held in the evening instead of the morning. Everything was going splendidly until something (I can't remember what) began to amuse me. The same thing amused Celestine and we both burst out laughing at the same time. We were helpless with laughter and, believe me, the Bishop was certainly not amused. We couldn't get out of the church quick enough after Mass and didn't stay for the buffet provided as we were mortified. The Cinderford congregation wanted to know how it all went and Celestine and I just looked at each other without uttering a word. After the usual tea and goodies, we went to bed but, as chance would have it, I was on the morning bell the following week.

I stupidly thought if I drew the alarm time on my forehead I would automatically wake up early enough to knock on the sisters' doors, but the following morning I was woken to the panic-stricken voice of a nun calling out to me that we had all overslept. I was reminded of the Angelus bell episode at Merrylee when the nuns were praying as if they were on steroids, only this time there was a Mass, breakfast and a school to run albeit somewhat late. When Celestine asked me why I had overslept, I had to confess to forgetting my alarm clock. She gave me hers and the remainder of the week went by hassle-free.

All good things come to an end, and my departure from Cinderford was no exception. Celestine saw me off at the train station, and I made the journey back to Glasgow with very mixed emotions. I had the time of my life at Cinderford, and I think everyone was genuinely sorry to see me leave. This was more than reciprocated and it struck me that not being part of the Mother House brought with it a great deal of freedom. On reflection, that was probably a good thing but, as a 19-year-old girl, I did not have the insight or maturity to comprehend this. I knew I would see some of the Cinderford crowd during the month of July when the summer holidays came, and was looking forward to that, but there was a restlessness in me that I just could not shake off or understand.

Once back at Merrylee, I got back into the usual routine, but I was still unsettled. Mother Gabriel was going on holiday during the month of July, and she tasked all the younger sisters with various little jobs. I loved the Abbess but when she mentioned I was to be in charge of her precious plants I just about fainted on the spot. The younger sisters had all been gathered round to find out what their respective duties would be so we all knew who was to do what. I kept thinking I would rather have been swinging on the Angelus bell than going into the greenhouse to water plants. As previously mentioned, Mother Gabriel was really protective of her plants and I hadn't a clue about gardening. That night in the juniorate, Sister Kevin looked over at me and, as she did, I remember saying, "Bloody plant pots", to which she burst out laughing saying, with a gleeful tone, "I knew you'd be pleased."

The summer months at Merrylee Convent saw many of the sisters come and go as they pleased. There was certainly a relaxed atmosphere, and I was introduced to a lovely nun called Sister Mary Gerard. Gerard had come over from America with the intention of going to see Sister Ninian's parents in Saltcoats. I never knew I had a furry face until Gerard told me I had a face like a peach. Unknown to me, she went to my Novice Mistress to ask if I could accompany her to Saltcoats, after which I was immediately summoned to Paul's office. Sister Paul must have been in a bad mood that day because she didn't mince her words when she told me about Gerard's request. She was raging mad that a finally professed sister should ask for a novice to go with her to Saltcoats, and she brought up the Adelaide incident about doing a reading for her final profession. I was lost for words and felt that the scolding was unjust. However, prior to leaving her office, Mother Paul said that I could go to Saltcoats with Sister Gerard. We went the following day and were made most welcome by Sister Ninian's family. I really liked Sister Gerard and I am so thankful that I got that opportunity.

As I have mentioned, during the summer months many of the sisters visited the Mother House. The sister I met in Lourdes came up from London to see me, and I felt quite privileged that she had kept her promise. When she left, I felt quite sad because I had the feeling I would never see her again, but I was buoyed up by the fact that I was going to see Celestine again.

I thought that because we had been so close in Cinderford, when she came to Merrylee, there would have been the same closeness. I knew that particular friendships were not encouraged, but Celestine and I were always laughing about one thing or another and I had thoroughly enjoyed her company. However, when she arrived at Merrylee, her cell was in the main part of the building which accommodated all the finally professed nuns. Logistically, it wasn't as easy for me to converse with her except during mealtimes or walking around the grounds, but I felt quite hurt that Celestine seemed to go out of her way to avoid me.

On one occasion when she did speak to me, she said that she had terrible back pain, and I immediately went to the local chemist to get her some pain relief. It turned out to be a stone in her kidneys. I have had kidney stones and, believe me, it's like being in labour without the break between contractions.

The summer months passed quickly, but I still couldn't shake off that feeling of restlessness I mentioned.

The Abbess came back from her holidays (thankfully, her plants were still alive), and she decided I should have piano lessons. I can hardly play a note now but my music lessons were going really well, and I dare say, if I had continued, I would have achieved a lifelong goal, but this was not to be because I had finally arrived at my decision.

In early September in 1973, in the evening, I told the Abbess that I wanted to leave. Her first response was, "Methinks the lady doth protesteth too much." She then said that she would give me a month's leave of absence (something she had never granted to anyone else) because she felt I was making the biggest mistake of my life. I could hardly believe that they wanted to keep me after all the high jinks I'd been up to, but those lovely nuns did not want to lose me. My heart was breaking when the date of 9 September 1973 was set for my departure.

CHAPTER 32 –
LEAVING THE CONVENT

I have to say, at this juncture, that it is far easier to enter a religious order than to leave. This was made evident to me when my cousin Bernadette and her husband John came to collect me and gave me the silent treatment all the way back to Appin Road. I was really confused about the decision I had made and, to top it all, I wasn't just going home to my mum but I had to accept that I now had a stepfather in my life. I do remember telling myself that if I disliked Michael Donnelly, I would never show it.

Thankfully, my fears were completely unfounded because this white, curly-haired gentleman welcomed me with open arms. I immediately liked him and called him Curly. He called me Tiny and then gave me money to go and buy myself some clothes. The next day I hit the shops in Glasgow and came home with three different outfits. Curly was a really generous man, and he had a couple of sons who worked in Tennent Caledonian Breweries in Duke Street, Glasgow, which meant many crates of free beer. My mum enjoyed her beer, and I was glad to see that Curly seemed to make her happy because she had become so much more relaxed. This was something I had never really seen in my mum throughout the years, as she always had to work so very hard to keep us going.

During that month's leave of absence, I didn't know what my decision was going to be.

I dreamt about being in the convent and, although my dreams were both happy and sad, I would try to convince myself that it was a sign for me **not** to permanently return. In the light of day, I would then convince myself to go **back** to Merrylee. It was a real dilemma for me and I was torn apart inside.

This continued until I had to return to Merrylee and give the nuns my verdict, and I believe my decision was based on words of advice that Peter in the hairdresser's had given me when he said, "When in doubt, leave it out." I returned to Merrylee with a very heavy heart but just in time for my final dinner. I smiled round at everyone and Mother Paul asked me if my smile meant I was staying, but I replied in the negative followed through with profuse thanks at having me in the first place. After dinner, I said my final goodbyes but felt as though a weight had been lifted off my shoulders.

As the years go by, I sometimes wonder if I made the wrong decision because a supernatural life is far easier than being in the real world, but I can honestly say that I have never regretted being part of that life in the year I was there. My opinion of the Franciscan Sisters of the Immaculate Conception has never wavered, and I hope and pray that God continues to guide them as they carry out their wonderful Mission.

CHAPTER 33 –
PARISH LIFE

A sad incident happened at a parish I attended. Although St Anne's RC Church was my local parish, I would often go to St Thomas' purely for nostalgic reasons. At that time, the parish priest was Father N. and I have to say he was always really pleasant whenever he spoke to me. A couple of times, he stopped by my house when I was out, and my mum told me she didn't really trust him. I was a bit shocked about that and decided that, in order to avoid any conflict, I would go to St Anne's Church on a regular basis instead of St Thomas'. Little did I know then that my mum was right to feel uncomfortable around Father N. because, in 2007, he admitted being intimate with a Polish student named Angelika Kluk. This poor girl was a victim of the serial killer Peter Tobin who worked as a handyman in Father N.'s parish in the Anderston area of Glasgow. At Tobin's trial in 2007, Father N. admitted inappropriate behaviour towards Angelika and, of course, this opened up a massive can of worms where more women stated that they had been sexually assaulted as far back as the 1970s. When I heard that news, I realised that I could have been one of those victims because the timeline fitted in with my departure from the convent in 1973. Father N. (a self-confessed alcoholic) died in 2010 after suffering a suspected heart attack. Although I felt relief at not having had too much to do with him, I just remember feeling really sorry for a priest who, through a weakness for alcohol, had lost his way in life. As my mum would say, "When the drink is in the wit is out."

CHAPTER 34 –
POST-CONVENT CAREER PLAN

After deciding I wasn't going back to the convent, I now had to have a career plan, but before I decided I signed on at my local Job Centre to give my mum some money towards food. I loved libraries and thought a job as a library assistant would be the way forward, but I was torn between working in a library and becoming a policewoman. At that time, the height for female officers was 5'4" and I was a quarter of an inch over the restriction. I remember poring over booklets about the work policewomen were involved in, which was mainly missing persons, indecency cases and the care and protection of children. To be honest, I think the uniform appealed to me and in 1973 policewomen were glamorised in the glossy brochures that were freely available. I also have to point out that jobs in the early seventies were plentiful and I was really spoiled for choice. I decided to apply for the City of Glasgow Police and went to Oxford Street (near Glasgow city centre) to sit the entrance examination. After the exam, those present were told by the examiner that whoever failed would receive a letter within a few days, but those who had passed the exam would be notified a few weeks later.

CHAPTER 35 –
JOINING THE POLICE FORCE

I decided to keep my options open. At the same time as I had sat my police entrance exam, I applied for a library assistant position in my local library. As you can imagine, I feverishly checked the post every day to find out if there was a letter for me.

I'm not great at knowing how I have performed in an exam and the police test was no different. After a few weeks, however, I did receive a letter from the library to attend an interview but, within a couple of days of that, I was invited to attend an interview at Oxford Street because I had passed my police exam.

I looked at the salary the library was offering and compared it with the police salary which, at that time, was slightly more than what the library paid. The grand sum of £19.67 per week was the dangling carrot and, for that reason, I decided to forego the library interview and attend the police one. I was thrilled, as I made my way to Oxford Street, to meet the interview panel. The interview was going well until I was asked *why* I wanted to join the police.

I knew I couldn't say that it was because of the money so I managed to flannel something about helping the public. After the interview, I was escorted upstairs where a female superintendent by the name of Miss Kay continued with the interview. This was the very last hurdle, because I had passed the exam, met the height requirement and was reasonably fit and healthy. A police officer told me that I should address Miss Kay as ma'am and at that moment the nerves were kicking in big time.

Miss Kay and I chatted for quite some time, and it was inevitable the question about what job I had been doing after I left school would be asked. I told Miss Kay that I initially wanted to become a nun and she immediately replied, "Eunice, you are going from the sublime to the ridiculous." She then warned me about the kind of people I would be dealing with and the danger of being spat upon or even assaulted. I just kept reinforcing that I thought I would make a good policewoman.

After questions and answers going back and forth like a ping-pong ball, Miss Kay said to me, "Eunice, you have a quality of innocence about you, which is a good quality, but I really don't know if you would fit in with police life." My heart sank, but my spirits soon rose again when Miss Kay told me she wanted to give me a chance and would make arrangements for me to be fitted out with a uniform from the police outfitters in Albion Street, Glasgow.

I was as happy as a lark on my road home and couldn't wait to tell my mum how I got on. Much to the annoyance of other people, when I am regaling a story to anyone, I start at the beginning and put in every single detail about my story prior to reaching a conclusion. My mum must have felt the frustration other people feel because when I reached the part about the 'quality of innocence', my mum immediately interjected calling me all the fools of the day for coming across as 'too innocent'. The stubborn part of me felt like keeping the end result to myself, but I just carried on and saw the relief on my mum's face when she realised I'd bagged myself a good career.

After being measured and subsequently picking up my police uniform, we new recruits did some of our training at Oxford Street in Glasgow. This was to finalise a few issues, a chance to ask questions and getting the important BCG vaccine to prevent tuberculosis. We formed an orderly queue prior to the injection, and one new male recruit was absolutely slated for passing out when he saw the size of the doctor's needle. I laughed with everyone else but, when it came my turn, I did likewise. I was mortified but delighted when I was told that since I had already been vaccinated for TB, I wouldn't have to get a second inoculation.

Oxford Street is quite near the city centre and, one day at lunchtime, I decided to get my lunch from one of the nearby takeaway shops. The city centre was really busy and, as I walked towards Argyle Street, thinking I was the bee's knees in my uniform, a driver crashed into a parked car. He was drunk and I had no way of alerting anyone to assist me. I hadn't a clue what to do because I had never had any formal police training. I could smell the alcohol off the driver, but he must have realised I was a police rookie and he took off. I was annoyed with myself but that accident was to prove a very valuable lesson for me when I dealt with a road traffic accident a few years later.

CHAPTER 36 –
FIRST STAGE TULLIALLAN
POLICE COLLEGE

In 1973, police officers did their First Stage training for one month at Tulliallan Police College in Kincardineshire. This is a residential establishment with more than adequate accommodation, a good size gym and a swimming pool. The female officers resided in the castle part of the building and the males within the main body.

I loved my time at Tulliallan and made some great friends. I was aware that females were not equal to their male counterparts, but I am not saying that was a bad thing because, when it came to training, and in particular doing press-ups, we females had it a whole lot easier. Nevertheless, I can remember literally crawling up the stairs to my dormitory after a session of PE. If I had considered myself fit prior to joining the police, I soon realised that it was certainly not the case. Every bone in my body ached and I was certainly not alone. As the weeks went by, the weary bones hurt no more due to the amount of time we spent in the gym. I don't remember swimming in my First Stage at Tulliallan – that was something to look forward to in Second Stage.

The role of a policewoman in 1973 had primarily to do with missing persons and taking indecency statements, as well as cot deaths. We did not get any of the heavy duties that were expected of male officers. Furthermore, night shift consisted of a couple of weeks a year. We were paid less than the male officers but, in my opinion, we were a whole lot better off. Policewomen were truly respected, something I didn't fully appreciate until we became Strathclyde Police.

After First Stage at Tulliallan, I had been assigned to the Tobago Street Police Office in Glasgow, which is near the famous Barras Market. Tobago Street and the surrounding areas were really rough back then but, having spent most of my life in Dennistoun, I knew the area like the back of my hand and was grateful to be stationed somewhere close to home.

I was excited and nervous at the same time when I first entered the Tobago Street building but was soon at ease when introduced to my fellow colleagues. I immediately liked a couple of girls, namely Agnes Brown and Jean Swinton. Agnes and Jean were great fun and already had one month's service under their belt. There was a senior policewoman called Sheila who asked me to accompany her to the mortuary because she was dealing with a baby death.

I tried to convince myself that I was quite happy to accompany Sheila to the mortuary, because I knew that it would be a good training exercise. The first thing that hit me inside the mortuary was the clinical smell. Sheila explained to the mortician why we were there and gave the required information to the mortician who led us to the room were the baby was.

Baby death

Nothing, absolutely nothing could have prepared me for what I was about to witness. I could not stop staring at this little, stone-cold baby lying on a mortuary slab, an image which still upsets me. The little girl had a thin head of hair and she was beautiful. I had to stick my glove over my mouth to stop myself screaming, and I knew that if Sheila saw how upset I was she would have told our superiors, Sergeant Bell or Sergeant Wardrope, and I was quite sure that my reaction would have been written on my six-months' assessment. I couldn't wait to get out of the mortuary and couldn't trust myself to speak to Sheila on the road back to Tobago Street. She kept asking me if I was okay, and I told her I hadn't slept the previous night. She seemed to accept this explanation, and we walked back to the office in silence.

All of this had happened in my first week at Tobago Street and, when I got home that evening, I told my mum all about it. I burst into tears whilst I was telling her and, during my sobs, I told my mum that I thought I had made the biggest mistake of my life by joining the police force. If I thought I was going to get any sympathy from my mum I was very much mistaken. She truly believed in tough love and reminded me that I had a good job and shouldn't take things to heart.

Thankfully, my mum stopped me from resigning there and then, and I told myself that I would give the police force six months and if I still felt as bad as I did that first day, I would resign knowing that I'd given my job a fair shot.

I look upon the first few months of my police career as the halcyon days. The east end of Glasgow had its fair share of criminals, but the policewomen were shielded from all of that. Whilst in the Tobago Street Office, I became very familiar with procedure and a great way to learn was going through the many files stacked on shelves.

Naturally, I was keen to find a copy of my own indecency report about the man who had sexually assaulted me in Appin Road. Once I had found my file, I looked closely to see if anything had been missed, but my statement was very accurate despite the fact that the culprit had never been caught. Nowadays, it would be so different because of DNA. The pieces of flesh and blood that I had spat out after the attack would have nailed the perpetrator. I often wonder how many times that man had attacked young women, but I guess I'll never know.

Prior to joining the police, the last formality was a visit to my house by an inspector called Chris C. She was lovely, and I was delighted when I found out that she worked from the Tobago Street Office. One day, she called me into her office and asked me if I would be willing to work from the Shettleston Police Office. She wanted a policewoman she could trust to assist a senior police woman called Ruth who had worked on her own at Shettleston for quite some time. I was already familiar with that office because I had been there a few times, going out on Truancy Patrol. Nevertheless, I loved my time at Tobago Street and had some great laughs with Jean and Agnes, but we always caught up for a night out at weekends so I knew I'd still see them one way or another.

Shettleston Police Office

Just before going to Shettleston, Jean told me that a Mr Lyons had requested a call from me. It wasn't a name I was familiar with but I looked at the piece of paper Jean had in her hand and took it from her. I dialled the number and the person on the receiving end said, "Good afternoon. Calderpark Zoo. How can I help you?" I immediately burst out laughing and told the guy I'd dialled the wrong number.

I enjoyed my time at Shettleston Police Station. Ruth and I worked our socks off, but we had a lot of fun moments. Some days we would accompany the driver and crew in the station's police van. We were seated on wooden benches on either side of the back of the van which was handy when we needed to be somewhere on official police business, but we also had a great deal of fun. When things were quiet, the crew would ask us if we wanted to go on a wee run, and if we didn't have much on it was brilliant. We'd stop at the chippie, crack jokes and generally have a good laugh. Moments I will always treasure.

We policewomen were issued with new hats as part of the standard uniform and, whenever we had to go out during the first week or so, we were extremely self-conscious. The first time we wore them, the Shettleston cops who were on early shift all lined up as we were walking in through the door and *sang* "Where did you get that hat, where did you get that hat?" Ruth and I were mortified but it didn't stop us laughing.

Ruth was engaged at the time and was soon to be married. In those days, the life expectancy for a policewoman was all of six years which was considered a long life. Female officers normally got married, became pregnant and subsequently left the force to take care of their baby. Married officers were shuffled around like a deck of cards, something which was just accepted. After Ruth got married, she returned to Tobago Street and I found myself running the Shettleston Office.

Quite often, I would get a new recruit to assist me and, one day, I was working with a policewoman called Mary Goff. Mary was gorgeous looking but earned herself the nickname 'Jaws' because she was always chewing gum. I'll touch more on police nicknames later in my book, but hardly anyone escaped being called something other than their birth name. I will also tell you more about Mary later on but, suffice to say, I thoroughly enjoyed her company.

The Baillieston Office

One day, I received a phone call from Inspector C. asking me how I was getting on. She would pop in now and again to the Shettleston Office, but her visits were few and far between. Her phone call came as a surprise, but I was a bit gutted when she asked me if I would set up a department in Baillieston. Inspector C. sweetened the news somewhat when she said I would only be there for six months or less. Baillieston had been part of the Lanarkshire Police and not the city of Glasgow and, although it is a part of the east end of Glasgow, in my mind's eye, I wrongly considered them as country bumpkins. I knew I would have my work cut out for me, but nothing prepared me for the mess I had to clean up.

Truth was, if someone went missing in Baillieston, there was no follow-up procedure. A name and contact number was taken and shelved until the missing person returned. I can't say I enjoyed my time at Baillieston, because there was a mindset about female officers and I felt that I was very much the outsider. I felt lonely when I was there, although my work didn't suffer, but I was only too glad when my time was up and I could go back to Tobago Street. Back there, I immersed myself in taking as many witness statements as I could and that mainly involved rape or some other form of indecency. I knew what to ask a victim, I knew how to act around a victim but, being an ex-convent girl, I hadn't a clue what the sexual connotations meant. There was a hockey team which a few of the other policewomen were members of, and I think if I had been part of that group my sex education would have improved greatly because, after a hockey match, it was the norm to get drunk and sing some rather sexually explicit songs. However, for the time being, I was forced to wing it.

Night shift
The policewomen did night shift about twice a year. The shift would start at 11 p.m. and finish at 7 a.m. and involved a stint at 'A' Division, St Andrews Street in the city centre of Glasgow. Normally, there would be a sergeant and a policewoman from a completely separate divisional police office and a policewoman from the Eastern Division, depending on whose turn it was on the rota. I didn't know what to expect during my week of night shift, and this may come as a shock to those who know me, but I was quite shy in front of strangers.

I was well aware that my performance would be scrutinised and reported back to my sergeant or inspector. I turned up at 'A' Division for the night shift and was introduced to a sergeant by the name of

Gwen. I thought at the time the sergeant had an unusual surname, and for the life of me I can't remember the name of her policewoman, but I know that she had a few more years police service than me. As luck would have it, the sergeant was a police driver and we policed all of the city of Glasgow divisions in the comfort of a panda car. I was really quiet for the first few nights, both in the patrol car and back at the office.

I had never seen any evidence of bigotry until one night when all three of us were in the London Road area of Glasgow. The sergeant in her lovely Aberdeen accent said to the other policewoman, "I wonder whit fit she kicks wi'?" (This comment alludes to whether or not you are Catholic or Protestant.) My heart sank because we were only a few nights into night shift, and I was only too aware that being a Catholic would not bode well for me. The sergeant asked me what school I had gone to, and I was never so glad to truthfully say that I had gone to Charlotte Street. She seemed quite happy with this explanation, and I felt I'd had a lucky escape. (If I had said that my high school was Our Lady and St Francis, I think that week of night shift would have been unbearable.) As we were approaching the end of the night shift, the sergeant said to me, "Eunice, you have really come out of your little box, haven't you?" I had become more familiar with my colleagues and, as the week progressed, we all got on well but, if I'm being honest, I was glad when the night shift ended.

About a month later, I got a phone call from the lovely Aberdeen sergeant saying that she had enjoyed working with me and would happily have had me in her division. I was chuffed about that phone call and immediately dismissed the thought that if the sergeant had known my background she may not have been so lavish in her praise.

It was soon time for me to go back to Tulliallan Police College Second Stage which involved three full months and weekends at home. I was excited about going back and sleeping in the castle area of the building, but there was an unusually large amount of policewomen on that course and we were put in dormitories quite near our male counterparts.

CHAPTER 37 –
SECOND STAGE TULLIALLAN

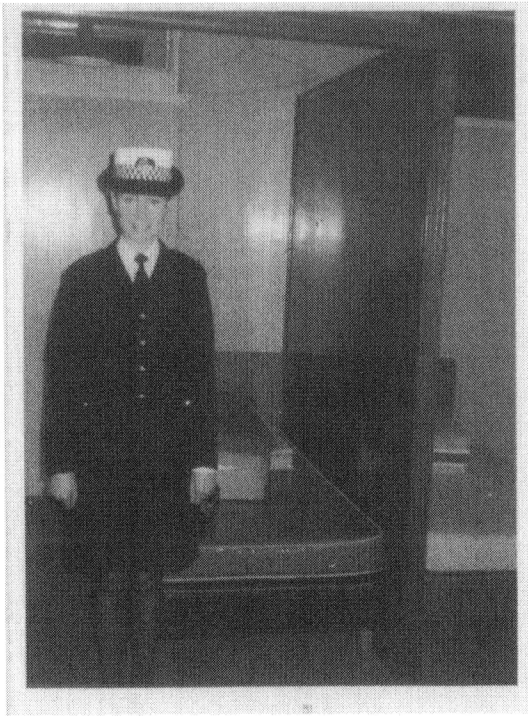

Tulliallan police college second stage

Life at Tulliallan was far more intense. First off, we had to study like crazy and respect for our senior officers was paramount. I recall thinking that a sergeant in my own 'C' Division commanded less respect than a sergeant at the police college.

Training was exhaustive, and we had very little time to go from being in the swimming pool to attending class. We found out that if we didn't change in double quick time we were in trouble. Whilst on the subject of swimming, I was delighted when I passed my Elementary exam and was put forward for Intermediate which required jumping off a diving board and treading water, some basic life-saving skills and diving for a brick six feet under water. At the end, the instructor told me that I had passed my Intermediate exam but would not be putting me through to the Advanced Stage because he felt that I had reached my potential. This was all fine by me, because I had come a long way from when I was that girl in Belfast thrown into a swimming pool by her cousin.

Tulliallan police college

It was winter in Second Stage training and absolutely freezing, but we were still expected to go for long runs in shorts and a T-shirt. I could see the reasoning behind this because due to the freezing cold you ran as fast as you could in order to get back to the warmth of the gym department. I came in first every time when competing against my female colleagues but was accused of taking a shortcut because my face wasn't bright red from exertion! Thankfully, the instructor believed that I was just one of those people whose face remains the same colour before and after a run.

Drill was an important discipline for recruits. Our uniform was inspected and it had to be pristine. Many of the girls got the male officers to bull their shoes so that the toecap came up like black patent. What that involved was spitting into a black polish tin, dipping a duster into the polish and intermittently holding a lighter to the shoe to melt the polish. This was one thing I didn't need to worry about, because my shoes were shiny faux leather, not real leather.

After drill and inspection, we were dismissed from the parade square and, depending on where you were on the inspection line, a recruit led his fellow colleagues back to the main building. I dreaded my turn because my sense of direction is terrible. The due day came and, as I walked off, everyone followed me like sheep and, lo and behold, before I knew it we were in a ditch!

All I could hear was the sergeant in charge shouting, "Where the hell are you going?" I could only mumble an excuse and apologise to my colleagues for causing their footwear to get so dirty.

During the first month in Second Stage, we had a little icebreaker session whereby we stood at the front of the class and told everyone about ourselves including where we worked prior to joining the police. This was another dreaded moment, because I didn't know what the reaction would be when I said that I had entered a convent for a year. In hindsight, I should have just mentioned working in the hairdressing salon but instead I told the truth. Obviously, a lot of questions were asked but, to be honest, it really wasn't the big apocalyptic deal I had expected it to be.

The food was brilliant at the police college and each table took it in turn to say grace. The sergeants and the remaining hierarchy sat at the top table whilst the rest of us sat at round tables of eight. It gave us all an opportunity to get to know one another and dinner discussions were often about the day we had or the forthcoming exams which were held on a monthly basis. However, going back to the subject of saying grace, I heard some weird and wonderful ways to thank God for our food including the famous and great Bard of Scotland, Rabbie Burns' words for the grace before meals prayer, which starts with 'Some hae meat and cannae eat ...'. On one occasion, after the commanding officer asked whose table's turn it was to say grace, no one responded. I was frantically looking around the tables and not one person stood up. I knew this reflected really badly on our training instructors so, in the absence of anyone else, I stood and asked everyone to join me in grace. My contribution to the cause!

At the end of the day, it was expected that we socialise in the club at Tulliallan and the bar area was always busy. I resented my time away from studying, but I didn't want to appear antisocial, so I would get up every morning at 6 a.m., have a quick shower, get dressed and then take my books into the toilet where I locked the door, sat on the toilet seat and crammed in some studying. My exam marks thus far had been quite high and I wanted to maintain this. We had outside lecturers coming into the assembly unit, and I never wasted an opportunity to get a bit of shut-eye somewhere at the back of the hall. Being at the police college was truly rewarding but also exhausting (in a good way).

I've mentioned before that we only spent weekdays at Tulliallan, and I was never short of an offer of a lift home. Many of the cops were married and couldn't wait to get home to their wives and family, but it was a different story for me.

One of Curly's sons would bring crates upon crates of beer from his workplace at Tennent Caledonian Breweries, and there was nothing unlawful in it as it was a perk of the job. However, some of the lager tins had a high volume of alcohol and my mum, being a beer lover, was unable to help herself. I don't think she fully realised that after more than a few cans she became intoxicated, and I just hated seeing her like that.

My mum was not an alcoholic, but I was seriously worried that she would end up one. The only thing that kept me going at weekends was going back to the police college on a Sunday night. I was friendly with a girl called Lorna. She was pretty and had the sweetest nature. I decided to stay one weekend at Tulliallan instead of going home, and I asked Lorna if she would stay too. It was the third month at Tulliallan and, apart from the reasons for my not going home, I felt we could put in some serious studying.

Moreover, the college was prepared for Second Stage recruits that lived too far away to travel home at weekends and supplied all our meals. For me, it was bliss. Lorna and I studied like crazy during the day and went out to the local pub at night. However, Lorna really missed her family, and I knew that I'd be 'on to plums' if I asked her to stay another weekend.

Exam time

Exams were coming up fast and furious and that included a first aid exam. I was fine with the theory but dreaded the practical test. Unfortunately, because of my theory mark, I was put into a group with a very strict instructor. Out of a hundred or so recruits, I was the only police officer to fail the exam. The sweetener was that I would get a second chance but with the same examiner. I knew I really had to concentrate on the practical part or risk the humiliation of failing a second time. The odd thing was that, despite all the policewomen in my dormitory passing the exam, I was the only one who knew what to do when a girl in our dormitory fainted. I had suffered fainting attacks and I knew the first thing was to put her head between her legs to allow her blood to circulate. Once I had done this, Kate was fine and carried on as though nothing had happened. A few of the policewomen said it seemed unfair that I failed the practical exam, but if the truth be told I just wasn't prepared.

My repeat exam was set for the following week, and the group included those who had missed the exam through no fault of their own as well as me. Thankfully, I did manage to pass it but only by the skin of my teeth!

We had a female sergeant called Kathleen Jones who was not only our mentor for Police Studies but also for some of the sports activities. I had played netball at school, and knew the rules, but couldn't seem to score a single goal at the police college.

I began to think I was a complete dough ball and, when Sergeant Jones sent for me one evening, my heart sank. She took me along a corridor to see some of the inspectors and chief inspectors on the course and, at this point, I truly thought I was getting my marching orders. She led me by the arm into a large office and said, "I want you to meet Miss Graham. Miss Graham can charm the birds off the trees." I could not believe my ears and my face was scarlet. I just grinned and said hello and then asked if I could go back to my dormitory. What I did not know was that Sergeant Jones was putting my name forward for the Endeavour Trophy. I returned to my dormitory feeling chuffed but when my friends asked me why my face was so red, I just said I'd been in a bit of a rush. I never mentioned my encounter with the police hierarchy to anyone.

As well as a final exam, we were expected to entertain our superiors by putting on a concert and funny skits (within limits, of course). I had my guitar with me, as did many other officers, and apart from singing a few well-rehearsed songs ('Paper Roses' by Marie Osmond comes to mind) we had a great laugh poking fun at some of the senior officers. It was a great performance and, being a large Second Stage course, the talents were wide and diverse. After the evening's entertainment, we had some very well-deserved drinks before bed.

Passing-out parade

The next thing on the agenda was the final exam and the seamless drill required for our passing-out parade. In my First Stage at Tulliallan, my exam marks were just average and I was determined not to make that mistake twice. I was growing in confidence as a scholar and a police officer. I was quite confident about the exam and managed to score above 80%. By the time our drill instructors were finished with us, our moves were nothing short of perfect. There was great unity on that course and the fact that the commandant, staff of all ranks and ages, as well as visitors, were going to watch our passing-out parade made us determined to give the performance of a lifetime. On special occasions, white gloves were worn and female officers wore white bands around their hats which was a stark contrast to our black uniforms.

Once the parade was over, we all went to the assembly hall where the commandant announced the winner of the Baton of Honour and the Endeavour Trophy. A female officer from Aberdeen won the Baton of Honour, one of the most prestigious awards in the police force, and a male officer from one of the counties won the Endeavour Trophy. It was at that ceremony I realised Sergeant Jones had put me forward for the Endeavour Trophy and, although I didn't win it, I was flabbergasted to be runner-up. Once all the excitement had ended, it was time to say goodbye to Tulliallan and, with very mixed emotions, I returned home.

I was due a fortnight's annual leave and decided to take this just after I returned from Tulliallan. After a day or so, I woke up with really severe back pain and it just got worse as the day went on. My mum decided to call a doctor and, since we didn't have the privilege of a house phone, she went to a phone box down the road. The doctor duly arrived and, after examination, he said that I had slipped a disc. He gave me some strong painkillers and told me that my back should be alright in a couple of weeks. I could have claimed back my annual leave but I didn't. I was just so thankful that I hadn't had a slipped disc at Tulliallan. The pain was excruciating, and I couldn't even go to the toilet unassisted. I lay on the living room carpet because the hard surface seemed to ease my back. After a fortnight, I felt ready to return to Tobago Street. It was great to see my friends again although I met up with them at weekends.

CHAPTER 38 –
A CRY FOR HELP

One evening when I was on back shift, I answered a telephone call that had come through to the policewomen's department. I was surprised to hear a little girl talking on the other end of the phone, and I will never forget her words. She said, "I am nine years old and my daddy has left me and my little brother in the house by ourselves again. He goes to the pub all the time and leaves me to look after my wee brother."

I asked the child her name and address and, accompanied by another officer, attended the house in Dennistoun. After a couple of flights of stairs, we knocked on the door and the little girl answered.

Child neglect cases were referred to as Section 32s, and there was no doubt in my mind that this is what I was dealing with. The little boy was about two years old and still in nappies. In fact, that's all he was wearing. The little girl didn't look too unkempt but the flat she stayed in certainly was. I checked the food cupboards to see what was stocked and couldn't find anything substantial to eat. It was about 9.30 p.m. and my colleague and I called for a panda car to take us all back to Tobago Street. I left a note for the father to let him know what had happened and to ring the office as soon as he got back from the pub.

My main priority was making sure the children were okay, and I quickly dressed the little boy in something more suitable prior to going back to the office. The little girl was chatty, but her brother was very subdued. Once we reached the office, some of the male officers went out for chips and juice because the wee ones were famished. I called Social Services for the children to be released into their custody, but I still had to deal with the father.

As well as feeling really sad for the children, I was furious that any human being could abandon his children not only once but on several occasions which I had noted when taking the little girl's statement. The father phoned me the next day, and I asked him to come to the Police Office. He was not in the least remorseful, and the fact I was charging him under Section 32 of the Children and Young Persons (Scotland) Act didn't seem to faze him.

I could not believe it when the man pleaded not guilty and the case was going to trial at the Sheriff Court in Ingram Street. The accused had hired a very good lawyer and he did a fair job at trying to discredit me whilst I was on the witness stand, but the father was found guilty and the children remained under the care of Social Services.

My colleague Agnes Brown had a similar case and, like me, she was really upset, but this time the brother and sister were to be separated and neither child wanted that to happen. It was heartbreaking but, nevertheless, we had to accept it as part and parcel of the job.

More incidents

One early shift, a policewoman and I saw a car crash into a mini. This incident happened in Dennistoun in Bellgrove Street just off Duke Street. These roads in Glasgow are heavy with traffic at peak times. However, it was not our remit to deal with RTA offences. Until our male colleagues arrived, I wanted to make sure that we noted every single detail of each vehicle as well as the drivers involved in the accident. My mind went back to that time when a drunk driver had managed to escape due to my inadequacy and lack of knowledge. On this occasion, I decided to err on the side of caution. By the time the cops on that beat attended, my colleague and I had jotted down pretty much everything in our notebooks. I was delighted when those beat cops informed Inspector C. about the incident and the efficient manner in which it had been dealt with. I felt somewhat exonerated after the embarrassing drunk driver episode when I was a rookie.

Fleeing the nest and back

I was approaching my 21st birthday and, although unexpected, my colleagues made an enormous fuss over me which I truly enjoyed. About a month earlier, my friend Jean asked if I fancied sharing a flat with her. I said I would, but it puzzled me that Jean was prepared to leave East Kilbride for Dennistoun.

I am a born and bred Glaswegian but I loved East Kilbride, and something about the area where Jean lived felt like home to me. We moved into the flat about a month prior to my 21st birthday. It was nice to have my own bedroom and a bit more freedom away from my mum and Curly. Before leaving, I had a phone installed at my mum's home and that gave me peace of mind.

My 21st celebrations at the flat were great, and my friend Jean had a cake made for me. I treasured the lovely adorned charm bracelet which she gave me, and that evening we celebrated with a bottle of Martini. To say my head was pounding the next day is an understatement. I had the mother and father of all headaches and, there and then, I decided I would never touch Martini again. I kept that promise to myself.

I remember we had a few parties and invited our male colleagues, but there was never anyone special that I was attracted to. There were a couple of gorgeous American Mormon guys that we met and invited them back to our flat. One of them had a crush on me and then spoke about leaving his partner whom he had just got engaged to. I advised him otherwise and, despite getting letters from him, I didn't answer in the hope that he would get the message.

In the flat, I was bothered by my mum's constant phone calls. She said she was against my moving into a flat and, on one hand I began to regret buying a telephone for her, and on the other hand I thought my mum was going through empty nest syndrome. I knew that the only way I would get any peace would be to return home. Jean was a great flatmate and I was dreading telling her about my decision, but she was very magnanimous and I think she decided it was cheaper to stay at home rather than pay property rental.

When I wasn't pubbing and clubbing with my friends, I would sometimes go to Old Drumchapel in Glasgow to visit my Aunt May. She had a lovely wee house and kept it immaculate. My godmother and I had an unshakeable bond and, although there was a large age gap, I felt I could tell her anything. She asked me to come and stay with her, and it was heart-wrenching for me to say that my first concern had to be my mum. It still makes me sad to think that I had to say no to my dear aunt. I never visited her home again because, shortly after, Bernadette told my mum and I that my Aunt May had suffered a stroke. It made me wonder if when she'd asked me to live with her she had been feeling unable to cope on her own. Bernadette took on the task of taking care of my Aunt May despite having a husband and (at that time) four children to deal with.

CHAPTER 39 –
TAKING MY GODMOTHER
TO GLENARM

I wanted to give Bernadette a wee break and therefore decided that I would take my Aunt May to Glenarm, so I wrote to Marie requesting permission to stay at her house for a week and received a letter saying I was welcome anytime. My Aunt May was really looking forward to going to Ireland, after all that's where she came from, and although she had lived in Scotland for a number of years, she never lost her Irish accent. We happily boarded the train for Stranraer and got on the ferry to take us across the Irish Sea. It seemed to me that my Aunt May had made a remarkable recovery from her stroke, and I truly thanked God for that. When we got off the ferry, we went to the bus station to catch the Glenarm bus. I think it was the last bus of the day because I remember it being quite dark albeit still warm due to the summer weather

Marie's house was fairly large and charmingly old-fashioned. The interior comprised of a kitchen, dining area with one of those old black ranges for cooking, a long hallway and a parlour. The only time visitors went into the parlour was if Marie was giving a music lesson or at night-time when the family said the Rosary followed by a cup of tea or hot chocolate and a biscuit. There was no television, but Kathleen Stuart (a distant cousin) and a lady called Cissie were frequent visitors in the evening.

In the dining area there was a settee which was used by the dog as a bed. Marie loved dogs and when Bracken died she immediately got another one. Upstairs there were three bedrooms. Marie had the large bedroom to herself and there were two smaller rooms.

On that August evening, my Aunt May and I knocked on Marie's door and, when she came to let us in, I thought she seemed a bit off. She led my Aunt May and me into the room where my wee Aunt

Cissie (the lady who sent me the dress and stole) had occupied until she died. By this point, my Aunt Martha and Uncle Tommy were also dead so Marie was now living alone. Anyway, Marie told us that is where we would be sleeping.

I wasn't used to luxury but I couldn't believe that, given the size of the house, we were expected to share the smallest room in the house. Marie returned to the parlour where Cissie and Kathleen were, and I felt really glad that Marie had company. I couldn't figure out her attitude, but I suspected she would act okay in front of her visitors. I unpacked my Aunt May's suitcase and my own and left my Aunt May to put her medication and other bits and pieces on the dressing table.

The parlour door was ajar and, as I was walking down the stairs, I heard Marie say, "She needn't think I'm going to be looking after May, I've had enough of looking after old people." I felt humiliated and was silently praying that my Aunt May hadn't heard that painful remark. I walked into the parlour as though nothing had happened but, before I sat down, Marie told me to go and get my Aunt May's jar. I hadn't a clue what she was talking about but apparently it's a hot-water bottle, so I duly boiled a kettle and put the ceramic jar under the bedcovers. By this point, my Aunt May was in the parlour and, after the usual hot chocolate and biscuits, the visitors left and we all went to bed.

My Aunt May had sleeping tablets but they caused restless leg syndrome and, needless to say, I hardly got a wink of sleep. I thought Marie would have been in a better mood the next day, so I mentioned the difficulties of the sleeping arrangements. I thought she would have said I could either sleep in the double room with her or go into the third bedroom, but I was horrified when she said that if I wasn't satisfied sleeping in the single bed with my Aunt May, I could have the dog's bed instead! Wow!

Things just went from bad to worse that week. I accidentally broke a plate and all hell broke loose. I offered to go into Larne – which is the nearest town – and pick up a similar plate, but I was told it was an antique and to forget it.

Kathleen next door was always a bundle of joy, and she had some saucy postcards which we both had a right good giggle at. She told me to show them to Marie and, when I did, she turned her head and said, "I've seen these before." Not once did I see her smile, and I gave up trying to engage her in conversation, but I earned myself the remark "being a martyr doesn't suit you".

Another time, when Marie was out, a lady came to the door. I had never seen the woman before and when I explained Marie had gone to the shops, the woman turned and walked away. When Marie came back she was livid with me and told me that I should have escorted the lady into the parlour. I simply could not win.

There was a bit of respite from Marie's attitude because, every day, my Aunt May and I would walk along the coastline and, occasionally, I would pop in to see Mona and other people that my Aunt May and I knew. I was glad of these moments because I didn't want to tire my Aunt May out, but I knew Marie did not want us in her house. Marie was a creature of habit and always went to Larne on a Wednesday which meant that we had one free day when we didn't need to go out. She was always a few hours in Larne and those days were far more relaxing. On the subject of Larne, I took my Aunt May to the shops and she loved that because, inevitably, we would end up in one of the many fancy tea rooms. I noticed some small side effects of her stroke but that didn't stop us having a great day out.

The most heartbreaking day of the week came when Kathleen asked if I'd like to go out for a ride in the car. Kathleen, Alec, and his son Michael and I all went out for dinner, followed by a lovely walk on the hills of Antrim with plenty of photographs taken at the most scenic spots. After an exhilarating day, I went into Marie's house and my Aunt May looked at me with tears in her eyes. I asked her what was wrong, and she told me that Marie had given her into trouble for accidentally letting the dog out.

I still feel my Aunt May's hurt and pain and thought about either going home early or staying in a hotel for the next few days prior to going home, but if we had gone home early, questions would have been asked and that would have caused a family rift.

On the other hand, questions from the locals would have been asked if we went to a hotel or boarding house. It was a no-win situation and we had to just suck it up. By that point, I was taking some of my Aunt May's sleeping tablets out of sheer desperation to escape her restless legs and, if I'm being honest, to escape my own thoughts.

Finally, it was time to leave and we arrived at the ferry port in Larne to be told that the evening ferry had been cancelled and we could only board the first morning ferry. There was no way on God's earth I would have taken my Aunt May back to Marie's house, so I made her as comfortable as possible and, after a very long night, we were finally homeward bound.

I had decided not to say anything negative about the terrible time we had in Glenarm because I thought it would cause a rift in the family. We got off the train at Central Station in Glasgow, and my cousin Bernadette said to me, "That was a nice thing you did for my mammy." I just smiled and there was no family breakdown. However, later on in life, Bernadette told me that my Aunt May had heard the comment Marie had made about looking after old people. I feel really sad as I write this because my Aunt May knew when I took her to Glenarm she would never be back and she wasn't. She predicted that she would have her three score years and ten on this earth. She ended up with dementia but, as predicted, God took her into His loving arms when she was almost 70 years of age. I still feel devastated at how she was treated by Marie and, although she herself is now deceased, sadly my opinion of Marie changed.

CHAPTER 40 –
THE POLICE CONCERT PARTY

In the seventies, I became very friendly with a policewoman called Wilma. Wilma was a Baptist and I was often invited to Praise and Worship in the Baptist Church. Over the years, I have had many Baptist friends, and I've always said that if I wasn't a Catholic, I would have been a Baptist.

Wilma and I were identical apart from the fact she had brown eyes and mine are blue. Wilma and I joined the police concert party, and at least once a month we would put on a performance in the Wellshot Halls, Shettleston, Glasgow. Wilma's party piece was 'The Old Rugged Cross', and the applause was deafening every time she sang it. We used to perform a duet and sing whilst I played guitar. The other song we sang was 'Sisters' from the musical *White Christmas*, and I think the audience truly believed that Wilma and I were blood-related. The concert party involved giving talks as well as music from different genres.

Another time when we were giving a concert, I was first on the stage to sing a song. There was a male officer who was really popular, and his party piece was 'Twa Heids are Better than Yin' (two heads are better than one), made famous by the Glasgow duo, Robin Hall and Jimmie MacGregor. If you ever get the chance to check out the lyrics please do so. It will give you a laugh if nothing else. The reason I'm telling you this is because the cop who sang it arrived just after the concert started, and as soon as the audience saw Jimmy walk through the door they all started clapping and cheering. I could have been Donald Duck up on that stage for all the audience cared, and I didn't know whether or not to walk off or carry on singing. It was one of the most humiliating moments of my life. In the end, I carried on singing because I didn't want anyone to think that it bothered me, but I don't ever remember going back to the Wellshot Halls as a member of the concert party.

CHAPTER 41 –
THE TRANSITION TO
STRATHCLYDE POLICE

On 15 May 1975, the City of Glasgow Police amalgamated with other divisions to become Strathclyde Police. This meant that policewomen had the same rights as their male counterparts. Even though we would now get the same wages and be treated equally, we were none too happy about the change because, in those days, policewomen were quite elite and did a specialised job. Unfortunately, this would no longer be the case. I don't know about other divisions, but certainly the Eastern Division of Tobago Street, Glasgow felt both anger and sadness that the chief constable had been instrumental in making this decision. It also meant that we could be transferred to Renfrew and Bute, Dunbartonshire, Stirling and Clackmannanshire or even as far as Argyll and the Isles. We couldn't go out without a bang, and a parade of all City of Glasgow Policewomen was arranged by senior female policewomen. I don't remember the exact date, but it must have been quite early in the month of May that we donned our best uniforms, wore our hats with white bands around them and our white gloves which were for special occasions only.

We formed a perfect line, with different rows, and marched in unison past the City Chambers in Glasgow. Photographers were on hand and, because I was on the outside of one of the rows, I got to see a clear picture of myself. We all felt enormously proud and I can honestly say, I never thought that my picture would end up as a museum piece. If you are ever in the City Centre of Glasgow, the Police Museum is worth a visit. Apart from the picture of the last ever policewomen's parade, there is a lot of interesting information and memorabilia.

CHAPTER 42 –
MY FIRST TRIP TO SPAIN

In the summer of 1975, Mary Goff and I decided we would go on holiday together to Spain. I had never been before and, after poring through brochures, we settled for Calella in the Costa Brava. We couldn't contain our excitement and decided that we would have a different outfit for every night of our 14-day holiday. I even went so far as to write down what outfits I would wear and itemise the list onto the inside lid of my suitcase. Mary invited me to her house to meet her mum and dad prior to the holiday. It was Mary's first time abroad as well as mine. Before leaving Mary's house, her mum told me to look after her. I told her not to worry and that I'd make sure we both got to Mass. It has always been really important to me to get to Mass on holiday, and one of the first things I do is check out the nearest Catholic Church.

I don't remember Mary and I going to Glasgow Airport, or even the flight itself, but I will never forget as we alighted the aircraft via the stairs the warmth that enveloped me. I also remember the Spanish smell and humidity and immediately felt exhilarated. Mary and I collected our luggage from the carousel, and there was a coach waiting to take us to our hotel. I was absolutely desperate to buy souvenirs and became quite despondent when the coach seemed to be taking us through rough terrain and there was no sign of a shop. However, as soon as we arrived in Calella, my spirits completely lifted. There was a plethora of souvenir shops, and I immediately loved this amazing town with its lively beach. We had arrived at our hotel quite early in the afternoon, so bikinis and sunbathing were the order of the day.

Being in our early twenties, Mary and I were checking out the 'talent' as we lazed about in our deckchairs around the pool. When the sun disappeared, we got all dolled up for dinner and were led by a waiter to a table for six people. There was an elderly couple and it was obvious that the man was the dominant one. His wife was scared to even order a glass of wine in case he disapproved.

Mary and I got into a routine of spending our days on the beach, buying souvenirs when the shops were open after siesta time and booking a few trips. We also managed to bag ourselves a couple of boyfriends. Obviously, we had been noticed by a couple of good-looking guys, but I think this was due to Mary going to a hairdresser to have her hair cut. Mary's new haircut really did the trick because it was a conversation starter. Her hair looked amazing, but it totally changed her appearance and made her look even prettier than before.

We booked a trip to go horse riding which was followed by a meal and sangria, the local Spanish drink. We were taken by coach to a ranch, and neither of us had ever been on a horse. I made the stupid mistake of wearing shorts and open-toed sandals because they looked fashionable. When we got to the ranch, one of the horse trainers said, "Anyone who has never ridden a horse before, please put their hands up." Mary and I immediately complied and that was one of the biggest mistakes of our lives. We were helped up on to the two biggest horses in the ranch. I thought I was going to have a heart attack. To crown it all, I couldn't steer the bloody horse and it ended up crashing into a wall, with my left leg and toes getting scraped alongside it. My leg and toes were bleeding, and the trainer was almost wetting himself laughing. I have never been so glad to get off a horse in all my life. Mary wasn't half as bad as me, but I was shaking like a jelly. I didn't have much of an appetite, and neither did Mary, but drank the sangria on offer like it was going out of fashion and, after the alcohol had the desired effect, we both agreed that we had had an amazing experience!

Another trip we paid for was a barbeque party. Mary and I got dolled up again and were taken by coach to the venue. There was plenty to eat and, because we were missing our evening meal, we had our fill of sausages, hamburgers and steaks as well as side salads. Again, the sangria was flowing, only this time there was a large stone fountain absolutely full of the stuff. It was almost like a round swimming pool and God alone knows what else was in that pool apart from the sangria, but we were given ladles of the stuff. Photographers didn't miss an opportunity to take pictures of the revellers, and Mary and I were totally inebriated. We had our photographs taken at the top of the stairs near the fountain, and poor Mary slipped and fell down them. She wasn't in the least bit hurt because, by that point, I think her body was just like rubber, and I have to confess I wasn't much better.

The next morning, we were both hungover to say the least and skipped breakfast but, by the afternoon, a good swim in the sea cured our sore heads. After sunbathing, we went for dinner and at our table we would regale the other guests about our adventures and vice versa. The woman who was really quite controlled by her husband became bolder as the nights went on, and I remember his eyes nearly popping out of his head when she ordered a bottle of wine for herself instead of a glass. After that, she just ignored the disdainful looks and carried on drinking whatever took her fancy.

As the holiday was coming to an end, Mary and I did some serious present shopping. In those days, lots of people brought toy donkeys back as gifts and the carousel at Glasgow Airport was full of them. Mary and I bought gifts for each other as well as the world and its auntie, but we never bought any donkeys. By the end of the fortnight, we both had an amazing tan and, believe me, we worked hard to get it. Fabulous holiday, great company, brilliant weather and, yes, we did go to Mass.

CHAPTER 43 –
MY 'BRUSH' WITH HER MAJESTY QUEEN ELIZABETH

Her Majesty, the late Queen Elizabeth, came to visit the Calton area of Glasgow which is near the famous Glasgow Barrowland and the Barras.

By this time, I had completed my probationary period and was classed as a senior policewoman which meant that I got to mentor some of the new probationers. Inspector C. called me into her office and advised me about the Queen's visit. She gave me the background detail, and I was like a nodding donkey hanging onto her every word, pretending I knew exactly what she was talking about. (Noddy was one of my nicknames in the police.) I remember wondering why I was being given information about times, dates, etc. until Inspector C. told me that, apart from there being a large police presence, she wanted me to take any flowers that the Queen was given from her lady-in-waiting. This was all about timing, and I was to take a probationer with me so I knew I couldn't mess things up. I felt honoured and scared witless at the same time. The due day arrived and, once again, it was a case of best bib and tucker in the uniform department. I was watching the Queen's every movement, so much so that I was oblivious to the large crowd that had gathered just to get the smallest glimpse of her. As soon as the Queen was given her flowers and she turned round to pass them to her lady-in-waiting, I nudged the young probationer and stepped in line with the Queen's entourage. The Queen received many bouquets of flowers which meant my probationer got her fair share of the action. I look back with pride and think I was so privileged to have been chosen to not only carry out an amazing duty but to have one of the most beautiful memories of my life.

A new wee dog

Being a police officer and living where I did brought more than its fair share of problems. I was despised by the local neds because of my job, and they would vandalise my car at every opportunity, as well as shout and swear at me whenever they saw me on the street. Since my first dog Roy was dead, I went to the nearest cat and dog home and came home with a beautiful Border collie. Suzy was in a filthy condition when I picked her up and, because I had gone to the cat and dog home on a bus, I naturally had to take a bus home. I had a cream-coloured coat on and had to take Suzy upstairs on the bus due to Glasgow Corporation rules. Suzy had bonded with me immediately, and I stupidly forgot to take a collar and lead for her. The dog decided to make herself comfortable by sitting on my knee, so you can imagine what my coat looked like when I got off the bus. The reason I'm telling you about Suzy is that, just like my dog Roy, she had her own personality. She seemed to sense when I was in trouble, because whenever I got flack from the local neds she chased them along Appin Road. She was relentless in her pursuit and she knew her way home, so I left her to it and hoped to God that she managed to bite my troublemakers. I think something must have happened because, a few weeks later, someone knocked on my outside door to deliver a *wreath* with my name on it!

CHAPTER 44 –
THE COMMUNITY INVOLVEMENT
BRANCH OF THE POLICE

By this point of my police career, I was in the Community Involvement Department, and our duties involved teaching children in the local primary school about the difference between right and wrong. You may think that parents should have been responsible for this task, but these children came from some of the poorest backgrounds and quite often classrooms were fumigated prior to our arrival. We engaged the children by using puppets, and my colleague and I would set up a screen, hide behind it and make the puppets talk to each other. The children enthusiastically engaged in this activity and sometimes got completely carried away when one of the puppets misbehaved. Many of these children were used to shouting and swearing, and even violence, in their own homes and followed that through when watching the puppets. One occasion, when a puppet was misbehaving, a little boy shouted, "Stick the heid oan him!" This is typical Glaswegian lingo which calls for someone to hit the head of the other while they are fighting, i.e. with their own head. I was with a cop called Norrie and none of the two of us could carry on with the puppet show for laughing. The local radio station got news of children interacting with the puppets and, once more, I found myself in the limelight. I don't want to sound as if I'm blowing my own trumpet, and I may not be coming across as having any humility, but with the permission of the local head teachers I had worked so many puppets that I was starting to believe my hands could talk.

Again with the permission of head teachers, I would go to the local schools and show a film called *Never Go With Strangers*. I had to learn how to operate the old-fashioned reels which would now be considered as antiques. The children would gather in the assembly hall, I would set up the reel and the film which lasted between 20 and 30 minutes. This was an ingenious way of not only capturing the attention of the little ones but driving home the message that it was not okay to be lured away by a stranger, regardless of what goodies were on offer. At the end of the film, I would ask the children to describe what they thought a stranger was, and I got some weird and wonderful answers, from 'monsters' to 'ugly people'. Although I praised the children for their efforts, I never received the answer I was looking for which was that a stranger could be anyone. I truly hope that I managed to get the message across and none of these children came to any harm.

In the Community Involvement Department, we had an inspector called George. He was a great guy with a brilliant sense of humour. We also had a sergeant called Jack and a couple of policewomen, including myself, and a clerkess. The department ran quite smoothly, and since Sergeant Jack seemed to be such a grumpy character, I would always try to be nice and friendly in the hope it would bring a smile to his face.

After I had been on holiday with Mary, I came back with a golden tan, and Jack did remark a couple of times how well I looked. At this point, I did not know how my life would change from thereon in.

A wee trip doon the watter

Sometimes the Community Involvement would take pensioners on a day trip down the coast, and one day we all boarded a vessel called the 'sludge boat'. The purpose of the sludge boat was to dump the city's sewage sludge. In spite of this, they were enormously popular with thousands of citizens who fancied a wee freebie trip 'doon the watter'. Trippers were picked up at the sewage works in Glasgow, and the sludge boat sailed down the river to empty its tanks at Garroch Head, the south end of the Isle of Bute. Glasgow citizens were survivors but, like everyone, they needed a break, and even the sludge boat created happy memories in what could be very dark times. Let us not forget the backdrop of World War II and the devastation it caused to the Glasgow economy.

Sergeant Jack had quite a lot to drink and began overstepping the mark with me right in front of some of the pensioners. When we finally got back to Tobago Street, I hid in the ladies only to hear him persistently knocking on the door and telling me, in not so many words, that I was the best thing since sliced bread. He eventually left, and the next day he apologised profusely. I accepted it and thought that was the end of the matter.

I was thoroughly enjoying my time in Community Involvement. There was always a great atmosphere, we didn't have to wear uniforms (apart from giving talks at schools) and, as time went by, I was given more duties and responsibilities. There was a CID chief inspector whose office was near ours, and he constantly asked me to join the CID. His name was Chief Inspector Catchpole, affectionately known as 'Catch the Polis'. My hours in Community Involvement were day shift with weekends off, and I wasn't prepared to give that up.

The Community Involvement had a good relationship with the local social work department and had expanded to giving talks to local secondary schools. One of these schools was Eastbank Academy and there we decided to form a weekly after-school youth group.

That was great fun and the pupils were wonderful. In fact, the department made the decision to take some of the older pupils to Millport. The due day arrived and, fortunately, it was sunny. Because it was the weekend, there was plenty of police supervision from our department, and I was looking forward to just curling up on the coach and having a wee, cheeky sleep, but a couple of the girls came back for me and wanted me to hang around with them. I thought it was a lovely, kind gesture and I hadn't the heart to say I would stay on the coach and sleep.

Still going down memory lane, I recall taking a class of primary schoolchildren to the Mounted Branch. The children loved stroking the horses and brought apples for them to eat. There were many funny anecdotes, one of which was about a mounted officer who invited the children to ask questions. I heard the word 'Dobbin' and I said, "Now children, say hello to the nice horse, Dobbin" only to be disdainfully told by the mounted officer that *his* name was Dobbin! After my grovelling apology, he saw the funny side.

CHAPTER 45 –
MY ACTIVE PART IN THE
EDINBURGH TATTOO

The world-famous Edinburgh Tattoo is always held in the month of August and in 1976 there was a huge police presence and not just for security purposes, but anyone with any talent was expected to participate. Some very senior police officers picked a dozen or so policewomen to perform country dancing. I was one of them and, prior to the event, hardly a night went by when I wasn't involved in dance practice. There was one particular dance (can't remember which one) where I kept making the same mistake over and over again. It was a nightmare because I knew how important the Tattoo was and everything about our dance moves had to be perfect. The Tattoo has a time slot of approximately three weeks and with audiences of around 20,000, combined with the price tag attached to this event, people naturally wanted value for money. I was sick with worry, but I managed to overcome my dancing blip prior to the start of the event.

The Police Pipe Band led off the celebration, and cops from Denmark came over to play various instruments. I have to say the Danes are really handsome and extremely courteous. The policewomen wore white dresses with tartan sashes and black dancing pumps and, when it was our turn to perform, our dancing sets went without a hitch. After the performance, we were treated to finger food, nibbles and drinks and that allowed us to get to know each other better. Thankfully, our part in the Tattoo only lasted about three days, but I enjoyed the small part I played in such a prestigious event.

The romance that followed the Tattoo
I was never short of a lift to and from the event. By this point, I was really friendly with all my colleagues in Community Involvement but particularly Jack. On Monday 23 August 1976, Jack took me home.

We were alone in the car together and, just as I arrived home, he gave me a really passionate embrace. He told me that he had fallen in love with me. He was almost 18 years older than me, but for the first time in my life (albeit having had boyfriends) I really fell in love. The big problem was that Jack was married with two children. When I got into the house, my feelings were all over the place.

How could something that was so wrong feel so right? No surprise that I hardly slept a wink that night. I was 23 years of age and should have been mature enough to know my own mind, but it is true that love is blind and I was both dreading and looking forward to seeing Jack the next day.

I must admit the whole affair was truly illicit but, no matter what, we couldn't seem to break it off. The thing is, when I get worried I lose weight and everyone I came in contact with kept remarking on it. My dear mum actually thought I was dying, and I couldn't tell her the real reason for the weight loss. Please don't think I'm looking for sympathy, I deserve none. What I was doing was completely abhorrent and shameful.

Jack told me he had never been truly happy in his marriage and, prior to getting hitched, he had tried to break if off with his wife. However, both Amelia (name changed) and Jack's mothers did a bit of matchmaking. Jack had been going out with a woman called Susan but, because she was a non-Catholic, the relationship was frowned upon. Jack's own mother was very religious and felt that her son should get married in the Catholic Church hence the encouragement from both sides for a Catholic wedding.

For the sake of his own children who were in their early teens or thereabouts, Jack said he could no longer go on seeing me. I was heartbroken but knew in my heart that it was the right thing to do. I remember my last words that night being, "God bless."

However, within a week Jack said he couldn't be without me. It is true that people who get involved with married men or women try to justify the relationship in every way possible, and I was no different. Sadly and wrongfully, I pushed thoughts of Jack's children to the back of my mind. It wouldn't have taken Sherlock Holmes to work out the fact that Jack was having an affair, and his wife would follow Jack's every move. One time, I left an earring in his car and that merited the third degree from his wife who seemed to pop up everywhere we went. The poor woman must have been breaking inside and, to this day, I can only say that I am truly sorry.

Police assessments

In the police, we had annual assessments and obviously the news of my affair with Jack had reached high-ranking officers.

One day, Chief Inspector McDonald called me into his office for my assessment. He was a lovely man and later down the line we worked alongside each other. I went in for my assessment at the appointed time and, as I had guessed, it was awful. I was accused of being lazy and slipshod in my work and that I had absolutely no ambition.

I remember thinking it was definitely payback time for me, but the assessment was really harsh and quite frankly untrue. Inspector George had retired by this point and was replaced with an inspector who ruled with a rod of iron. The chief inspector had to sign the assessment off after completion by our new Community Involvement inspector called Mr R. Chief Inspector McDonald simply refused to accept Inspector R's comments and said that anyone who had just sat and passed their promotion exam definitely had ambition. I think he already knew that, despite everything going on in my personal life, I did have a real work ethic.

A short time later, I was called in again by the chief inspector who advised me that my assessment had changed to reflect my own competencies. I should have been happy about that but I have a very determined streak in me and I decided I would make an appointment with the superintendent in charge of Tobago Street Police Office. I demanded that he go through all my assessments. I knew by his manner and body language he was feeling uncomfortable about it and wanted me to speedily exit his office, but I stayed until he read out every single remark about me. He never cracked a smile at any point in that interview and neither did I, but when I left his office I felt vindicated.

CHAPTER 46 –
TRANSFER TO SHETTLESTON
CRIME PREVENTION UNIT

About a month later, I was transferred to the Crime Prevention Department in the Shettleston Office. I was working alongside a sergeant called Charlie and, apart from general administration duties, my remit was to investigate burglaries that had taken place and give the relevant advice such as getting an alarm fitted. It was up to the shop owner, or whoever had been a victim of burglary, to take our advice, it was their choice. Every Thursday, the superintendent held a warning court for juvenile offenders. Glue-sniffing was really prevalent in the seventies and, after a few sessions of sitting in with the superintendent, I was allowed to take these courts myself. On one occasion, a man brought his son and was not prepared to listen to any advice. The father became quite abusive and he and his son ended up being escorted out of the building. I remember thinking that the man's son would definitely end up a victim of the criminal justice system with a father like that.

The Crime Prevention Office operated 9 a.m. until 5 p.m. (except for the Thursday warning courts), and during my lunch breaks, I'm ashamed to say, I was still seeing Jack. I kept wondering what Jack saw in his wife but, then again, she was a lot older than me, and I suppose having a couple of children is not always easy. Furthermore the fact I was seeing her husband must have cost her many sleepless nights. One day, I bumped into Jack's wife in Chester Street immediately outside of the Shettleston Office. She demanded an explanation from me about my affair with Jack and was visibly upset. I was so arrogant (and I am truly ashamed of this) that I said to her, "Your husband is no oil painting but I happen to love him." After this unkind remark, I walked into the police office and burst out crying in the toilet. The toilet was just next to the sergeant's office, and I had only just composed myself when I heard one of the sergeants saying, "She's a nice-looking girl, what on earth does she see in him?" I knew I was the topic of discussion and of course that set off more waterworks. It was a hard and confusing time for me but, then again, I deserved it.

I was then approached by the parish priest of St Anne's Church and the first thing he said was, "Who's the boyfriend?" I felt dreadful because I had known that priest since my schooldays, and I just couldn't come up with an answer. I don't know who went to see my parish priest, but I did know that he was going to advise me to stop seeing Jack. I knew that was the right thing to do and my conscience was screaming at me, but I wasn't prepared to listen to it.

Confession time

My mother needed to know what was going on, and it was one of the worst conversations of my life. I asked her to sit down before I broke the news to her but was surprised when she said to me that Jack needed to get a separation. I don't think Curly really heard much of the conversation, if he did, it wasn't obvious. Please don't think my mother was condoning the affair – she certainly wasn't – but her words about Jack and his wife getting a separation are the ones most prominent in my mind.

I still kept in touch with Sister Celestine and whenever she came to visit her parents in the Barlanark area of Glasgow, I would go and see her. Her mum and dad were lovely people, but sadly her mother ended up in a home because she had dementia. Celestine was the next one on my tick list regarding Jack and, obviously, she was none too happy about the bombshell I dropped on her. A few days later, I received a letter from her telling me to stop seeing Jack. I knew in my heart that it was either Jack or Celestine and, it was too late for me to stop seeing my future husband. I didn't reply to Celestine because under no circumstances did I want her to feel compromised. It was many years later when I decided to get back in touch with her.

At home, things were semi-normal. My mum wasn't drinking much beer, and any time she fell out with Curly I would take him to his favourite pub which was the Kirkhouse Inn in Shettleston Road. Curly was registered blind and he looked forward to his weekly visits to the pub. By this point, I was driving. It took me three attempts to pass my test, but on the first occasion I only had ten lessons prior to my test and there was no way I would have passed. Not only that, I had no car to practise on, so my lessons were of paramount importance. The second time I went for my test, my instructor told me the name of one of the examiners. He also told me that if I got that examiner I would definitely fail. This was just prior to the test, so no pressure! Lo and behold, I did get that examiner and he failed me on one thing. I immediately booked my third test and, I don't know if you have noticed, but a driving examiner doesn't say very much apart from giving instructions. I hated the silences between the examiner and pupil, so I vowed to myself that I would just talk about everything and anything in the hope the examiner wouldn't know if I made any mistakes. When it came to the third driving test, the examiner's ears must have been ringing because by the time the test was over (apart from his instructions), the only two words he managed to get out of his mouth were, "You've passed." That very same day, I went to the Royal Bank of Scotland and asked if I could take out a loan for £100 and, with it, I bought myself a wee Ford Anglia (Harry-Potter-style). Needless to say, I was teased unmercifully by my fellow colleagues to the extent that they wrote the following poem:

Off oan a wee jaunt went Eunice
In her ain wee caur it was bliss
But God help the poor pedestrians
That Eunice tried to miss.

I can't remember the rest of the poem, but I think four lines are probably about as much as you can take. However, I did have the pleasure of offering Miss Fitzpatrick a lift home after Mass one Sunday. My driving must have been awful – either that or she was a very nervous passenger – because at every junction we came to she would ask me to wait until a car went past and, for the first time ever, I completely disobeyed her, because I felt there was more than enough room to get out of the junction. I got the impression she was very relieved when she arrived home safe and sound.

CHAPTER 47 –
A WEE BIT MORE ABOUT CURLY

Back to Curly. As I've said, he was registered blind. I used that to play little tricks on him, as we had such a good relationship and I thought I would make him laugh. My hair was always long and dark, but one day I bought a blonde, curly wig and put it on before I went to talk to him. Because of his eyesight he didn't notice I was wearing a wig and he kept shouting, "Tiny, Tiny, what the hell have you done to your hair?" I quite nonchalantly said I'd had it cut, coloured and curled. I honestly thought that Curly was going to burst into tears. After I realised I was taking the joke too far, I pulled the wig off and my dark hair fell down over my shoulders. Thankfully, Curly saw the funny side of it. I think I would have had the silent treatment for a very long time if I'd been bold enough to change my appearance so dramatically.

Curly smoked a pipe and was always saying the best pipe you could buy was a meerschaum. Apparently, these are now an antique dealer's dream, and Curly had told me he would love one but they were too expensive.

I went to a tobacconist shop in Glasgow city centre and, when I saw that meerschaum pipes were on sale, I bought one for Curly. I think it must have been for his Christmas or birthday, but he was totally overjoyed and any person who came to the house was shown the meerschaum even before they could remove their coat. I am so glad I bought that pipe because it was to be my last gift to him.

Being quite a bit older than my mum made it almost inevitable that he would die before her. One morning circa 1977, Curly was complaining about chest and back pains and the doctor immediately sent for an ambulance to take him to Belvidere Hospital on London Road.

The hospital has now been raised to the ground for housing purposes, but Belvidere was originally an infectious diseases hospital.

After Curly had been in hospital a few days, my mum said that he kept asking to see me. I honestly thought whatever was wrong would have been cured and he would be back sitting on his chair at home puffing on his pipe. I had all this business going on with Jack at the time and to say I was selfish would have been an understatement. Nothing and no one else mattered to me more than Jack. I should have gone to see Curly sooner and not four days after he had been in hospital. When I walked into the ward, he was truly delighted and I felt very ashamed. I knew he cared about me and vice versa, but his reaction that day was just indescribable. I gave him a massive hug and kiss before I left, and the next day my mum received a phone call from the hospital to tell her that Michael (Curly) had passed away during the night. His sons took over the funeral arrangements and, to this day, I still regret not going to see him every night during visiting hours. I felt that the only 'father' I had ever known had been taken from me. Curly once said to me, "Do you like me, Tiny?" to which I replied, "I love you, Curly."

After working in crime prevention for about two years, I knew my stint was coming to an end. It was no surprise that because of the situation between Jack and me that I would end up working early, back shift and night shifts on the beat. I hated it and, at every opportunity, I would remain in the office to write up crime reports. I just kept turning up for work, doing the job to the best of my ability and waiting for my shift to end. Early shift began at 6.45 a.m. and ended at 1.45 p.m. There is a reason why I am being specific about these times.

The curse of the menopause

Since Curly had passed away, my mum and I put two single beds in the bedroom. I can't remember where I slept when Curly was alive but it was probably on the living room settee. Anyway, I was back in the bedroom with my mum who was not a great sleeper (runs in the family). She was also going through the menopause at the time and, night after night, for hours on end, she hurled insults at me. I never said one word back to her.

I totally dreaded going to bed, knowing that I was doing the early shift the next day. When my mum was finished verbally attacking me, she would then say in the sweetest voice, "Eunice, Eunice love, can you make me a wee cup of tea?" I would diligently go and make the tea and then get ready for work. I don't want to paint a horrible picture of my mum; it was only later that I came to realise that she was having menopausal symptoms and I don't think my mum knew what was wrong with her, but it was relentless.

Night shift hours were fine because I could sleep during the day, and when I was on back shift I didn't start until 2 p.m. so I managed to get some shut-eye. One day when I was working early shift and had taken all the verbal abuse my mum had thrown at me, she started on me again as soon as I came home. I have a very placid nature and I can't believe I'm actually writing this, but my mum was so in my face that I slapped her across the cheek. I immediately jumped back and thought, *Oh my God she'll kill me*, but my mum didn't say a word. I was apologising like there was no tomorrow, but that one slap must have made my mum realise that she was taking things too far with me because I never received nasty comments during the night again and, later on in life, my mum apologised for "putting me through hell" (her words).

CHAPTER 48 –
BACK ON THE BEAT

Before I knew it, and just as I suspected, I was put on the beat. No more cushy numbers for me. Not only was I patrolling the streets, but I was put on Group 3, headed up by Inspector Finnie who had earned himself the reputation of being a man who ruled with a rod of iron. I dreaded it but, at that time (not now), I saw that as a way of God punishing me for my relationship with Jack and, in some skewed way, that's how I managed to accept it.

I have to say that Inspector Finnie was great with me. He gave me a great neighbour, a young guy called John (nicknamed 'the Claw'), and the two of us were always on the beat in the Tollcross area of Glasgow. We were known as the Tollcross Patrol and before the commencement of each shift, the Claw would check the register to see what beat we were on. John and I had great fun. We managed to find a wee bakery and, when we were on early shift, we'd go into the kitchen for a cuppa and rolls and sausage. Once we were fed and watered, we would go to a large park just off Tollcross Road which housed a mini zoo. The streets were quiet so we took the opportunity to have a look at the goats – one of which we decided to call 'Finnie'. There was also a myna bird in the zoo and the zookeeper – a Glasgow Rangers supporter – spoke with a burr in his voice which meant the 'R' sounding words were more prominent.

The myna bird never shut up and kept shouting "Good old Rrrrangers" at every opportunity. It never ceased to amuse us, but we had a job to do and an inspector who was fanatical about statistics, so we had to get on with some good old-fashioned police work and produce results.

A cheeky wee cuppa
On the night shift, and to a certain degree on the back shift, our 'doss' (a place you could go for a cuppa) was a home for the elderly

in Braidfauld Street. The staff were brilliant with the police and it was a great way to keep warm in winter. The only downside was that Braidfauld Street was near Wellshot Road which was next to Tollcross Road and we had our notebooks signed at least twice during our shift. The minute we gave our location, Finnie and his sergeant would know we had been dossing, so the Claw and I had to come up with something else. We managed to find a secluded street, but it meant climbing fences to get there at short notice before our notebooks were signed. It worked a treat because it took Finnie and his sergeant longer to find us. I began to enjoy my shift and at break time in the muster room, our time was spent playing pool which I became really good at.

The shift totally accepted me, knew that I was a reliable witness in court and was good for doing the dirty dishes left by other shifts. The Claw and I became great pals, but he was never happy when I was taken off the beat to help out with incidents that required a policewoman. I was fine because I got transported about in a panda car.

One night, an Indian takeaway in Tollcross Road went on fire. We summoned the fire brigade and more officers to try and extinguish it and prevent damage to other properties. In cases like that, the CID looked at all the evidence to know whether or not the fire was accidental or deliberate. It was eventually established that the fire had been deliberate and was an insurance job. The wee Asian guy had started it because his business was declining. I had spoken to the man in the past and his English was really broken so I couldn't wait to see what was written in the CID report. I burst out laughing when I read what the man said. It was "Not only do I set fire to shop but I make screaming c...t of it".

At one point on my inspector's shift, I decided to apply for a job as court officer, but Finnie had to oversee it and put his comments on the application. He summoned me to his office and said, "Eunice, are you really sure about this job? If you're not, on a personal note, I don't want to lose you." I thought long and hard about it and, although having a 9 a.m. to 5 p.m. with weekends off would have been cushy, I don't think I would have been as happy as I was on Inspector Finnie's shift.

In the seventies and eighties, the police had a heavy drinking culture to the extent that some officers became alcoholics. The shifts played a huge part in this, and getting free drink for making sure pubs and off-sale premises were secure simply added to the alcohol culture. Sadly, I witnessed with my own eyes, a really nice inspector, who was promoted to the Eastern Division, going from being a social drinker to an alcoholic in six months. It got to the stage he would steal drink that had been confiscated from prisoners or even money to buy alcohol. At his Long Service and Good Conduct Medal Ceremony, he could hardly walk in a straight line. It was tragic.

Another time, two police officers who had escorted a prisoner from England to Scotland had a couple of pints on the train and ended up being dismissed. One of them I felt particularly sorry for because he was a great officer, and I was relieved when he managed to get a job in the fire service. I was quite friendly with a sergeant who was having marital problems and resorted to drinking during the night shift. He had been a Baton of Honour winner at Tulliallan and that is a truly prestigious award. He asked me not to cover up for him if the night shift superintendent was about but, although that never happened on my shift, I would have probably covered up regardless. The other thing about the police is that men and women can become seriously attracted to one another, as was the case with myself.

Whilst I was still on Tollcross Patrol, the Claw was off one night and a guy called Jimmy (drop-dead gorgeous) was John's replacement for the night. Jimmy and I got on like a house on fire at break times but, that particular night, when we went to check in on one of the pubs in Tollcross Road we were offered a drink. We declined, but Jimmy said afterwards that he had been sorely tempted, as was I. We were both gasping with thirst but losing your job for a pint of beer simply wasn't worth it. There was mutual chemistry between Jimmy and me, but I was engaged to Jack by then and I really had to rein it in. Later in life, I heard that Jimmy had left his wife for a policewoman. It's possible that if I had remained on Finnie's shift, I could have been that policewoman and somewhat responsible for not only breaking up one marriage but two. Thankfully that never happened.

Superintendent Cunningham to the rescue

There was a new superintendent that came to the Eastern Division, and Inspector Finnie called me in one early shift and said that Superintendent Cunningham wanted a word with me. I had a serious attack of the drips because I thought I was in trouble for something, but it was quite the opposite. Superintendent Cunningham had been going through staff records and, when he came to mine and he saw that I had passed my Sergeants' Exam, he was raging that I was out on the beat. He said that I would be leaving Finnie's shift to be appointed bar officer in the Shettleston Office. That didn't fill me with delight because I was so happy on Inspector Finnie's shift, but there was no way I was going to refuse the offer. My shift planned a night out for me in Glasgow town where I drank Babycham like there was no tomorrow. I chose that drink because it was low in alcohol and thought I wouldn't get drunk, but one of my colleagues pointed out that he had lost count of the amount of alcohol I had and needless to say alcohol in small measures should have been applied!

Board and lodgings for Jack

Before I tell you about the next stage of my career, I need to give you a little update about Jack. In the late seventies, Jack left his semi-detached house to his wife and children. After thrashing out financial arrangements, a divorce was agreed. For a short while, Jack went to live with his sister who had a large bungalow in Glasgow. After a few weeks, however, Jack felt it was a bit unfair to be staying with his sister, because she was friendly with Jack's ex-wife and was getting caught in the crossfire of the whole sorry business.

It was common practice at that time for widows (mainly) to offer a spare room to a police officer. This came in really handy for officers who were travelling long distances considering that we were now Strathclyde Police and it covered a wide area. Jack managed to find digs with a lovely, wee lady but, within a few months, he decided we should buy a house in the Dennistoun area. I helped him decorate because it had been previously inhabited by an elderly gentleman and the flat needed a lot of work. Jack was a good handyman and, between us, we managed to get the flat to a really good standard. The added bonus for us was that one of the Shettleston typists lived next door and, although she knew Jack well, she used to do my typing for me and we also became friends. Cathy was one of those kinds of people who are age defiant. When Cathy was in her forties, we all thought she was in her twenties. She had a great nature and used to call me 'little one'. Cathy was very mild-mannered but warned me repeatedly not to go into the CID. She said I would have been "swallowed up".

CHAPTER 49 –
UNIFORM BAR OFFICER
AT SHETTLESTON

The hoose and me taken outside Shettleston police office

Back to work. My predecessor at Shettleston was a guy called John. He was now bar officer in Tobago Street and, as bar officer at Shettleston, my supervisor was a man called Sergeant Johnston (affectionately known as 'The Hoose'). The story goes that not long after he had moved house, Sergeant Johnston would look in all the nearby skips and pick up objects saying, "That'll day fur the hoose" (this will do for my house) hence the nickname. When I first started working with Sergeant Johnston I wasn't too sure about him, because I was always being compared to the previous bar officer. I would get 'John Mack did this, Johnny Mack did that', but as soon as it was discovered that I could touch-type (self-taught on the old typewriters) my uniform bar sergeant could not praise me highly enough. I managed to get court cases done in double quick time and was very efficient at dealing with customers. I was nicknamed 'Fingers' because of my typing speed.

In the Chester Street Office, we didn't have an awful lot of room to detain prisoners so, as soon as they were processed, they were put in a cell until I had enough information to type up the necessary report. Prisoners were then escorted to Tobago Street until the next court day. Night shifts tended to be busier at weekends so, during the week when all the work was completed, Sergeant Johnston would send for a panda car to take me home. No one ever seemed resentful that I got away at least three hours earlier than them – it just seemed that's what Sergeant Johnston did, and I'm guessing John Mack received the same perk.

Luggy

One night, a cop brought an Irish man to the bar because he was drunk and incapable. The layout of the bar was such that when anyone came through the door to report something they were immediately at the reception desk, but prisoners were brought round to the side because they could then be popped in a cell when dealt with. This officer had really sticky-out ears but nobody dared mention it because it was such a touchy subject. The drunk he brought in fell down onto his back, looked up at the constable and shouted, "LUGGY, LUGGY, you're the ugliest big bastard I've ever seen in me life." To say the staff exploded laughing would be an understatement. The cop was purple in the face, and I thought the poor drunk was going to get a breach of the peace charge thrown in for his cheek!

Sergeant Johnston was always singing and he would make up songs about different types of offences. For example, when someone was being charged with assault, Sergeant Johnston would sing, to the tune of 'You Were Made for Me':

You assaulted me,
I assaulted you,
We both assaulted each other.

I think the prisoners thought he was stark raving mad!

One day, a woman came into the uniform bar to produce her driving documents. She had been given an HORT(1) Form after being in an accident. At that time, you were allowed five days (now seven) to show your driving licence, insurance and MOT if required. Sergeant Johnston started to sing and dance in the office to the tune of 'Hound Dog' by Elvis Presley, only his words were:

It ain't nothing but a HORTI
and you've had your five days,
It ain't nothing but a HORTI
And that's just the way it stays.

The woman looked at me as if she had walked into a madhouse.

Shortly afterwards, the telephone rang and Sergeant Johnston answered it. The woman calling said, "I know you'll think I'm mad." Sergeant Johnston replied, "Tell me what it is, but I'll still think you're mad." The woman then said, "But you don't know what I'm about to say." Sergeant Johnston said, "Whatever you say, I'm still going to think you're mad." The woman started laughing so loudly that she forgot what she was phoning about in the first place and eventually she and 'The Hoose' hung up.

It was a laugh a minute working in the Shettleston Bar. Sergeant Johnston put a spin on every offence. A breach of the peace became a 'Bop of the Poss', and whenever the cops brought in someone who had urinated in a public place it was the ultimate cue for song. As soon as the cops told Sergeant Johnston that they had brought in a urinator, Sergeant Johnston would give a rendition of 'See You Later Alligator' only he would put his own spin on it by singing:

See you later urinator.
In the jail with a pail.
See you later urinator,
No, no you won't get out on bail.

Oftentimes, I was absolutely helpless with laughter. I can honestly say I have never met anyone in my life like Sergeant Johnston. He was an absolute gem of a guy and never took himself or anyone else too seriously. Like a lot of police officers who liked a drink, Sergeant Johnston was no exception. When night shift was reasonably quiet, and I hadn't been sent home, Sergeant Johnston would go have a drink in the sergeant's office with fellow colleagues, but there was always the danger of being caught by the night shift superintendent who came from another division without any warning whatsoever.

One such night when Sergeant Johnston was through the back having a wee bevvy, the night shift superintendent walked through the door. I was standing at the reception of the uniform bar, but the place smelled like a whisky distillery. The first thing the superintendent barked at me was, "Where is the bar, sergeant?" I said he was in the sergeants' room and offered to go get him, but the superintendent was adamant he would go himself. I asked if he would hold the fort whilst I went to the toilet – I did this to prevent him from going anywhere near the sergeants' room which allowed me a few seconds to warn 'The Hoose', and indeed the others, that the superintendent was on the warpath.

I just managed to get the message across in time and, as I was returning from 'the toilet', I bumped into the night shift superintendent making his way down the corridor. My heart was going like the clappers. I hadn't imbibed, but I was hoping to God there was plenty of chewing gum in the sergeants' room.

The following day, Sergeant Johnston phoned me at home to find out what had happened the previous night. I explained everything to him, and I am assuming that Sergeant Johnston got away with his drinking escapade because he remained the bar sergeant at Chester Street. I don't know what the night shift superintendent's comments were, because that was strictly confidential, but that night was to be my very last night shift at Chester Street, albeit I just thought I'd be going off on annual leave and return to Shettleston.

CHAPTER 50 –
YUGOSLAVIA

Jack and I went on holiday to Yugoslavia that year. A female colleague had recommended it to me, and I was excited to be going somewhere other than Spain. Jack and I duly arrived at our hotel and, although it was clean enough, I instinctively felt that there was something wrong with it. I didn't say anything to Jack, but we unpacked and decided to go for a walk. As we were exiting the reception area, most of the holidaymakers had a deck of playing cards. I remember thinking it was a boring thing to be doing but, as I looked around, it was mainly pensioners playing rummy or whatever and that kind of alleviated the negativity I was experiencing. Jack and I walked along the shoreline, and unlike Spain there wasn't a tourist shop in sight. I kept chastising myself because of that comparison and decided I would embrace the Yugoslavian culture as much as I could. The beach nearest us was a shingle beach and not conducive to lying on. I was a complete sun worshipper (as you may have realised when I told you about going on holiday with Mary), and I said to Jack that we should just keep walking until we could find a sandy beach. A few hundred yards further to the right of our hotel, I could see lots of holidaymakers in and around the same area, but I was looking from a distance, and my spirits rose because I thought that I would get my tan, some snacks, souvenirs and all the touristy things you normally do. As we got closer, you could have struck me down with a feather. The beach was a nudist colony and talk about flaunting your assets! I thought those people were completely shameless. I was a bit prudish, and I know you are probably thinking that's rich coming from someone who had been involved with a married man. Jack and I simply turned around and walked back towards our hotel.

The other thing that struck me was that, every so often, we would pass by a lamp post with a 'Silence after 2200 hours' sign. We got back to our hotel and sat down with other guests at the dinner table.

There was the usual chit-chat, but I found out that whatever meal was served in our hotel was exactly the same in every other hotel in Poreč. I could not believe how regimented things were.

After dinner, Jack and I had to queue up for drinks tickets and then return to another queue to produce our drinks ticket to a bartender to get what we ordered. The staff were very cold and barked out orders about the different queues we should line up in. I became more and more dismayed at the thought of spending a fortnight in Poreč but decided to keep my options open about some night-time entertainment.

Jack and I had our drinks, left the hotel and, instead of walking to the right of the hotel, we thought we'd explore what was available to the left of it. We duly turned left and, being a bit of a gannet, I felt quite peckish. I thought there would be a chip or burger van or anything (you can hear how desperate I was becoming), but the only thing for eating was a vendor selling corn on the cob roasted over hot coals. It was better than nothing, so I bought some. As I was munching on my delicacy, I saw a crowd of people in the distance and most looked relatively young. I could feel my spirits soaring again and thought I was about to hit the jackpot only to discover that, the closer we got to the crowd, it was a display to see who would win the Miss Topless competition. You can imagine my dismay. I told Jack I just wanted to go back to the hotel, and I bought a pack of playing cards!

A trip to Venice

The weather was nice on the day we arrived in Poreč but really temperamental for the next 13 days, and the only thing keeping me sane was the one trip we were allowed to book for Venice. We were advised that we could only change a certain amount of Yugoslavian currency into lira and that if we had any spare lira after the Venice trip they would be confiscated. Thankfully, it was a sunny day when we boarded the small ship to take us to Venice. The ship itself wasn't all that comfortable and was packed tight, but I would have swum to Venice if I had to, just to get out of Yugoslavia. As we embarked the ship we changed currency, and the relief and freedom I felt inside was indescribable. If you have never been to Venice, I thoroughly recommend it. I was overawed by the stunning waterways, architecture and the liveliness of the place. There are so many famous places like Doge's Palace, St Mark's Square and of course the Grand Central Canal. Just looking at all the gondoliers fascinated me, and I kept reminiscing about my schooldays when I had been studying *The Merchant of Venice*. Jack and I packed as much as we could into that day trip. We found a little restaurant just at the back of St Mark's Square and had spaghetti bolognese. Perhaps it was because I was having such a great time, but that spaghetti was the best I'd ever tasted. Venice wouldn't be complete without a coffee in St Mark's Square and a ride on a gondola. We hopped on a gondola and were given a guided tour with all the architectural history explained as we slowly moved along the canal. When the ride was over, we went for a coffee in St Mark's Square. It is the most expensive place in Venice to eat or drink, but we were certainly not going to have our leftover lira confiscated and decided to spend the last of our lira currency on coffee. Whilst we were enjoying our coffee, Jack said to me, "If we ever have a son, Eunice, we will call him Mark." I loved the name and that was just fine by me. It was a wonderful end to a jam-packed, fulfilling, beautiful day.

We duly returned to our ship to take us back to Poreč, but I wasn't too fussed. My head was full of lovely memories, and I barely noticed the time going by. Besides, I knew that I would soon be going home to Scotland and would never return to Yugoslavia.

Jack and I did not live together in our Dennistoun flat until we were married, so he dropped me off at my mum's and returned to his flat. I told my mum about my adventures and went to bed.

CHAPTER 51 –
THE FIRST FEMALE TURNKEY IN
STRATHCLYDE POLICE

The following morning, I received a call from Inspector Barrie telling me that I was to report to Tobago Street Police Office as I had now been appointed turnkey. I couldn't believe my ears. If I thought the holiday was bad, this was even worse. I was happy at Shettleston and assumed I was going back there. I immediately called Jack, and he had also heard the news. It was with a very heavy heart that day when I put on my uniform to return to work. As soon as the overlapping shifts had settled, I approached Inspector Barrie, who was the duty officer at Tobago Street, and my exact words to him were, "How on earth is this going to work?" His reply was, "Eunice, you are the first female officer in Strathclyde Police to be put in charge of male prisoners. We have to make this work."

There are four things I recall from my time as turnkey at Tobago Street, and you might be thinking that's not much, but Tobago Street Police Office was closing and we were moving to a brand new office in London Road, just along from Celtic Park Football Club. Looking back on my time at Tobago Street, there were 30 holding cells. I can't remember how many specific female cells there were but, at that time, it was predominantly males who offended. Drugs were not as prevalent as they are now, but alcohol was widely misused. Tragically, some would drink methylated spirits to get some kind of high and, on those occasions, it tended to be people who were really scraping the barrel, God help them. The most horrendous thing for all of us was when a police colleague was in the cells. We could tell immediately by the atmosphere in the office, and it happened on one occasion when I was on night shift. My other colleagues spoke in hushed tones and, instead of the usual banter, we all felt flat to be honest. I remember speaking to the officer in question who had been charged with theft, and I asked him why he did it. He gave me a lopsided smile and said he "just felt like it". All night, I kept asking myself why someone would risk a good career only to be caught thieving. It made absolutely no sense whatsoever.

On another occasion, when I was back shift, a man came in with a dog in his arms and asked me to phone a vet. The man was crying, and the poor animal had been run over by a car. I phoned the vet but, by the time he came, the creature had died in the man's arms. I remember feeling outraged that a call-out fee was charged. It just seemed so unfair, but I suppose that's a vet's policy, and without any argument the man paid the fee. The image of that dog is ingrained in me.

Desperate for shelter

One time when I was on night shift, a man came to the uniform bar and asked me to lock him up because he needed a bed for the night. It was the weekend and, culturally in Scotland, people frequented the pubs at weekends which resulted in more breaches of the peace, assaults and drunk and incapable charges being pressed. We were in the east end of Glasgow and in the rough area of the Carlton which meant that any spare cells would be used up by prisoners who were normally held until the Monday morning when they would go to their respective courts. At this stage, I'm not going to give you many details about the duties expected of a turnkey. I want to wait until you come with me to London Road.

Anyway, back to the wee man who wanted shelter. I explained that he hadn't done anything wrong and I couldn't lock him up without reason. He then gave me a cheeky wink and walked back out the door only to return 30 minutes later with two police officers who were charging him with vandalism. The man had put a brick through one of the shop windows in the Gallowgate and, by all accounts, had caused quite a bit of damage. When I accompanied him to his cell, he gave me the biggest grin and said, "Now you'll have to give me a bed for the night", the bed being a plastic mattress and a blanket. I just shook my head but had a wee giggle to myself after I'd locked him up. One happy prisoner!

Truth or loyalty

The fourth thing was unpleasant. A police officer, who shall remain anonymous, came in with his colleague and a prisoner who was being charged with a breach of the peace. The prisoner looked badly beaten up, and I knew the officer concerned had a real temper. The accused wanted the officer charged with police assault on him, and Inspector Barrie handled the matter. The whole thing disturbed me, because I felt that the man was telling the truth but I was torn with that feeling of loyalty to my colleague. Again, it was on the night shift. The man was taken to the Royal Infirmary Hospital in Glasgow to have his wounds attended to and let out on bail for the breach of the peace charge. Little did I know, at that time, that this unpleasant incident would come back to haunt me, because I later received a Citation for the Defence (of the police officer) to attend the Sheriff and Jury Court in Glasgow. The man had reported the matter to his solicitor, the policeman was charged with serious assault, and I was asked to go as his witness. What a dilemma. I didn't want my colleague to lose his job. Being suspended was bad enough, but a job loss? However, I was livid that my colleague had put me in that position. The officers on duty that night knew what had happened, and no one doubted that the policeman in question was guilty.

My due date arrived for the court hearing and I felt physically sick. I had already been seen by a precognitions officer (a person who takes a statement from a witness for the defence) and had given a statement with the time, date and place where his client had been charged with the crime. I thought the matter was never going to end, and being a witness really loomed over me. I was duly called to give evidence, and I stuck to the facts and no more. I was relieved when the ordeal was over, but I knew that the evidence I had given was strictly factual without being too damning. The officer in question was found not guilty, and he came out of the court punching the air. I can't say that I had the same sentiments. I never had to go through that experience again, thank God, and I really have to say that whilst in the police, my colleagues were really good and fair officers. I suppose in all walks of life you get a few bad eggs and, in that respect, the police force is no different.

CHAPTER 52 –
MOVING TO NEW PREMISES

In early 1981, I was on night shift and that was when we moved from Tobago Street to London Road Police Office. Thankfully, the night shift was quiet which meant I could label drawers and make sure they were full of the relevant paperwork which made it easy for the early shift. Moreover, since I was an avid perfectionist, everything had to be in its proper place. I also had time to have a good look around this new office, and I immediately felt comfortable.

The bar area had a desk for the duty inspector (in my case Inspector Barrie), a couple of desks for myself and a colleague called Alan. The bar officer, John Mack, had taken the opportunity to transfer to Edinburgh, so I was doing the job of bar officer as well as turnkey. In those days, we had teleprinters which we used to communicate to warrants officers in the event that a prisoner had a warrant out for his arrest. The old-fashioned typewriters weren't even electric so when you got to the end of a sentence you would swing the typewriter back to the correct position to type another sentence – that as well as constantly having to change the ribbon on it. Leading off the bar office was the control room which was all about communication between those on patrol and jobs that needed allocated. At the front of the bar, there was a glass panel separating the bar office from the reception area, and to the rear of the bar office there was an area where prisoners came through a side door and brought to another desk where they were charged and their possessions bagged and labelled.

The CID office was on the ground floor. The CID clerk was probably in his late forties and, although he didn't do CID investigations, he attended to people who were victims of fraud and other CID matters. When I think about fraud today, all that springs to mind now is the amount of scammers operating from various call centres.

George, the CID clerk, was a lovely guy and had a beautiful wife whom he truly loved. Jack and I would go to the Police Club in

Coatbridge, where alcohol was relatively cheap and monthly dances were held. George and his wife were very professional dancers and when they danced it put the rest of us on the dance floor to shame. They were both immaculately dressed, and it was obvious that this was a match made in heaven. Unfortunately, George had fallen victim to cancer, which must have been aggressive, because within a few months he was dead. I couldn't believe my ears and constantly thought and prayed for his poor wife. I saw her one more time at the Police Club, had a wee chat with her, but what do you say in circumstances such as these? I truly believe that his wife had decided to go one last time to the Police Club, almost to say goodbye, because the following morning, I was told by a sergeant that the poor woman had committed suicide. I was so shocked, I remember saying, "Is she dead?" What a stupid remark! I was informed that she had taken an overdose of pills, phoned her daughter to say her final goodbyes and, unfortunately, rigor mortis was already setting in by the time her daughter got to her. The painful thing is that after receiving that terrible news, we had to carry on as if nothing had happened. There was a job to be done and being emotional wasn't part of the job.

At the London Road Office, there was a gym and a typist room. Upstairs was the administration office which was occupied by a chief inspector and a constable. It was a 9–5 job and considered a cushy number. The divisional commander had his own office, there was a muster room (kitchen area) where the cops had their tea, and a storeroom where a civilian had a desk and paid out any necessary expenses; there was also a small room just to relax in – a room where I inevitably fell asleep during my breaks and, of course, many more offices.

Everything went smoothly my first night shift at London Road but, because the prisoner bar desk was quite high, I could hardly see over the top of it. I was grateful that Inspector Barrie managed to find a stool for me which was ideal for my height. God help me if I was doing that job now, because I have osteoporosis and have shrunk four inches.

When the early shift came on at 6.30 the next morning, I showed them where all the paperwork was and gave them a tour of the office. We had 40 holding cells for male prisoners (cell number 40 for dangerous or suicidal men) and we had six female prison cells. There was a small kitchen just off the cell area where meals were cooked.

The casualty surgeon's office was also on the ground floor but far enough away from the prisoner area. The casualty surgeon was normally called out whenever a rape took place and also to take blood or urine from drunk drivers. Just opposite the prisoner bar area were two rooms for anyone who had absconded from one of the social work homes. It was normally a home called Beechwood which housed girls who were outwith parental control.

When I was on Tollcross Patrol, I hated being called to Beechwood. The best words that summed up that place was complete pandemonium.

After this little briefing on London Road Police Office, I would like to describe some of the work I did. The station was an extremely busy one, but that suited me just fine because I was a complete workaholic. Apart from processing prisoners, taking fingerprints and being in the company of the casualty surgeon when required, I had to type up cases for court on the Monday morning.

Celtic and Rangers matches and busy cells

Obviously, the weekends were the busiest and there was no shortage of prisoners in the cells. As mentioned, we had 40 male cells in London Road, but after a Celtic/Rangers match we had in excess of one hundred prisoners! This meant doubling up and some, and the rule of thumb was that you couldn't have an even number of prisoners in a cell. On these busy occasions, we had as many as five to a cell. The cells themselves weren't all that large but managed to house five mattresses and blankets. There was also a toilet inside the cells and had to be flushed from the outside. I frequently flushed the toilets, made sure there was no fighting (although most prisoners were drunk and fell asleep) and, on the morning when they were due to go to court, I would make sure each prisoner had a wash from the sink at the rear of the cells. Another thing I did was ensure that if cigarettes or sweets were handed in for a prisoner, I would take time to hand out whatever goodies were on offer. Many of the prisoners were regular offenders and, if I was early shift, the minute I checked on my prisoners they gave me a clap. If a prisoner dared to be abusive to me, the other prisoners would go apeshit.

If you think of a hundred prisoners or more, you can imagine the paperwork that would generate, but I typed fast and had the cases done and dusted in no time. It got to the stage that I knew my job so well that I would help out Inspector Barrie or remind him of duties that required doing prior to the next shift handover.

Being good at my job came with its downfalls because, if on the odd occasion we were quiet and I needed to get home earlier than 6.30 a.m., I would ask Inspector Barrie to let me leave around 4 a.m. especially when I was going to a wedding which was taking place early afternoon. To my dismay, the most time off I got was finishing half an hour early. I didn't ask for time off unless it was absolutely necessary and I was rarely off sick, but I suppose, realistically speaking, I was getting paid to do a full shift.

On the early shift, we had to make sure that the divisional commander had access to the 'Book to the Force'. This had to be on his desk the minute he walked through the door. At that time, the chief constable was a man called Pat and in the divisional commander's office there was a large, framed picture of him. Usually, myself and another officer would check over the 'Book to the Force' to ensure there were no inaccuracies regarding custody cases and other incidents. The names we shouted at the chief constable's picture were simply unrepeatable, and I would be in stitches laughing at the little bit of 'power' we had over him.

Nicknames and pranks

At this juncture, I want to explain that everyone had a nickname of some description. These names were never intended to insult or hurt anyone but having a nickname meant that your colleagues were quite fond of you and in the early seventies through to mid-eighties, *PC* meant Police Constable and not political correctness. I had more than my fair share of them. When I was at Oxford Street, prior to my initial training at Tulliallan, I used to get called 'Eunice Wolf It'. The reason being that not only do I love my food but my plate was scraped clean when most people were only halfway through their meal.

Another name I was labelled with was 'Sooky' because, apparently, I used to suck up to sergeants and inspectors but, to be honest, I don't really believe that. None of my nicknames were particularly cruel, but that wasn't the case for everyone. I remember a cop bringing in a prisoner on a breach of the peace charge and even Inspector Barrie called him by his nickname. The cop had a massive space between his front teeth and earned the name of 'Space Face'. The odd thing was that he just accepted it, and I don't have a clue what his Christian name was.

At one point, a lovely cop who had a bad stammer was leaving the force after completing his 30 years' service. There was a whip-round to get him a gift and one of those gifts was a cake. Not just any old cake. On the top of it the inscription was 'Ch, ch, ch, cheerio Davy'! Davy just burst out laughing and wired into the cake.

There was a dedicated divisional van driver on my shift. He and I had a love/hate relationship. Because he lived quite near East Kilbride, he would give me a run home at the end of my shift. He had a sports car which was a bit of a banger, but as long as I got home in one piece, I was quite happy. Jim would show off by driving his sports car as fast as it would go and, honest to God, it was like being on a roller-coaster ride. Jim had a bit of a stutter which would be more prominent if he got overexcited. He had no idea that behind his back we affectionately called him 'Marble Mouth'. One early shift, he was really getting on my nerves and I completely lost the plot with him. I can't remember what he said to get me so riled up but without thinking, I said, "Listen Marble Mouth, enough is enough." His eyes nearly popped out of his head and he said, "M-m-m-m-marble mouth? Did you call me m-m-marble mouth?" Honest to God, I started to back-pedal like crazy and just kept digging myself deeper into the very large hole I had already created. My punishment to myself was to be nice to him for the rest of the day, but I will never forget the look on his face when I uttered those words.

More often than not, just as we were finishing a night shift at 6.30 a.m., someone would come to the reception desk. The worst thing paperwork-wise was dealing with a road traffic accident. There was loads of information to fill in and you knew you would be held up for the best part of an hour. Quite often, one of the cops would go to the reception desk and then tell me that someone wanted to speak to me. Just my luck because, inevitably the minute I went to deal with the customer, they would tell me that they wanted to report a road traffic accident. My shift would be behind the glass screen absolutely gutting themselves laughing. Eventually, after being het and not getting home on time, I would tell the customer to have a seat and then informed the early shift that a customer wanted to see them. You can imagine how popular I was when the early shift ended up dealing with an RTA (road traffic accident).

Sad incidents

Sometimes, we would get psychiatric patients in the office who were placed in a locked room until a psychiatric nurse or doctor came to assess them. I had dealt with situations like this when I was on Tollcross Patrol and called away because a female was involved. On one such occasion, a beautiful, young girl was a total wreck in front of her parents. The parents lived in a really nice house which was calming and relaxing but nothing would calm their daughter down. The girl's mother informed me that her daughter had never had a history of mental illness until she got married. A fellow officer and I stayed until nurses came to the house, and I don't know if the girl felt safer in their company but she immediately calmed down. She was then taken to a psychiatric unit. Her mother informed me that the girl's husband was to blame and this was not the first time her daughter had to be sectioned under the Mental Health (Scotland) Act. I often wondered why the husband was to blame, but it was really none of my business and therefore I didn't press the girl's mother for any more information. I just hoped and prayed to God that the girl would eventually recover.

Another time, a young woman was brought to the police station and, after being placed in the holding room, she started punching at the door and screaming at the top of her voice. I hadn't seen her when she was brought in, but I thought if I stood outside the door I could maybe talk her down. Her name was Mary and I immediately recognised her as a girl I used to play with. My mum and her mum were great friends and it was natural that Mary and I became friendly. She recognised me and I spoke about some of the good times we had together, but the minute I walked away to attend to my prisoners all hell broke loose. The door was getting battered so much that I thought it was going to break and she was screaming like a banshee. It was tragic. I found it so hard to believe that someone whom I had played with, and appeared to be perfectly normal, had turned into a mental wreck. I reflected deeply with regard to some questions about life – why and how does a person reach this stage? Do we help those who are struggling or do we simply turn away?

When the nurses eventually came to fetch her, I remember one of them saying, "Oh, it's Mary again." The poor soul was obviously well known in the psychiatric unit, and I kept asking myself how her mum and dad must have felt. I often wondered what happened to Mary, but at the time I knew that getting involved was not an option.

On another occasion, a cop on my shift had suffered a sudden cardiac arrest. It was decided that I should accompany a couple of police officers to pick up his wife and take her to the Royal Infirmary to see her husband. I don't know why, but I was told to tell the cop's wife that her husband had been taken ill and not mention the sudden cardiac arrest. My stomach was churning at the thought but, eventually, we reached the officer's home and I told his wife what I had been told to say. The woman responded by saying, "I have a chicken in the oven for my husband when he comes home." I remember thinking, *That chicken will never be eaten.* She continued to ask me how her husband was, and I could only downplay the situation as much as possible. However, just as we were approaching the Royal Infirmary, the officer who was driving the panda car turned round and told the lady that her husband had had a cardiac arrest. She immediately turned to me and said, "He's arrested?" It was a terrible moment, because her husband was only in his forties.

CHAPTER 53 –
WEDDING BELLS

Jack and I planned to get married in 1981 and set a date for 20 November. I decided I was having two bridesmaids – a fellow police officer Mhairi and Cathy whom I've previously mentioned. Cathy was a bit reluctant because she was in her forties, but she was so young-looking for her age that I thought she was an excellent choice. Mhairi and I had become friends when I was stationed in Shettleston. We instantly clicked, and I was a regular visitor at her house in Bothwell. Her sister was also a policewoman, as was her brother. I was so close to Mhairi that Jack and I received a full invitation for her sister's wedding. Mhairi made me laugh, particularly when she burst into song and quite nonchalantly sang to the tune of 'Magic Moments', "it wasn't the grass that tickled her ass it was the grasshopper". I think because she sang it with such a serious face that it made me laugh even more. Mhairi was delighted to be my bridesmaid, and we would regularly meet up whenever we had some free time to have a drink and a bit of a blether. She regaled me about the time that she and her neighbouring cop attended a housebreaking just off Edinburgh Road in the east end of Glasgow. Although I say housebreaking, it could be any type of building that someone was trying to break into and steal whatever goods were on offer. On this particular occasion, I think it was licensed premises, but I don't really remember. The offender was a man about six feet tall and he was certainly not surrendering without a fight. Backup was called for, and it so happened that I was in a panda car with my neighbouring driver.

As soon as I saw Mhairi and the mannerisms of the criminal, I knew she was getting dog's abuse. I don't think I even waited for our panda car to come to a halt before I jumped out. I was livid that anyone would treat my friend and colleague in that manner and, before I knew it, I had grabbed the man by the throat, lifted him up and had him pinned against the wall of the premises he was trying to rob. I remember clearly shouting at him, "Don't you dare treat my pal like that." I was so angry that I think I must have had the strength of a lion because, after letting the guy slide down the wall, he meekly allowed handcuffs to be put on and then be taken to the panda car that Mhairi and her neighbour were in. Mhairi later told me that the three of them in the car sat in silence, because they could not believe that 'Titch' (one of my other nicknames) had managed to pin the criminal to the wall.

Wedding prep

In the 1980s, it was the custom to have a show of presents instead of a hen night. Some people would dress up the bride-to-be and take her around their nearby pubs to collect money from the punters who would put it in a container that the bride carried. That wasn't something that appealed to me, so I settled for a night in the house where people could come and have a drink and a bite to eat as well as seeing the presents displayed on the bed.

I arranged with Mhairi for her to come and help me pick my wedding dress. The problem was that we were on different shifts, and on the day when I was due to go wedding dress shopping in Glasgow, Mhairi had just come off a night shift and was far too tired to come with me. My mum stepped in to fill the breach, and we eventually found a wedding shop in Sauchiehall Street that seemed to have a nice selection of dresses which suited my budget. Because I had no alternative but to get married in a registry office, I didn't have the sense of excitement you feel when wedding shopping. I told a member of staff that it was just a registry office affair, but she managed to convince me that this was one of the most important days in my life and that I should at least have a look at white wedding dresses, headdresses and veils. I picked out a designer dress that was very reasonably priced, tried it on with a veil and headdress and it looked beautiful. Nowadays, I think wedding dresses are far nicer and they do not have to be just white.

Naturally, I was delighted with the fact that my mum wanted to come wedding shopping with me but that was it. I'm not blaming my mum because I am very self-sufficient, but she had decided to go to Spain for a couple of weeks with her sister – my Aunt Vera – and she wouldn't be home until two days before my wedding. My mum asked me if I minded and I said no because I wanted my mum to have her holiday, but I thought the timing was a bit off and I could have done with a bit more support.

However, it was what it was, so I carried on regardless and picked out my bridesmaid dresses and my mother's outfit. Jack and I were paying for the wedding, and the one thing I insisted on was that the wedding reception would take place in a really lovely hotel. I therefore booked a hotel called the Silvertrees in Bothwell which I think has been renamed the Bothwell Bridge Hotel. The grounds are lovely and the inside was very tastefully decorated, but more importantly, I knew we would have a delicious meal. From experience, most people who are invited to a wedding ask what the bride looked like and how the meal was.

Jack and I had been at a registry office wedding in East Kilbride a few months previous. He was the best man and I was the bridesmaid. It was nothing short of disastrous. During the ceremony, the bride had a fit of the giggles which set me off and then the wedding party went back to the groom's house in East Kilbride for some nibbles and cheap wine. That sounds so horrible, but I really didn't want anything remotely like that and that's why I settled for our marriage to be in Motherwell (North Lanarkshire) Registry Office and then the reception at the Silvertrees.

The due date of 20 November 1981 arrived, and I went to my local hairdresser's to get my hair done prior to putting on my wedding dress. I did my own make-up and I guess I looked as good as I could. Jack and I met at the registry office and made our vows after which the registrar said to me, "You are allowed to smile, you know." The East Kilbride wedding experience where the bride couldn't stop giggling had the opposite effect on me and I think I looked a bit too serious.

However, it was smiles all round for the photographs, and the meal at the Silvertrees was amazing. My mum's outfit was a plum-coloured, velvet skirt and jacket with a matching hat. She had come back from Spain looking tanned, but she must have been subjected to the 'Birdie Song' written by the Tweets because she sang it constantly. I think it was played at least five times on my wedding day and every time she heard it my mum got up to dance, actions included. It was as if she heard it for the first time, because her face lit up when I suggested it to the band that consisted of some of my very talented colleagues who so generously offered their services free of charge.

My first husband and me on our wedding day

Honeymoon

In those days, it was traditional for the bride to slip away from the reception area and get changed into another outfit prior to escape from the wedding party to wherever the honeymoon would take place. I had a lovely checked skirt and jacket which I removed from a suitcase covered in confetti, courtesy of Mhairi and Cathy. My colleagues had tied tin cans to the back of Jack's car and a 'Just Married' sign was splattered across the back window. We had booked the honeymoon suite in a hotel complex at Aviemore. Although it is a small town, Aviemore is a major holiday resort with absolutely stunning scenery. It is situated in the Cairngorm Highlands and is renowned for being one of the best ski resorts as well as local tourist attractions.

The hotel was stunning, as were the facilities, and Jack and I packed a lot into that week. We did lots of walking in the Cairngorm Mountains and took a trip on the Strathspey Railway. Since it was late November, the Cairngorms were blanketed with snow, so Jack and I hopped on to the funicular railway which took us up to the ski resort where we hired our skiing equipment. Jack was much better on skis than me even though we'd both practised on the dry ski slope situated around our hotel.

All too soon, the week came to an end and it was time to go home, only this time my home would be at Bannatyne Avenue instead of my mum's house. Credit where it is due, Jack completely transformed the flat which was far more modern than when the elderly gentleman had it.

I was really content in our home and, as a music lover, the record player was on constantly. I have to confess that I am a bit OCD (not as bad now) but, at that time, the house was immaculate. The good thing about living in Dennistoun was the plethora of shops and I was spoiled for choice when doing the shopping. I wasn't too far away from my mum either and made it my mission to see her as often as I could. My mum had told me that when someone was just married, they would wear nice outfits so, taking that advice, I put on a lovely suit on my first visit to her house just after my honeymoon. Big mistake! My mum took one look at me and said that the weather was far too cold for me to be wearing something so flimsy, although she did say I looked nice, so I suppose that was something.

CHAPTER 54 –
LIVING AT BANNATYNE AVENUE
AND EAST KILBRIDE

When we were first married, Jack and I were on different shifts. It was a police policy that married couples did not work in the same division or on the same shifts. I expected one of us to be moved, but I was kept at London Road and Jack remained in Shettleston. Jack took advantage of the fact that our working hours were different and, after one night shift, I came home to find a pile of cops lying drunk on the living room floor (including Jack). Empty cans and bottles were everywhere and I went ballistic. I physically lifted the cops one by one and threw them out of the flat. I then cleaned the place and told Jack, in no uncertain terms, that if that happened again I would leave him. Sounds really dramatic but I was livid and Jack got the brunt of a temper that I rarely lose, but when I lose it, I lose it big time! Needless to say, I didn't earn myself any brownie points from my drunken colleagues.

We had been at Bannatyne Avenue for a year when Jack suggested we sell the flat and move. At first I was very reluctant, but we did need bigger accommodation because our bed was in a recess in the kitchen and, although it did the job, the idea of having a proper bedroom was very appealing. We advertised the flat and it was sold within a week. We then bought a three-bedroom, mid-terraced house in Tarbolton, East Kilbride – the exact area I had wanted to live in.

I had already told Jack where I wanted to stay when we agreed to sell the flat, and he said to me, "Eunice, I think your expectations are too high. You not only want to live in East Kilbride, but you've decided on the area. What if those expectations can't be fulfilled?" I just told him a house would come up, and I put my faith and trust in God.

Eventually, Jack was transferred onto the same shift as me but remained at Shettleston. In those days, that was unheard of and we couldn't believe our luck. It meant that Jack could pick me up after every shift and I was guaranteed a lift home.

I often pondered over my wedding and it hurt me that none of my relatives came except my mum and Aunt Vera. My other relatives, whom I looked upon as sisters and brothers, sent negative replies to their wedding invitation and, although it wasn't specific, I knew that it was because I was being married in a registry office instead of a Catholic church.

I had never thought I would get married in a registry office and it didn't fill me with excitement, particularly when I had recently been to the wedding of a girl called Helen (clerkess in Community Involvement) who had the full nuptial Mass. It made me realise what I was missing out on, and Jack and I left the wedding earlier than we should have. I made an excuse about stomach pains, but it just felt far too raw.

The other thing that was a bit disjointed were my own wedding photographs when they finally arrived. I had contacted a renowned photographer in Hamilton, and I think they sent the most inexperienced wedding photographer because a lot of the pictures were hazy. I didn't complain – some were alright but some were sketchy to say the least.

CHAPTER 55 –
OLD FIRM GAMES AND MORE
ABOUT LONDON ROAD OFFICE

Back at London Road Police Office, shifts carried on as normal. Some were really busy particularly due to the Old Firm games. Prior to being turnkey, I did football duty myself and met many famous players and managers but, other than managing to bag a free pie and gravy at half-time and arresting the usual suspects, I wasn't in the least bit interested in football. It didn't matter to me who won. I was just glad when the match was over.

On one occasion, an absconder from Beechwood Girls Home had been put in one of the locked side rooms until her social workers arrived. She seemed perfectly calm and, when her social workers arrived, they stayed in the reception area whilst I escorted her along the corridor to release her into their custody. All of a sudden, the girl went totally crazy. She started battering me senseless and, before I knew it, I was on the ground whilst my hair was being pulled out at the roots. My hair was long and was always tied up in a bun, but I think I must have lost half of it during that assault. It took four very strong police officers to get her off me. The girl had gone totally ballistic, and I felt pain in almost every part of my body. As soon as the cops had her on her feet and a bit calmer, I charged her with a breach of the peace and police assault to which she pleaded guilty. I will never forget that totally unexpected incident.

Dealing with a hundred or so male prisoners was a doddle compared to some of the females we had. Obviously, male prisoners were strip-searched by male police officers, and vice versa for females, prior to fingerprinting which was done by both male and female bar staff. Female prisoners tended to be much more aggressive.

It was a different scenario when it was a genuine rape case, because the poor victim was only too happy to be rid of clothes that were stinking of semen. Rape was hard to prove, due to the lack of DNA evidence in those days, but you instantly got a feeling when someone was telling the truth or lying because they'd had sex with some random person whilst being married to someone else. The casualty surgeon immediately knew by internal examinations and, although it was not the most pleasant part of his job, it was unavoidable. In such cases, there was always loads of paperwork to be filled in as well as statements to be typed up, but we were there to do a job and get on with it.

One night shift, as well as quite a few male prisoners, I had two female prisoners. One of them asked me if I had a sleeping tablet, so I asked the inspector for an aspirin and gave it to the prisoner pretending that I had managed to secure something to help her sleep. I told her to snuggle up on her mattress, made sure she had enough blankets and within five minutes she was snoring like a pig!

When I approached the other female prisoner, I noticed she was only about 19 or 20 years of age. She had been arrested for prostitution in Glasgow Green near to the Winter Gardens. Obviously, that was in the east end, but 'higher class' prostitutes normally frequented Blythswood Square located in the city centre of Glasgow, also known as the red-light district. Prostitutes had clientele who had more money than those around the Glasgow Green and it was on the tip of my tongue to ask the young prisoner why she hadn't gone there instead. However, I no sooner thought it when I remembered that prostitution is an offence, no matter which area, so instead I asked the young girl why she had prostituted herself. Sadly, her answer was, "I need to pay my university fees and I can't afford them, so the only way of making easy money is to have paid sex." There was absolutely nothing I could say to that. She was a lovely girl but to her, the end justified the means. I just remember feeling sad that she was in that situation, and I think there are arguments on both sides for the legalities of prostitution.

One night, when I was walking down Dalmarnock Road (just down from London Road Police Office), a man started kerb-crawling. He must have just seen the dark skirt and jacket and thought he was on to something because, the minute he popped his head out the passenger window, I showed him my warrant card and he hightailed it up the road. I should have taken his car registration number, but I was so astounded at what had just happened and subsequently disappointed in myself that I neglected to do so. I remember cursing Jack for being off sick.

As mentioned, cell 40 was reserved for people who were suicidal or were likely to harm themselves in some way. One night, a young man in his twenties was brought into the station. After processing him, I was told to put him in cell 40. To be honest, he didn't seem suicidal and I didn't get the impression that he would harm himself, but it wasn't my place to argue so I just did as I was told.

It was a night shift and, during the night, I checked on him constantly, but he appeared to be sleeping and I couldn't see anything untoward. One of the times, when I flushed his toilet, he came over to the cell bars for a chat and, having already processed him, I knew that he was in custody due to drug offences. In the early eighties, it was quite unusual to have someone detained for taking heroin. He appeared perfectly fine to me and was very well spoken. I'm not decrying the east end of Glasgow, but most of the time the language was choice to say the least, particularly if someone lived in Barrowfield. I was curious to know why the young guy was taking drugs, and when I asked him his reply was, "It makes me feel normal."

I didn't quite understand then, but nowadays there is a much greater awareness around drugs and I totally get it if someone who is depressed, anxious, afraid to leave the house, or just feels totally worthless, resorting to something that makes them feel better can be tempting if only for a short while. I am not in any way advocating heroin or any other type of Class A drugs but, as I get older, I can totally understand why people advocate the legalisation of drugs such as cannabis, particularly for pain relief.

CHAPTER 56 –
A JEALOUS HUSBAND

Being part of the uniform bar at London Road also meant planning for nights out. We would have a kitty where we put money in as soon as we got paid and treat ourselves to a slap-up meal somewhere in a posh part of the city centre. This was nothing new, and I had been out before with my colleagues. I certainly didn't think things would be any different on this occasion. We would meet up about 7.30 p.m. for an 8 p.m. meal and then have a few drinks and a good gab before leaving around 10.30 p.m. On one occasion, we decided to go for our meal in January rather than the busy festive period, and I got myself dolled up for a night that I was really looking forward to. The night was brilliant and I got home about 11 p.m. When I tried to open the front door of the house, I found it locked. I thought Jack must have locked it by mistake because the key was still in the door, so I went through the garden gate towards the patio doors. I found that they were locked as well. I was trying to figure out in my mind what was going on. I had a key for the front door but not the patio door, so I wandered back round to the front and started firing pebbles at the bedroom window. Jack eventually opened the door, but to say he was furious was an understatement. I got a lecture about how late it was when I came home and that normally a meal would last an hour at the most. I tried to explain that we had taken our time over our meal and had a bit of banter, but Jack was having none of it. My heart was sinking by the minute, but that was nothing compared to what met me in our bedroom. The bed, mattress, bedclothes and everything else that could be uplifted was overturned onto the bedroom floor.

I just stood speechless. Eventually, I cleared everything up, by which time Jack had gone through to one of the other bedrooms. I cleaned myself up, got into my nightdress and went into bed but couldn't sleep a wink all night wondering what the hell I had done that was so wrong. I had seen a very jealous side to Jack on one previous occasion, which I just can't talk about, but I truly thought it was a one-off and never expected it to happen again. Jack obviously did not trust me as much as I trusted myself and that hurt. The next day, when things had calmed down, I explained as logically as I could every single account of my actions from when I went out until I came home. Alarm bells should have been ringing, because I remember telling Jack that I would never go out with my shift again. He had calmed down considerably but never disagreed with my statement about the shift outings. It took me ages to get over that incident, but at that time I truly loved Jack and felt that perhaps it was just a blip in my marriage.

Tenerife

After that, things calmed down somewhat. Jack and I always had our annual holiday abroad. On one occasion, we went to Tenerife, and instead of the hotel we had booked we were transferred to a higher-class hotel. It was a hotel that the famous lawyer Joe Beltrami used to go to, and I didn't fit in there. I guess you can take the girl out of Dennistoun but not Dennistoun out of the girl. It was a very lavish hotel and instead of selling postcards and little souvenirs, this hotel sold fur coats. The clientele even got staff members to lick their stamps prior to putting their postcards in the hotel post box, and the only real highlight of the holiday was a fashion competition where contestants came from far and wide. There was also a great concert on that occasion and people were paying a fortune for tickets for both events, but Jack and I had a bird's-eye view from our balcony.

We were in the cloudy part of Tenerife, namely Puerto de la Cruz, and most holidaymakers took the cable car up Mount Teide and back down again. We were no exception but, although it was warm, the clouds far outweighed the sun and I was disappointed. We went out walking quite a lot, and one day, just after our Mount Teide experience, we were walking along a country road, Jack was in front of me and I was slightly behind. Before I knew it, a couple of bikers passed by and were about to grab my handbag when a police car came alongside them. The bikers fled into the distance but, although I couldn't speak Spanish, I was all too aware that the police were conveying to me that I would have been the subject of theft or even more. I was really shaken up by the experience, and I have never been back to Tenerife since.

CHAPTER 57 –
ALCOHOL ADDICTION IS A DISEASE

Back in my house at Tarbolton, East Kilbride, we had excellent neighbours, particularly Peter and Betty Brogan (RIP). Every Friday night, their large family would have a get-together and, although it was noisy, it was nice to listen to the laughter. They were a happy family and Peter and Betty were a great couple. They both loved playing bowls and would go to Jersey every year for their holidays, mainly for the bowling. One time, they invited Jack and me to go with them to the west of Scotland indoor bowling centre which is quite near Glasgow city centre. We readily agreed and a date was set for the following Saturday when we both had a day off.

However, something happened in the meantime which was very disturbing. In our living room, we had an old-fashioned glass cabinet. A part of the cabinet had a pull-down handle where we kept bottles of alcohol. There was a bottle of vodka inside the cabinet and, when I looked at it, I knew something was wrong. I tried unscrewing the top but it came off immediately and, when I dipped my finger in the bottle, it was water. There was only Jack and myself in the house and we hadn't been entertaining, so it didn't take a rocket scientist to know who the culprit was. Jack was out at the time and, as soon as he came through the door, I questioned him about it. He told me that he had opened the bottle ages ago and had been taking small sips now and again, but I simply didn't believe him and told him I wasn't going with him to the bowling centre. I was more upset than angry because, after that incident, the thought of acting normal in front of the Brogans just filled me with dread. Jack begged me to go and told me he would never do anything like that again. He admitted it was a bit dishonest and eventually convinced me to go out as planned. The Brogans were great bowling players and so was Jack, but I was absolutely rubbish and, although I'm okay at tenpin bowling, I never ventured indoor or even outdoor bowling again in case I made a complete fool of myself. I suppose nowadays I would just laugh it off but, in my twenties, I wanted nothing short of perfection of myself and, of course, that rarely happens.

Back to London Road

At London Road, I always enjoyed my job. You could throw anything at me and I would have just got on with it. However, there was one thing that has always bothered me and it was one back shift when a mother brought her daughter to the reception desk and told me she had taken 'smack'. I hadn't a clue that it was a slang term for heroin and I was completely flummoxed. I decided I would go and have a word with my colleagues for guidance, but by the time I got back to the reception area, the woman and her daughter had gone. I had not even taken down a name or address which, of course, could have been passed on to the Drugs Squad. I didn't just let myself down that night, but I also left that young girl and her mother to deal with something which could have been prevented in the future.

I hope to God that was her first and last time but the common-sense part of me tells me that it wasn't and, with just some proper intervention, I could perhaps have stopped another statistic. I was inexperienced, but I still beat myself up.

Another evening, a woman was brought in and charged with being drunk and incapable. Her family came to the reception desk, and I immediately recognised them because they had lived in Appin Road whilst I was there with my mum. I tried to hide away from the reception area, because I was worried that the family would be embarrassed. Quite the opposite! They started shouting, "Eunice, Eunice do you remember us?" I went out to speak to them, but I know I would have been totally mortified if I had been in their situation. I felt that, under those circumstances, there is no way I would have wanted someone to recognise me, let alone shout out my name.

CHAPTER 58 –
HOBBIES AND INTERESTS

Back at home, life was good. Jack and I would go jogging together around Strathclyde Country Park and go on camping holidays. The first camping trip was to Cornwall, and I bought a tent that was so psychedelic in colour that you could see it for miles. Jack laughed when he saw it, but it was sturdy enough to do the job. Cornwall is beautiful and has a great climate, so our week away was one full of sunshine. However, the first night we slept in the tent and it was all zipped up, I realised I was claustrophobic. I panicked like mad, because I felt I couldn't breathe properly, so the compromise was keeping the zip halfway down the tent to let in fresh air. Despite the tent, the holiday itself was thoroughly enjoyable.

We did a lot of hill walking in Arrochar and usually stayed at a youth hostel. I'm not sure if it's gone now, but it was cheap and certainly served the purpose. As well as hill walking around Loch Lomond, Jack and I decided to climb Ben Nevis. We had the tent in the back of the car and that was our accommodation for the night. Jack took me to a lovely restaurant and it was the first time I tasted trout. I have never had it since, despite the fact I found it delicious. I suppose I just wanted to hold on to that special memory.

The weather was lovely to begin with but, during the night, the heavens opened and we were totally drenched. That was the night that I discovered the tent was not waterproof and couldn't wait to get in the car for a change of clothes and set off home.

Whilst I am reminiscing, I think every couple have their own song. Our song was one by England Dan and John Ford Coley, a song called, 'I'd Really Love to See You Tonight'. The ironic thing about that song was the lyric said, "I'm not talking about moving in and I don't want to change your life but there's a warm wind blowing around the sky and I'd really love to see you tonight". Well, if ever a song wasn't meant to be for us it was that one because marrying Jack certainly changed my life and, to be truly honest, not for the better.

CHAPTER 59 –
RE-EDUCATING MYSELF

At this point in my life, I felt it necessary to get myself some more qualifications. Jack and I went to night school to do Italian, but Jack dropped out halfway through the course. I found the language really easy to learn and passed the O level without any trouble.

Once I had the Italian out of the way, I went to night school and enrolled in Higher French and Higher economic organisation. The Higher French class was cancelled due to lack of numbers and I was devastated. The Higher economics was also cancelled, but four of us decided that we would pay the teacher if the school would facilitate the use of a room in Duncanrig Secondary School, East Kilbride. We all got on great and kept in touch for many years after the Higher Examination but I suppose life gets in the way and we all eventually went our separate ways.

Police courses

In the police, I was sent on quite a few courses. One of the courses was the Teleprinter Course which, for me, was easy because I was so used to using it and I didn't really see the need to be sent on the course, but it was mandatory. The **control room** in London Road was always really busy and that was something I wasn't so familiar with. It was mandatory to go on the Police National Computer (PNC) course, and to be honest, I avoided it like the plague. It was inevitable that I would end up going on that course which meant that, if necessary, you could end up being in the control room when we were really busy. This was a course I totally dreaded but the inevitable happened and, before I knew it, I found myself in Oxford Street, Glasgow for the week's training. I sure as hell did not want to fail the course, so I listened to every word my instructor said, wrote as much down as possible and obviously had to do the practical stuff as well.

The PNC course coincided with Holy Week which was the week before Easter. During the practical training of the course, we were placed into booths in order to respond to any calls that were generated. Another police officer started an 'emergency' call and it was my turn to respond. The cop shouted, "There's a fire in the local convent and it is surrounded by hot, cross nuns." As we all know, hot cross buns are plentiful in shops leading up to Easter but, when that cop made the emergency call, I was bowled over with laughter. When I finally managed to compose myself I said, "The divisional van is attending."

For once in my life, I was quiet in the classroom to the extent that the instructor accused me of daydreaming. I remember saying to him, "I will surprise you", but I don't think for a minute he actually believed me. On these courses, there was an exam at the end, and guess what? I got the highest mark in the class. The instructor was flabbergasted, but I just said to him, "I told you I would surprise you." I had worked my socks off during that course and was determined to get a high mark, but it came as much of a surprise to me as it did to the instructor that I got the highest mark.

My time in the Administration Department
In London Road, the Administration Department dealt with football crowd control, the Glasgow Marathon (not the half-marathon), school-crossing patrol wardens, personnel records and many other duties that escape my memory. The head of that department was Chief Inspector McDonald whom I have previously alluded to. In that department, Chief Inspector McDonald was assisted by a uniformed constable and it was a 9–5 job, Monday to Friday. Everyone called it a cushy number simply because of the hours and getting weekends off. The cop who was in admin was either promoted or left to go to another division, and Chief Inspector McDonald requested that I replace him on a temporary basis. I didn't want to leave my bar duties or my turnkey duties, in fact, I much preferred working shifts, bizarre as that might seem, but when Chief Inspector McDonald called me into his office and told me that he thought I was the best person for the interim gap, I couldn't refuse. He was so nice to me and I wanted to help him out, so reluctantly I agreed to be part of that department for what I thought was going to be a temporary job. I knew Inspector Barrie didn't want me to change departments, but he was an inspector and had no clout when it came to a higher-ranking officer.

When I went into the department there was a filing store which was nothing short of a terrible mess. My OCD kicked in big time and, within a few days, the store was immaculate. I soon got into the swing of things and even managed to get my mum and her neighbour a job as lollipop ladies. I know that's not politically correct nowadays but back then it was. I found that organising the Old Firm games easy enough, I just needed to follow the instructions that were already in place but, on the other hand, the Glasgow Marathon was a complete disaster. I was asked to organise that and there had only been one marathon the previous year. I naturally thought that all I had to do was copy the previous year's instructions but it was completely and utterly shambolic. Cops were on points duty (something I was more than familiar with when I was a younger police officer) but they were in the wrong place. The marathon started at the Glasgow Green and, obviously, police were dotted about all over the place because it was such a big event. I cannot honestly tell you what went wrong, but I think the instructions were all askew, and the next day complaints were coming in from many senior officers about the mess of the Glasgow Marathon. Chief Inspector McDonald didn't seem in any way troubled and, if he didn't give a damn, I was happy to be the fall guy. The marathon was over and done with. I couldn't change what happened but I think, in retrospect, I should have realised that the marathon requires careful planning. Back then, I too was still learning.

At one point, Chief Inspector McDonald said to me, "Eunice, I didn't know you worked in Personnel." I had worked in Personnel for a week which gave me access to everyone's records. There were only a handful of policewomen chosen to do this because of sensitivity issues but, naturally, I had a sneaky peak at my own record and the thing that stood out for me was "The girl with the ready smile". I was chuffed to read that.

I still had the 'Higher' bug and working 9–5 p.m. in administration was a real bonus, because it allowed me to attend St Bride's High School in East Kilbride where I studied anatomy, physiology and health (APH). The Higher Exam wasn't the easiest I've studied for, but I managed to pass with a B mark. I've come to realise over the years that I am one of those people who has to always be doing something which normally involves studying, work and housework.

CHAPTER 60 –
THE DAY I HAD A MISCARRIAGE

I was rarely off sick when I was in the police but, by this point, I was 30 years old and trying for a baby. I did fall pregnant but, as hard to believe as this sounds, I was totally ignorant when it came to knowing about miscarriage. I started to bleed quite heavily after I was ten weeks pregnant, but I carried on regardless and put on my uniform for the back shift. However, I decided to go to the doctor's surgery to find out if they could help the bleeding. The receptionist looked at me as if I had horns on my head and said, "You're not thinking of going to work, are you?" I said I was, but she immediately phoned an ambulance to take me to Hairmyres Hospital in East Kilbride. When I was in the ambulance, the realisation dawned on me that I might be losing my child, despite the reassurances of the ambulance crew.

I arrived at Hairmyres and a doctor attended to me. He told me I had lost my child and showed me the afterbirth. I felt sick to the stomach. Besides the devastating news, his manner was terrible, and I remember asking myself what I could have done differently to prevent the miscarriage.

I returned to work a week later after pretending I had come down with a cold. In those days when you were in the police, a pregnancy was seen as a self-inflicted injury. Thankfully, things have changed for the better but back then, if you returned to work after having a baby the fact that you had passed your sergeant's exam counted for nothing. Being realistic, you were put on a crap beat. I then fell pregnant again, quite soon after, and was delighted. I had read books on miscarriages, just to make myself more aware than I was first time round, and I decided that I would not work through my pregnancy.

I had to let Chief Inspector McDonald know. He told me that he had suspected when I was off with a 'cold' that I was pregnant, but there was one other person who needed to know and that was the divisional commander, Mr R.

I have mentioned him before when I had been in Community Involvement and, quite frankly, I found the man a pompous and arrogant individual. He was not the easiest to talk to, but I think he nearly had a heart attack when I walked in front of him into his office, told him to sit down before I announced my news.

Because I was off work for so long, I had to make an appointment with the casualty surgeon. At first he was quite hostile and told me that I wouldn't get sick pay, but I explained that I had lost a baby previously and I wasn't prepared to lose another child. His attitude changed completely, and he gave me a hug and wished me luck as I was leaving. A little humanity goes a long way and that casualty surgeon was delighted for me.

CHAPTER 61 –
THE BIRTH OF MY
BEAUTIFUL LITTLE GIRL

My friend Jean became pregnant at the same time and we would go to mother and baby classes together. She was my regular driver, and I always sat in the back seat of the car because I was paranoid that I would miscarry again. We ended up in Rutherglen Maternity Hospital (which no longer exists) at the same time. During my first trimester, I had been terribly sick and could not even watch a television advert without spewing up. However, my appetite did get better and by the time I had fully reached my gestation period, my stomach was enormous.

My beautiful little girl was born in 1985, and I cried tears of joy when I saw her. However, with me nothing is ever straightforward, and my delivery was so difficult the surgeon in charge of me was called out from his home address. I remember him saying, "We have to get that baby out of there, it is suffering from foetal distress." In those days, you didn't know the sex of your child and I had refused an amniocentesis test because I do not believe in abortion and didn't see the point of the test.

When I was in labour, I was scared witless. I had heard all these horror stories regarding childbirth. I had an epidural, but I was in so much pain I just wanted to die. Before I knew it, my legs were in stirrups, I had cramp in one of my legs and the surgeon had a large pair of forceps. I felt he was ripping my baby out of me. Thankfully, she was alive and well, but the stitches the surgeon gave me seemed endless. It was the first time I had medical stitches and I asked the surgeon how many there were. He kindly replied, "You would only boast."

I wanted to breastfeed my daughter and she took to it like a duck to water, but it was very painful for me. She unfortunately had jaundice and was put into an incubator with little goggles on. I was in a room on my own, and Jean came to visit me with her daughter Pamela. Jean had a normal birth, but I had to take salt baths to try and heal myself.

My friend Josephine Boyle came to visit me and gave me cream for cracked nipples, which was amazing. At the mother and baby classes, I was told that one of the worst things someone could say to you after you had a child was, 'When is your baby due?' Guess what? I was so fat that it looked like I was having triplets. After I had given birth, I was asked that very same question.

My mum obviously came to visit me and, believe it or not, my little girl tried to crawl on the first day she was born. My mother was as astounded as me, but I was in too much pain to be overly impressed.

Whilst in hospital, there was an Asian woman who had given birth to twin girls, but because she wasn't blessed with two sons she rejected her children. She refused to feed them or change their nappies, so the nurses had to do everything for her. Eventually, she accepted one of the babies, but I don't know what happened after that. To say I was shocked is an understatement, but I suppose her culture frowned on her and the poor woman felt under pressure to keep the cultural tradition going.

In the 1980s, you were kept in a maternity unit for almost a week, and I believe that a week away from home life allows you to bond with your baby. I was totally in love with my little girl and couldn't wait to play games with her and teach her through singing.

Elizabeth and her mum came to visit me, and I couldn't help but reflect on my relationship with someone who has been more like a sister to me than anything else. The little girl who my mum looked after from Monday until Friday was always around me. Whenever I took her back home on a Friday, she wanted to come back and stay with me at the weekend. My mum probably thought she was due a break, but I was delighted with this arrangement and Elizabeth used to hide behind my back to give my mum a surprise.

She was an adorable child and has been the one constant in my life that I can always rely on. On the day she came to visit me after I had delivered my little girl, I said to Elizabeth, "Would you like to hold your Godchild?" Elizabeth and her mum were genuinely surprised, but I would never have chosen anyone else.

When I was finally allowed to take my daughter home, I very quickly discovered that, unless she was breastfeeding, things became relentless. I was constantly tired because my daughter would only sleep on my chest instead of her crib, and most nights, if I got four hours' sleep it was a bonus. Because of my OCD, the housework never suffered, but I had gone from ten and a half stone (including pregnancy weight) to six and a half stone within a matter of months. My daughter was not one of those babies who liked a lot of sleep which meant breastfeeding made things difficult for Jack to take turns at putting her to sleep.

I was dead on my feet and would have given anything just to get one night's undisturbed sleep. Then a thought popped into my head. I made a deal with God that, no matter how tired I felt, I would go to 10 a.m. Mass every day and take my baby with me.

CHAPTER 62 –
GOD REALLY DOES WORK
MIRACLES

The next day, I kept up my end of the bargain and arrived at St Leonard's Church ten minutes prior to Mass. The first thing I saw on one of the benches was a handwritten note. At first I thought someone had forgotten to take it with them, but I felt compelled to read the contents which stated, "Come to me all you who are weary and burdened and I will give you rest" (Matthew 11:28-30). I could hardly believe what I was reading and truly saw this as a sign from God. My daughter went to sleep early that night and, for the first time in a few months, I actually managed to get some rest.

I continued with my promise to God but, having married a divorced Catholic, I was not allowed to receive the Sacrament of Holy Communion. This went on day after day until, one day, a priest who was only short term at St Leonard's RC Church came up to me and said, "You come to Mass every day, but I have noticed that you never take Holy Communion." I told him that it wasn't permissible due to my marital circumstances and had been refused an annulment. The priest said he would have a think about it and then get back to me.

Shortly after, that same priest came to me and suggested that I receive the Sacrament of Confession. He told me that my confession really had to come from the heart and it did. I am not at liberty to tell you why I was then allowed to receive Communion because I made a promise to that priest, but all I can say is if you pray hard enough for something, and I truly mean this, miracles will happen. I felt an indescribable peace in my soul.

When my daughter was six months old, I woke up one morning with severe back pains. It was a pain I had never experienced before, and I now know that they call it, 'labour without the break of contractions'. The pain was awful, and Jack told me to spend the day in bed. I was screaming in agony and asked him to call a doctor who confirmed that I had kidney stones. The doctor prescribed morphine for me and told me that if I were to be admitted to hospital that's the treatment I would get. I was more than happy to stay at home and, whilst in bed, I would play games with my wee one. I had a big hat with various little objects around the bed and whenever I asked my daughter to pick up an object and put it in the hat she got it right every single time. I think at that point I started to realise just how intelligent she was.

I have told you how thin I became, and my mum was extremely concerned. Even when I went to my local bakery, one of the assistants told me that I didn't look well. Jack, my mum and I decided to go abroad on holiday. We managed to get a really cheap apartment and flight for £100 and so off we went to Ibiza. There was a little cot in the apartment, and by this point my baby girl was eight months old. I had a really proud moment when she pulled herself onto her feet assisted by the wooden cot rails. However, the hot sun did not agree with her. She would cry constantly and the only thing that stopped her was when I carried her on my shoulders. I did this until the end of the holiday.

CHAPTER 63 –
THE BIRTH OF MY
BEAUTIFUL BABY BOY

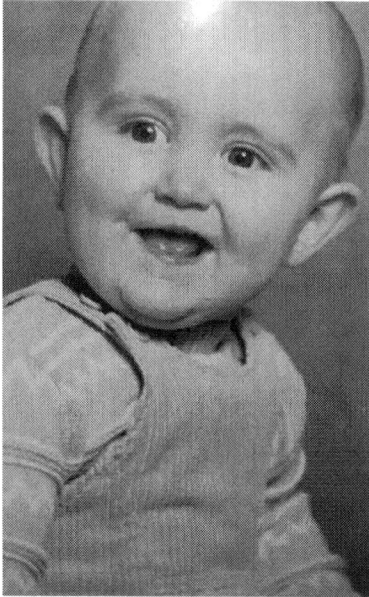

My baby boy Mark

After we returned home, I went to the doctor for a routine check-up. I'm not sure if it was a smear test or not, but the doctor asked me if I could give him a urine sample. I couldn't believe what I was hearing when a very smiley doctor came back to tell me I was pregnant. I had walked to the surgery, which took around 20 minutes, and on the road back, I alternated by running, walking, crying and laughing. My emotions were all over the place. I was already one month pregnant. When I got home, I burst into tears when I told Jack the news. I'm not really sure if my tears were joyous or otherwise. All I can say is that I couldn't believe it.

For a few years, Jack was doing a Bachelor of Arts degree with the Open University and he wanted our daughter to be there when he graduated. My mum and Jack's sister Agnes (RIP) and her husband came along and we had a brilliant day. The sun was shining, the ceremony was a first for me and the meal we had afterwards was amazing. Agnes and her husband Jim really spoiled both our children and for every gift received, I am truly grateful.

Whilst pregnant with my next child, I never gained any weight whatsoever. I was a size 10 and you would never have thought I was pregnant. I came to the conclusion that our second baby was going to be an unhealthy weight. As my third trimester approached, my mum came to stay with us in East Kilbride. It was January 1987 and one of the worst winters on record in East Kilbride. There was no way anyone could drive because the roads were covered in snow, but Jack would walk to the local supermarket to ensure we didn't run out of food. On 23 January, my labour pains started, but I was remarkably calm. I had written out meal plans and sealed them to the freezer to make things easier for my mum and Jack whilst I was in hospital. I clearly remember my mum almost spilling her tea and boiled egg when I told her that I was in labour.

The weather had much improved on 23 January, but a helicopter was on standby just in case I went into labour early. Jack drove me to Rutherglen Maternity Unit, and one of the nurses told me that if I was as calm in labour as I was when she did an internal examination, I would do just fine. The nurse was completely right because, not long after being admitted, I was in a hospital bed feeling the urge to push. It was so much better second time round.

A Chinese doctor delivered my little boy, and I remember him crying with joy before he put my son in my arms. Mark weighed in at 8lbs 1.5oz, a good, healthy weight and only one ounce less than my daughter. I breastfed my son for six weeks but was advised by the midwife to bottle-feed after that because, although there was quantity in my breast milk, the quality wasn't there. I don't know if that was because there were only 16 months between my two children, but at least I had given my son antibodies.

Mark was the least troublesome baby you could ever have clapped eyes on. He rarely cried and slept through the night without disturbing me. At this point, my daughter's sleeping pattern was good, and I really thanked God for that. Believe me; I felt that it would have been easier coping with twins instead of two children who were only 16 months apart.

The night before Mark's christening

I decided it would be more prudent for Jack to look after Mark (who was sleeping) whilst I went to the vigil Mass with my daughter. For the first time in many years, I was allowed to receive the Sacrament of Holy Communion. It was a precious moment for me because not only was I at one with God, but I was determined that I would set a good example for my children.

When I returned home, I rattled the letter box and Jack opened the door. He was like a raging bull when I arrived home despite being okay with my taking my daughter to the vigil. He accused me of receiving the Blessed Sacrament before him, and whenever I tried to explain that it made sense for me to go to Vigil Mass he just shot me down in flames.

I could not believe his attitude and I felt unbelievably hurt, especially when Jack stormed upstairs. I was left to put my daughter to sleep and then get everything ready for the following day. Over and over I pondered all this in my mind, but I had a job to do because quite a few relatives and friends were coming back to my house when the service finished. Jack's sister had been invited to be my son's godmother. Jack never offered an explanation as to what had happened the previous night and something in me told me not to pursue it.

The christening itself was lovely and, just as had happened when my daughter was christened, I was given Mark's Baptismal Certificate and a candle to light each year on the baptismal day of the children. This was a tradition I kept up for many years, and the children loved it because they always managed to get a toy or two as well as the edible goodies that went along with the celebration.

CHAPTER 64 –
THE NEED TO WORK

As mentioned, I have always been a workaholic and nothing changed when my children were young. The house was pristine and, as well as looking after the children, I found myself looking for things to do. One day, I decided I would take a part-time job. Although Jack and I had a joint bank account, I never felt comfortable using it. I had always been so independent and used to dealing with my own finances that it just seemed alien for me not to be earning a wage. The first job was in telesales and there was only one other female in the office. It was horrible having to cold-call people about double glazing, and the method used was simply based on going through the phone book. That job lasted all of six weeks because the company went into liquidation which meant we didn't receive our wages.

My next venture was delivering telephone directories in my neighbourhood, and when I tell you there were hundreds of books to deliver, I am not exaggerating. The lock-up garage that we had was full to the brim but, in the 1980s, £100 was a lot of money and I was determined to earn it. Elizabeth came to my rescue, as always, and I duly received my £100.

Elizabeth was at university, and she would often bring her friends to my house to be fed and watered. I cannot praise her highly enough but, even now, many years later, I know that if something goes wrong in my life, Elizabeth is always there for me.

My next job was working in Glasgow in the evening and involved a typing test. I asked my friend Lesley if she would be interested, because I knew that she worked as a personal secretary and the typing test would be a doddle. We duly arrived at Union Street and took the test but, the odd thing was, I scored higher.

We both got the job and the work was computer based. We would chase up catalogue debts and, although the work was quite boring, I liked it. Before I left for work in the evening, I made sure my children had their bath and were fed and watered. It felt great to be earning some real money again, albeit part time.

Whilst I was working for the company in Union Street, I spotted an advert for an administration assistant in my local newspaper. The job involved a lot of court duties and I knew I was more than qualified to apply. Again, it was only part time, but it was with East Kilbride District Council and felt a lot more secure than the company I was with. I felt bad about telling Lesley that she would no longer be receiving a lift into town every night which, subsequently, meant that she too had to leave. The wages were fine if you had a car but bus and train fares on top just didn't make economic sense.

Just prior to being called for an interview, Chief Inspector McDonald phoned me at home. He was one of my referees for the job and had already been contacted about my reference. When he telephoned me at home, he stated that the head of legal service asked if I could be trusted, to which he instantly replied, "You can trust that girl with your life."

My due date came for my interview and, although I didn't have a successful feeling about it, I do remember one of the questions was whether or not I had worked with computers. I explained about my job in Union Street and that seemed to satisfy Dan, the head of legal services, who was to be my immediate boss.

I told Jack all about it, and since my little daughter was now four years of age and Mark almost three, they were both eligible for private nursery. This was completely ideal because, if I did get that part-time job, it meant that Jack and I could take them there just prior to 9.30 and he would pick them up at 1.30 p.m. and then collect me.

CHAPTER 65 –
WORKIING WITH EAST KILBRIDE
DISTRICT COUNCIL

A few days later, a large envelope came through my door, and I remember Jack saying to me that the council would not send such a bulky envelope if I hadn't got the job. I opened the envelope, signed on the various dotted lines and I had an offer to start with legal services the following Monday.

On my first day, Anne (the court administrator) gave me a guided tour of the East Kilbride District Council building and the various departments I would be dealing with. I know I told you that, as a policewoman, I had applied for a court job and then thought better of it, but when I saw East Kilbride District Court, I immediately felt at home. The court was next to the Ballerup Hall where many activities took place including Christmas dances. Because the legal office had too many bodies, I had to do my work with the admin staff and then let Anne cast a glance at it before it went to the public. I was tasked with unpaid road traffic fixed penalties and, believe me, they came in their hundreds, but I quickly understood my role and churned out hundreds of letters, all courtesy of the typist department. East Kilbride District Council office was a bit of a maze to begin with, and it took a while to get used to all the various departments because I normally spent the four hours of my shift just doing unpaid fixed penalties.

Legal services, the chief executive's offices, typist and licensing administration were all on the first floor of the council building. There was a reception desk manned by staff who dealt with customer enquiries as well as printing and photocopying. It was a very neat set-up and completely seamless. My own head of legal, Dan, and his deputy head had an office to themselves.

Whilst working in the licensing office, I overheard the type of duties that were involved in being part of that specialist kind of job but, as a policewoman, I hated talks on licensing and it was even worse when that subject came up in an exam. I simply had no interest in it and thanked my lucky stars for being part of a court department. The solicitor who held court was called the clerk of court and he/she would sit up on the bench alongside the Justice of the Peace. The clerical officer (in this case Anne) would take minutes of every case and, whenever time was up, she would process the necessary work. I was amazed when she showed me that side of the job but, since I was part time, I guessed it wouldn't really be something I would be expected to do.

By this point, I was due to go on a pre-booked holiday to Great Yarmouth with Jack, the family and my mum. I had told my employer about my holiday dates when I got the job but, just prior to going on holiday, my immediate boss Anne (who, by the way, was one of the most beautiful speakers I have ever met) dropped the bombshell that she had applied and been accepted for the tax office and would commence her employment a few months later at the beginning of July. It was fully expected that I would apply for Anne's job, and I just kept thinking I really didn't want it. I was used to my little routine, as were my children, but my daughter was due to go to school and, moreover, she would be at school full time after the October week of that year.

I can't recall putting in my application form in for the full-time post. The money wasn't great. I was a GS1 with a salary on a pro rata basis and Anne was a GS3. Anne was always stressed out, which didn't surprise me in the slightest, because there were two court days per week, namely Tuesdays and Thursdays, and the paperwork fallout from that would have made you run a mile. On top of that, Compensation Orders had to be dealt with and whenever Anne managed to get round to it (which wasn't very often), Means Enquiry Courts had to be held for those who had not paid their court fines. It was a complete circus and one which I wasn't entirely sure about playing the part of the juggler!

My colleagues kept telling me I would be ideal for the job and why would I think twice when flexible working hours were being fed to me on a plate. However, nothing anyone said seemed to help me make my mind up. I knew, by the time I got back from holiday, Anne would be gone, so I asked as many questions of her as I could whilst I still had her attention.

In the meantime, I cast off all my work fears and Jack drove us all down to Great Yarmouth. Although we were only supposed to be part of the holiday camp for a week and had paid up front, the entertainment and activities for the children were brilliant, and we were blessed with super weather. When the week was coming to an end, Jack and my mum hatched up a plan to take a less expensive caravan for a week which was a bit further away from the activities but near enough to be allowed to use them.

All good things come to an end and, as we were driving up to Scotland, I felt the sword of Damocles hanging over me. I began to feel irritated about everything and anything and, when we parked at one of service stations, my little daughter ran off in the wrong direction and, I am thoroughly ashamed to say, I bawled and shouted at her. Normally, I would have just run after her, took her hand and walked in the right direction. My mum became angry with me, and I knew that I had taken my job decision out on my little girl. I think my son Mark just kept out of my road, but what I did was wrong and I realised I was uptight about my job.

There had been 100 applicants for the junior clerical assistant job, so you can imagine what it was like second time round for a senior position. Back at East Kilbride District Council, it always fascinated me that employees had their names emblazoned on brass on the door. I was informed that I had been accepted for Anne's job which had really good flexible working hours. It was one of my finest moments when I had a plaque on the door too.

Just like Anne had needed an office junior, I also needed extra help and that help came in the form of a lady called Norma. She was a great wee worker and came from Broughty Ferry in Dundee and, just after six months, Norma announced that she was leaving as her husband had been promoted to another job. Just prior to that, the typing pool was hiring a permanent typist and a semi-permanent typist. I've previously alluded to having my own typist, and June (semi-permanent) would type up my work which was nothing short of immaculate.

There was a procurator fiscal's office just at the side of the courtroom where a woman by the name of Margaret worked. Margaret was a really jolly soul and it would have been very difficult not to like her. We decided to have a leaving night out for Anne at the local hotel. Anne had jokingly told me to bring notes with me because she hadn't had time to show me everything in the five days that remained prior to tendering her resignation.

Margaret, Anne and I all sat at a table and yes, I did have the notes with me. It must have seemed a bit desperate when my notebook fell out of my handbag. I don't remember what I ate, I just knew I wanted to learn as much about the district court as possible. In an earlier conversation, Anne had told me that whenever there were any team meetings she was never invited along, and I wondered why. I knew the lawyers were clerks of court and as well as doing conveyancing and other legal matters, the district court generated an enormous amount of work and the fact that no court representative attended a team meeting did not sit well with me at all.

One day, Dan called me into his office and asked if the district court merited two full-time positions. I affirmed without a shadow of a doubt that we needed another permanent member of staff and, once again, the applications came in their droves. The one person who stood out as the most likely candidate was June my typist. I remember the day like yesterday, when I knew who the successful candidate would be and June asking me the whole way down to the toilet if she had secured the job. The mischievous part of me let her wait a few more minutes before I threw my arms around her and welcomed her on board. One of the best decisions I have ever made.

CHAPTER 66 –
JUNE McSPORRAN, AN EXCELLENT
FRIEND AND COLLEAGUE

Because June became a GS3 band (my former position), it meant in effect that my own post merited some scrutiny. The highlights of the week were our Tuesday and Thursday court days which started at 10 a.m. on the dot. Every second Tuesday things all went a bit crazy, because that was known as the 'Pleading Diet'. This allowed the offender to plead guilty or not guilty either in person or via his/her solicitor. A Pleading Diet normally held over 100 cases and if any of those cases were statutory and not dealt with in the six months period allotted, they would automatically become 'Time Barred'.

This was great for the accused but not so for the prosecutor. I mentioned before that the justice and the clerk of court sat on the bench and during the interlude or even an adjournment, a particular case would be passed about like a ball until a decision was reached. Whenever a justice thought of sending someone to prison, it was the norm to order a social enquiry report which gave further background about the offender's personal details and also to see if any mitigating circumstances could be provided that ultimately led to a fine rather than incarceration.

Nobody liked it when a defence agent decided to appeal the decision of the court, because there was very limited time to do so. Unfortunately there was one such occasion and J. who was a solicitor in our department had been the clerk of court. She ran out for lunch as fast as her legs would carry her but the defence agent held his ground, waited until she came back and then said, "I think you and I have some talking to do." I was never involved in the appeals procedure, but I felt sorry for the solicitor who ended up having to get their trial notes typed up.

As mentioned, the Pleading Diet came around every fortnight

Tuesday, but the Thursday of that week was for trials – as was the following Tuesday and Thursday. That meant June and I could go through various files pertaining to those who had either made no payment or had only paid some of their fine. Some of the fines included things like not paying a road traffic fixed penalty which, if the offender did not pay or had paid only some of their fine, the alternative of a sentence in prison was calculated.

I recall a man who was never out of our local rag (*The Weekly East Kilbride News*). This man was always in court on breach of the peace charges, assault (normally his wife) and generally making a nuisance of himself wherever he went. On one of our Pleading Diet days, Margaret in the fiscal's office alerted me to a warrant regarding this gentleman. His case was calling in court, but there was also a means enquiry warrant for failing to turn up at a means court.

I can still see the man pleading with me not to send him to Barlinnie Prison. This was definitely not a man you could trust, but he begged me to give him 15 minutes to get the money owed and I nodded my head. I was scared witless that I'd end up losing my own job by taking a punt on this man, but lo and behold the man came back just in time to hear another one of the infamous breaches of the peace. When the judge told him he had a means enquiry warrant, the wee man piped up that he was just about to pay the money owed at the court reception desk. The justice agreed only if he showed him the fine receipt. The man paid his fine, I let out a very long sigh of relief and the next little gesture is one which will stay with me in my heart forever. With the few coins he had left over, the man handed me a tiny bar of chocolate, apologising that it wasn't a full box of chocs! I felt touched, really touched, and came to the conclusion that in most cases there is some good in everyone.

I'll give you a little flavour regarding the work we did. Fixed penalties were the order of the day when someone committed an offence if the charge was minor and they had no previous convictions. Well that was supposed to be the case, but more often than not the fiscal would give the offender a second chance. Apart from fixed penalties, June had general administration work to complete. East Kilbride was a very busy court and generated a lot of work.

I am quite feisty, and I took the decision upon myself to go to staff meetings. I was really passionate about my court work and felt that it was something that should be discussed at team meetings. I think our legal team were a bit shocked when I followed them from our office to the meeting room, but no one said anything and it just became the norm for me to give my input. My head of legal must have been quite impressed with my knowledge, because one evening he had a meeting with the justices of the peace and asked me if I would give them a talk about the work required of a court administrator. I have alluded to parking penalties in a previous chapter but, just as I was finishing my discourse, I passed round a parking penalty to let the justices see what one looked like. Obviously, the name of the offender was on the penalty, but my little nugget made them burst out laughing because someone with a sense of humour had put the name 'Jesus Christ' as the offender! The meeting ended on a high note but my downfall, on top of a very busy workload, was to be in charge of the Justices of the Peace from thereon in.

Like everything else, things changed and we ended up with computers. At my interview for the part-time job, I was asked if I knew anything about computers, and I think it swayed the decision on my getting the job when I told Dan that I was working with computers at my job in Glasgow. In addition to now having computers thrust on us, June and I were told that we would be moving from the Legal department on the first floor to a room next to the court itself.

We were not happy with the forthcoming move but had to accept it for what it was. It also irked me that my name would be taken down from the door and not transferred to the office downstairs. I know that seems really trivial but somehow, when I saw my name on its brass plate, I felt proud. Looking back, moving next to the court made complete sense, but that little name plate bolstered my ego and pride certainly comes before a fall.

CHAPTER 67 –
BEING IN CHARGE OF TRAINING JUSTICES OF THE PEACE

The due date arrived for moving, and June and I worked like mad to make sure everything was in its place. The computers were ready and waiting for us, but it was frustrating when we hadn't a clue about using a Word document and on many occasions we had to enlist the help of someone from the typing pool. Not long after we had become used to the computers, Dan did indeed put me in charge of training Justices of the Peace. It was mandatory for them to go to a Sheriff Court as well as do a prison visit. When I had organised a visit to Barlinnie Prison, we were warmly welcomed by the governor and shown around the various wings. When the tour was complete, tea/coffee and biscuits were the order of the day and created an opportunity for the Justices to ask questions. Everyone took advantage of the liquid break except me. The prisoners had made the tea/coffee and I knew, from being in the police, that if a Justice of the Peace put someone behind bars and a JP visit was scheduled, prisoners would spit in the tea/coffee prior to serving it. I don't think for one moment that every prisoner did this, but I certainly wasn't taking any chances. I just said that I wasn't thirsty and never told my Justices my reasons for passing up the offer.

One of my Justices of the Peace was also our Lord Provost. Because he held this position, Dan asked me to put together a personal training plan for him which I duly did. I was glad it worked out as well as it did and, because of that, I was given more and more control over Justice-related matters. One of the big events was hosting an annual meeting of Justices who came from far and wide. When it came to our turn to host, Dan put me in complete charge, and I truly couldn't have pulled it off without June's help. It involved setting a suitable time and date, hospitality and a degree of training. Expectations were high, and also there was some healthy rivalry from other district courts in order to see which court had pulled it out of the bag.

The due date arrived and, after meeting and greeting the Justices, I spoke about how the district court operated in East Kilbride. This seemed to go down well enough and, after discussions and a few comfort breaks, there was a three-course meal. Once dinner was over, the Justices had to read six case scenarios, which I had assembled, and when the allotted time was over a mixture of opinions was shared. That day went really well, and I was really proud of June's and my achievement. I am naturally competitive and I wanted that day to stand out which was evidenced by the amount of thank-you cards and phone calls sent to my head of legal. Dan called a staff meeting the following week and he was genuinely delighted by our efforts. At that time, there was an advert on television which I think was for Scottish Gas and Mr Russell winked at me before using the slogan, "Don't you just love being in control?" I just burst out laughing.

After the successful Justices' training day, Dan Russell passed me quite a lot of legal work and, to be honest, it didn't go down too well with the solicitors.

Dan was a member of COSLA, an organisation that champions the causes of local governments in Scotland. COSLA had contacted our head of legal to find out about his views on whether or not the 'not proven' verdict should be scrapped or retained.

For those of you who are not familiar with this terminology, the main verdicts in a Scottish Court of Law are guilty, not guilty and not proven. (Unfortunately the not proven verdict is due to be abolished.) Dan passed the correspondence to me in order that I could give him my opinion. I suppose in some ways that made sense because, by this time, my district court knowledge was excellent. I know that sounds big-headed, but I loved my work as well as the interaction I had with Justices, fiscals and defence agents.

I was able to weigh up both sides of the coin and, after a great deal of deliberation, I came to the conclusion that we should retain the 'not proven' verdict. My main reason being that court cases are not just black and white as my direct police work experience certainly taught me!

I drafted up all my reasons for retaining the not proven verdict, and my head of legal sent the necessary paperwork to COSLA. He didn't change any of the content (apart from his own signature) of the document and, about a month later, I was informed that yes it was in the best interest of an accused person to allow for discrepancies. I was really chuffed. It was the right decision and one which allowed both justice and fairness for the defendant. It saddens me that the not proven verdict will no longer exist in Scotland.

I got to know my Justices really well with all their different personalities. Whilst in court, the Justice would be in the centre, with the clerk of court (solicitor) and me on the left-hand side of the Justice. There was one particular Justice and her name always amused me because she never left us in any doubt that she was a practising Catholic – her name was Mrs Pagan.

Whenever the court would have an adjournment to consider a verdict, Justice Pagan (RIP) would request that I have some input into the decision. Again, this was something that didn't go down too well with some of the legal staff, but I duly put in my tuppence-worth prior to the verdict being reached. I'm not going to name all the Justices because I would bore you witless, but there were some I favoured over others. Mr Cadenhead and Jean Boyce were always brilliant at filling in when a Justice couldn't take their turn of the annual rota and for that I was really grateful. We had Scottish and mixed-race justices, one of whom was prone to falling asleep during a trial. I could never understand how he could arrive at a verdict when the trial was over, but somehow he pulled it off. At the time, I do not really think I appreciated their admirable work, because these pillars of the community gave up their spare time to help our court function and rarely claimed expenses. It would be remiss of me if I didn't give a special mention to a couple of Justices who are ingrained in my memory for very different reasons, and you'll understand why when I explain.

CHAPTER 68 – MY INVITATIONS TO THE ROYAL GARDEN PARTY

Mr Hamilton (RIP) was a millionaire and drove a beautiful Bentley car but a more humble man you could not meet. If anyone asked him what he worked at, he simply said that he was a milkman. This 'milkman' lived in a very large estate in East Kilbride and donated 32 acres of land including a 16-acre loch facilitating water sports, a lovely café and a children's playground. It is a beautiful scenic place and ideal for a stroll round on a summer's day. It was officially opened in 1996. I have quite a few favourite memories of Mr Hamilton.

We also had a justice called Jenny Auld who was made freeman of East Kilbride in 1993. She was quite formidable but worked tirelessly to shape my home town. I could go on and on but, just prior to Jenny retiring as a JP, Mr Hamilton asked me to accompany him to choose a piece of crystal as a leaving gift. Dan gave me permission, and I felt like the Queen travelling in that gorgeous Bentley. There was great banter that day, and we finally picked a beautifully fitting piece of crystal. Jenny was very principled and insisted that the council should not pay for a retirement party, so we raised some money to give her the send-off she deserved for her services.

A few months later, Mr Hamilton phoned me at the office and asked me if I would like to go to the Royal Garden Party. I said I would be delighted, and it was agreed that not only would he get me two tickets but he insisted on taking my husband and me for a meal. When I told Jack he honestly thought it was a wind-up, but lo and behold, the invitations arrived and I was thrilled. My mum looked after the children, and Jack and I, all suited and booted, headed off to Edinburgh. Mr Hamilton had invited other guests, and we all had a lovely three-course meal at a posh hotel in Bothwell after the garden party.

The following year, I received another phone call from Mr Hamilton asking me how many tickets I would like for the Royal Garden Party. I was gobsmacked but asked for three. This time, I thought it would be nice to take Cathy (my former bridesmaid) as well as Jack, and when the due date arrived the weather was gorgeous. Cathy was over the moon at the invitation and, once again courtesy of Mr Hamilton, we were treated to a fancy meal. I don't know what made me ask for three tickets but something instinctively told me it was the right thing to do.

The Royal Garden Party in Edinburgh is held in July and, on arrival, I noticed that Cathy's stomach seemed really swollen. I didn't give it too much thought at the time because the day was so enjoyable. I am so glad now that I asked for that third ticket because, a few months later, Cathy's sister phoned me to tell me that Cathy was in the Glasgow Royal Infirmary with leukaemia. Jack drove the children and myself to the hospital but declined to visit Cathy saying that he preferred to remember her as she was. The children and I duly went into the ward, and Cathy was really pleased to see us. As we were leaving and said our goodbyes, I saw a tear roll down Cathy's cheek. The following day, I found out that she had passed away. I was so glad of the time I had spent with her prior to her leaving this world.

CHAPTER 69 –
MY INTRODUCTION TO THE
FOCOLARE MOVEMENT

Jack and I saw an article in the *Scottish Catholic Observer* about something called 'the Mariapolis'. The article was excellent and promoted a little touch of Heaven for five days. With the attitude of nothing ventured nothing gained, I decided to phone the Focolare Centre based in Glasgow. Somewhere at the back of my mind, I had heard of this movement and knew that it was a religious organisation that was founded in the Catholic Church. The founder, Chiara Lubich, came from Trent in Italy and was still alive.

I discovered that Mariapolis meant 'City of Mary'. It was a good article and the Mariapolis gathering seemed to cater to everyone, and I felt that it might be something different for the children to enjoy.

We booked our accommodation for Bonskeid House and drove to Pitlochry when the due date arrived. As we entered the small town of Pitlochry, there was no mistaking the main reception area for the Mariapolis due to the many large banners hanging outside. We drove a bit further up the road and saw Bonskeid House. With its amazing woods, trees and country walks, it was the perfect place for a family holiday. After dropping off our luggage, we checked into the reception area, paid our dues and received the five-day itinerary. People from all denominations and faiths were welcomed at the Mariapolis and, during my time there, I found out more about what this movement was about and why it appealed to me. Chiara lived in Trent and it was during World War II that she thought God had called her to Himself in a special way. With her companions, she began living the Gospel in her daily life. The Focolare Movement was approved by the Catholic Church in 1962, and there was something fresh about this spirituality that attracted other religions.

Personally, I loved the ethos of starting every day afresh and living the present moment and, although that can be difficult, if you apply it in your life it takes away the stresses and strains that lie ahead. My daughter had the joy of actually meeting Chiara when she went to Rome for a youth convention. The days of the Mariapolis were wonderful for us and brought us great peace. Chiara died on 10 March 2008 at the centre for the Focolare Movement in Castel Gandolfo. Her beatification is due to take place and hopefully one day she will be canonised a saint.

For the moment, back to Pitlochry ...

There was always morning Mass and, as soon as it finished, we had tea/coffee which let us get to know each other. This was followed by plenty of activities and the children were split into their appropriate age groups. We adults would partake in whatever activity we were interested in. Weather-wise it was glorious and ideal for outdoor barbecues as well as ceilidh dancing. There was a concert on the final night. Those five days flew by, and I can honestly say that the little taste of Heaven which I remember to this day certainly met our expectations. I remember arriving home thinking that everything seemed so noisy, and Jack more than agreed with me.

CHAPTER 70 –
MIRACULOUS MEDAL AND
MY THIRD LIFE

At Easter time, I received a phone call from the father of a little girl who was a gen youth member in the Focolare. He asked if my daughter could come with their family to Ireland. My daughter and the little girl had become inseparable whilst we were at the Mariapolis. It was agreed that my daughter could go and she was very excited.

The downside was that the Irish ferry left from Fishguard in Wales, and this involved a very long drive from East Kilbride.

During the journey, the car skidded and spun so far round that we were facing oncoming traffic on a very busy road. It was a terrifying moment. I distinctly remember that I kept touching my Miraculous Medal – a medal that depicts the Mother of God. It is worn round the neck to protect you from danger.

Jack was driving at the time, and he managed to steer the car away from oncoming traffic. We decided to park the car for a few minutes because we were quite badly shaken up. I then discovered that my Miraculous Medal was no longer around my neck. We searched the car high and low to try and find the gold chain and medal, but it was nowhere to be found. It was like Our Blessed Lady was reminding me how dangerous that accident would have been if I had not been wearing the medal. I know some people will find this explanation sceptical, but I truly believe my wearing that medal stopped us from being killed. I quickly realised that I had used up **the third of my nine lives**. However, I have lived to tell the tale. There have been numerous healings attributed to those wearing the Miraculous Medal, and I personally will wear this precious medal until the day I die.

Sometime later, Mark and I went to another Mariapolis gathering in Stirling which was great. My mum, the children, my daughter's friend and I went to the Lake District. However, I think Bonskeid

House will always be my favourite. Although I dip my toe in and out of the Focolare Movement, I can honestly say that the charism of Chiara has remained part of my life. It's very difficult to start each day anew when various personalities are involved but, if you can do that, I suggest you give it a try. It will give you much peace – at least that was my experience.

CHAPTER 71 –
MY MUM TO THE RESCUE AND THE HOLIDAYS WE HAD

Things were really going well at work for me and, with June by my side, we were a formidable team. I wish I could have said the same about my home life, as my husband's drinking habits were worsening. I employed my mum to look after my children from Monday through to Wednesday. She would then come for Sunday dinner. She came on almost every family holiday with the exception of Florida. She was the grandmother of my children, my mother and a wonderful companion as I strived through life. I would never have dreamt of using my mum as a babysitter on holiday.

There are three holidays that I remember most with Jack, my mum and the children. One of them was L'Estartit and we stayed in an apartment. Not long after we had checked in, our children put on their bathing suits, jumped into the pool and then, totalling dripping wet, skated around the reception area. Needless to say, the reception staff were none too happy and, although I couldn't help laughing, I had to put paid to that incident.

There was a pub just round the corner where they had entertainment every night, and I never thought I would enjoy *The Rocky Horror Show* so much. During that holiday, it was the commemoration of my daughter's baptism day, so I put banners on the walls and organised a party for her. There was always a present to be had but obviously I wasn't going to leave my little son out, so excitement was had by all. The champagne was really cheap at the local supermarket, and my mum and I drank and bought plenty of it. We had a late checkout prior to going home and, as my mum and I lay on the veranda sipping champagne, Jack was the one who had to organise the packing. At the end of the holiday, I felt sad but the children only had one week off school and our family time together was special.

In the summer, we always went to mainland Spain or the islands – Menorca was the number one favourite. The local restaurants were amazing and we took great delight in choosing the fine cuisine on offer. During the school October holidays, we normally went to one of the caravan parks in England which had lots of facilities for children. I used to wonder why Jack would offer to go for any shopping we needed, particularly in Spain where tap water wasn't suitable for drinking, but over the years I realised that Jack probably had a few drinks before returning to our apartment.

Our second holiday in Spain involved coach travel. My mental health wasn't great but, for the sake of my children, I tried to appear as normal as possible. My mum loved the fact that she could buy cheap cigarettes and always bought them from the same shop. The thing is that my children and I had gone into a joke shop which sold small exploding sticks ideal for putting in cigarettes. My mum would be puffing away one minute and the next minute her cigarette exploded. This normally happened on the beach, and I don't know how on earth she never saw the children and me laughing, but she put it down to a bad batch of 200 cigarettes. We waited a few days and did the same thing over again, and my mum had steam coming out of her ears, as well as a cigarette that exploded after a few puffs. She threatened to go back to the shop where she bought them, but somehow we managed to dissuade her. The children were egging me on at every opportunity, but I had to wait a few days before I tricked her again, and it was only when she was so determined to walk into the offending shop, I knew it was time to admit the truth.

The third holiday was in Majorca, and by this time Jack's drinking was really out of control. So much so that I purchased four gala dinner tickets instead of the five that would have included Jack. I really didn't want to be shown up by him, and I knew that would definitely happen. There were quite a few funny moments on that holiday, because Mark bought himself a laser pen, would shine it on the apartment window when Jack was looking and then turn it off as if nothing had happened. Jack would become raging mad because he couldn't identify the source, and the rest of us would be stifling laughter. I can't remember just how old my children were but certainly old enough to have a good laugh, particularly when playing cards with their grandmother, but sadly Jack's conduct on that holiday was enough for me to say that I would never go on holiday with him again.

The following year, my mum, my two children and I went on holiday to Turkey. The hotel was lovely and the Turkish people genuinely like children. My son was no exception so, after a great deal of persuasion by a Turkish boat owner, I allowed Mark to go sailing with him. In later years, Mark told me that he felt really uncomfortable on that trip. My daughter is very fair-skinned and that attracted lots of unwanted attention whenever we were out shopping. On any holidays, I have always tried to get to Mass, but in Turkey you had to book a trip to Ephesus. Many people take that trip to see the wonderful ancient ruins there, but what came to my mind were St Paul and his Letters to the Ephesians. Whenever I read those letters, it is obvious that Saint Paul had an overwhelming love of Jesus Christ and, as a convert himself, he was zealous and passionate about the Gospel.

Apart from getting to Mass, one of the other reasons I wanted to visit Ephesus was because when Jesus was being crucified he entrusted his mother to St John and said those eternal words, "Son this is your mother, Mother this is your son." St John took the Mother of God to his home in Ephesus where she would remain during her final years on earth. We had two trips to Ephesus and, on the road there, we saw quite a few statues of Mary. I was told that because the Turkish people see Jesus as a prophet, they also venerate His mother.

The archaeology interested me, but I was more interested in seeing where Our Lady had lived prior to her Assumption into Heaven. Naturally, there was a bit of a queue to see this house which is now a small church, but eventually I managed to get inside, kneel down and say a few prayers. It was a wonderful, blessed moment.

CHAPTER 72 –
A MESSAGE FROM THE
MOTHER OF GOD

Before entering the church, I saw a priest from India chatting to some tourists before he was about to celebrate Mass. On exiting the church, the priest appeared to be engrossed in conversation with these same tourists, but he stopped mid sentence, walked over to me and his exact words were, "I have a message for you." I was stunned by this. I had never seen this priest in my life before and he certainly didn't know me. The priest said, "Mother Mary has heard your prayer. She is pleased with what you ask and says that she will remain with you always."

I love the Mother of God very much, and this amazing message gave me great joy and peace. I knew that it would be something I would never forget and hoped that, the following Sunday, I might be given another message, but I guess enough had been said.

Strangely enough, while we were still there, I dreamt that my mum's neighbour Suzie had died. My mum was close to her next-door neighbour who was kindness personified. The dream was so real that I sat upright in bed around 2.30 a.m. and then eventually dozed off. The next day, my mum decided to buy postcards and she told me she was sending one to Suzie. I told my mum about the dream and, for some strange reason, I wrote down the time and date and put it in my handbag. The dream was so real that I cautioned my mum about sending the postcard. I was more than convinced Suzie was dead but, since it was only a dream, my mum decided to send the postcard anyway.

After landing in Glasgow Airport, Jack picked us up, took my mum home and then took the children and me back to East Kilbride. Later that evening, I received a telephone call from my mum to say that Suzie's daughter had put a note through my mum's door to let her know that Suzie had died. It was the exact same date that was in my dream and her time of death was between two and three in the morning. Incredible!

God's message

I still had a few days annual leave prior to going back to work, so my mum and I met up in Glasgow for lunch and also to buy a sixtieth birthday card for my cousin Mary. I knew she would appreciate a Mass card. At that time, St Paul's bookshop was situated in Royal Exchange Square in Glasgow. It is now called the Pauline Media Centre and located elsewhere in Glasgow. During lunch, I asked my mum if she wanted to come with me to a show involving a medium in the Village Theatre, East Kilbride. My mum gave me a clear *no*, but I told her I thought it would be a bit of a laugh as well as a night out. We didn't discuss it further and duly went into St Paul's bookshop. I picked up a nice card for my cousin and then went to look at some of the books. I opened a book which really gave me goosebumps. The paragraph that literally jumped out at me was, "Look to the Spirit and not a Medium for Direction." I dropped the book like a hot potato and ran out of the shop. Mum was right!

Another incident that gave me goosebumps happened more recently. For some reason, I woke up in a right bad mood. Couldn't understand why but, on my way back from my kitchen, I looked at the crucifix in my bedroom and said to Jesus, "I'm not too happy with you either." The immediate voice that came into my head was, "What do you think it is like for me hanging on a cross?" I couldn't believe it. I promptly knelt before the crucifix and asked God to forgive me.

CHAPTER 73 – OPEN UNIVERSITY, CLOSE TO A BREAKDOWN, GLAD FOR A GOOD FRIEND AND HELPING OTHERS!

I never dreaded going back to work as June was more than capable at the helm. It was great to know that I wouldn't be coming back to a major backlog of work. I was in my late thirties and thought I was invincible. I lavished up all the praise I got from my colleagues because I was doing an Open University degree. It was the Bachelor of Arts foundation course and it covered a wide range of topics such as philosophy, history, music and at least three other subjects. Those were the days when we didn't have computers, resulting in handwritten essays. It was a crazy pace to keep up and, once the children were sleeping, I would stay up until 3 a.m. writing. I would sleep for a couple of hours and then I was up for work no later than 7.30 a.m. I was so tired one morning, and I couldn't find my essay anywhere. I couldn't believe my eyes when I noticed I had accidentally put it in the bin. That should have been a warning sign, but it wasn't. I was ambitious and getting good essay grades just fuelled the fire inside me.

Because we were allowed flexitime at work, I had accrued a few days' worth which meant I didn't need much annual leave to go to the Open University mandatory summer school in Stirling for a week. My son and daughter had been enrolled in a sports camp at Jordanhill in Glasgow which thankfully coincided with my summer school university dates. It was a great week and my fellow students were good company. It can be great to study at home, but a classroom atmosphere allows interaction with the tutor and I was far more knowledgeable by the end of that week. There was an impending exam in the autumn, and I wanted to achieve a good pass mark. We sat our exam at Glasgow University and, although I felt reasonably confident, I was unsure how well I had done. Between my exam and essay marks, I just fell short of a grade A by three marks. I had done my best and the break from the Open University was very welcome indeed.

I decided I would study psychology the following year, but I didn't feel as enthusiastic as I did in my foundation course and I thought that after the break I would feel better. However, something in me was off and I couldn't figure out what it was.

Second year was upon me before I knew it and, once again, I was back to writing essays. I was doing well enough, but I couldn't shake off the feeling of impending doom that seemed to be lurking inside me. I wasn't my usual smiley self and, with that in mind, I began to realise (too late as it happens) that I was doing way too much and the only one suffering was me. One night when I was lying in bed, I felt really claustrophobic and so anxious that I passed out. When I came to, I was shaking and panic attacks were coming at me every ten minutes or so. The following morning, I could hardly face getting out of bed. I told Jack what I was feeling, and he stood me on my head! He told me this was a way to get my blood circulation going. If you have never felt anxiety or panic attacks it is something that I wouldn't wish on my worst enemy. I made an appointment with one of the GPs at my surgery, told him what was happening to me and I distinctly remember saying that I was afraid that I was becoming depressed. He reassured me that this would not happen, but within a week I *was* severely depressed and saw another doctor who gave me medication. At work, I knew I had to confide in June who, thankfully, understood. It got to the stage I could hardly answer a phone call. It was a constant living hell and the only thing that kept me motivated were my children.

My head of legal had arranged for me to go on a clerk of court's course in Glasgow city and I dreaded it. Normally, I would have been quite proud of being sent on a course reserved for solicitors only and probably would have boasted about it, but on that occasion I was too depressed to enjoy it. I knew answers to the various questions asked, but all I could think of was getting home in one piece.

The horrible thing about depression is that you become impatient for the day when you feel just that tiny bit better, and I can only describe those moments as feeling like a ball that you just can't catch. I remember walking to the bus stop and glad that the course had gone well, but my antidepressants hadn't kicked in and I was barely functioning.

Holy Week was approaching and, as a practising Catholic, I wanted to attend as many services as possible. There was normally an early morning Mass to give workers the opportunity to attend a service, and I had gone to Mass as often as I could. I still carried on doing so, despite the panic attacks. I just wanted the stress, anxiety and depression to leave me, but every day without fail was like living in a black hole. Nothing seemed to shake it off.

My colleague June was brilliant during those dark times because, coincidentally, she was suffering as much as I was and hadn't wanted to mention it.

My birthday was on 1 May as you know. From a young child, I would dive into the new grass smell the May dew and rub it on my face. This has been traditional every year of my life except the day of my fortieth birthday. The legal team had gone all out with presents, balloons, birthday banners and dinner at a local hotel. How in the name of God was I going to cope with that! Anyone out there who has suffered stress and anxiety will know exactly what I mean. I really had to give the performance of a lifetime during that meal and, if I remember correctly, there would have been about eight of us. Thankfully, we had a late dinner and an early finish from work.

Jack took me to a youth hostel in Arrochar at the head of Loch Long to mark the occasion. There was beautiful weather, gorgeous scenery, great walks and a good time was had by everyone except me. I distinctly remember one of the hostellers trying to have a conversation with me in the kitchen, and I literally ran away from her mid sentence. I must have seemed really rude but, although I looked normal enough, I was struggling inside. I felt no joy whatsoever and the finale was yet to come.

Elizabeth's wedding was coming up, and my daughter was to be her flower girl. Elizabeth looked stunning and both my children behaved impeccably.

I was so grateful that when Jack was invited to a function, he was always the dedicated driver.

Mark's Confirmation was coming up in May and, after the Sacrament, we had quite a few guests back at the house. I managed my anxiety by constantly topping up glasses, making teas and coffees and ensuring everyone had enough to eat, but inside I felt totally dead. My mum noticed that I wasn't my usual happy self and, years later, she told me that she knew something was wrong with me. She wasn't a woman who cried easily, but I do know that the day she saw me like that, she went home and burst into tears as she told her neighbour how worried she was about me.

No one apart from June knew about the issues I was having, and I cannot thank her enough for her help. Years ago, mental health issues were a stigma. I am so glad that in this 21st century, people are more open about how they feel and they know that they are not alone. I knew that if I had stayed off work when it first happened, I would never have gone back. It took at least a month for the antidepressants to kick in. Slowly but surely, I began to function better.

Not long after June had started in the district court, a woman called Kate was the assistant head of legal. Kate was nothing short of a genius. I don't think I have ever met a more intelligent woman in my life. Moreover, despite my getting more legal work, all our solicitors were very nice about it which made me feel better. Kate asked Jack and me to be her son's Confirmation sponsors. You might wonder where I am going with all this, but Kate head hunted a woman called Susan. Kate had seen the quality of Susan's work and thought she would be an ideal candidate for the legal clerical work whilst we were still part of East Kilbride Council. I immediately liked Susan and we became firm friends. When I first met her, she was trying to hold down her full-time job as well as being a carer for her mother and her uncle who suffered from depression. My life (notwithstanding Jack's affliction/addiction to alcohol) seemed really peachy compared to what Susan was living through, and she would confide in me when we went to lunchtime Mass at St Bride's in East Kilbride during Lent.

Eventually, during the lunchtime breaks when June and I had just moved into the office beside the court, Susan would make sure, for security reasons, that the office was manned by two people. I knew how tough things were for Susan because, although she was outwardly happy, the strain of looking after two old people was starting to take its toll on her, to the extent that she felt (after much soul-searching) her mother would be better in a home in Lanark.

Sadly, Susan's mum had dementia and at the same time her Uncle Joe's depression seemed to be getting worse. I wanted to help Susan as much as I could. After my children came home from school, I was picked up from work and we would all have dinner. I would take the children with me to Susan's mum to give her a break. Sometimes this would be twice a week, and it tied in nicely with the arrangement I had with my mum. The downside for the children was my choice of music when I subjected them to Marilla Ness CDs (singer-songwriter of mainly Gospel music), but they were fine and it all worked out. St Mary's Home in Lanark had a very calm atmosphere, and the children never complained because the café was always open and they would get treated to the home baking on offer.

When Susan turned 50, we had a surprise party and it was all hands on deck. The party was brilliant and a good time was had by all. The next major thing was the death of Susan's Uncle Joe. Susan had her own council house, as did her Uncle Joe, but after he died a house in a better area came up. I couldn't have been more delighted for Susan when she got it, but there was a lot of work to be done. I decided to take some annual leave to help out with stripping wallpaper, scrubbing floorboards and basically any job that was needed. I then followed the same routine of taking the children to see Susan's mum in Lanark – a routine I committed to until Susan's mum died. I was glad to be of help to my great colleague and friend. It was always clear to me that life consists of joys and sorrows and, in those dark moments, I drew on my faith to keep me strong and focused.

One day, my head of legal called me into his office and asked me what I thought about having a computer in the actual courtroom. By this point, June and I were completely familiar with our own computers and I told Dan that I thought it was a great idea. He told me we would be the second court in Scotland to have this facility, and I remember thinking why couldn't we have been first? We discussed the pros and cons, and the only con we could think of was if the computer wasn't tied down in some way onto the table of the bench, it could be stolen. The district court facilitated weight-watching groups at night as well as a makeshift church on a Sunday and, believe me, it was the Sunday worshippers who would leave a right mess in the kitchen for June and I to clean up on the Monday.

The computer was duly delivered, and we had a Pleading Diet in excess of a hundred cases. It was agreed, as the court administrator, that I would be in control for a while and train June gradually, so I was in my element. Instead of having to type up warrants, social enquiry reports, issue fine letters and update court sheets after court finished, I could do it there and then. The printer was in the court office but as soon as (for example) a warrant was issued, June would bring it through. At the end of court proceedings, I could produce an updated and accurate court sheet to the court police officer, procurators fiscal, the *East Kilbride News* journalist, as well as having one for filing in the office. The difference that computer made was unbelievable and, before long, the relevant heads of legal services were writing to Mr Russell to arrange a suitable time and date for their own staff to see this in action. I was well and truly in my element and could not impress enough just how advantageous this new venture was.

June and I got on well with the fiscals and when anyone was leaving or there was a Christmas night out, they very generously invited us. The defence agents gave chocolates to us at Christmas, but I suspect that was more down to us not charging a fortune for a copy complaint that could be done in an instance!

CHAPTER 74 –
HOMOPHOBIA

There was one fiscal night out that ended in tragedy; a night that neither June or I had attended, thank God. There was a fiscal by the name of Marshall. He was a great-looking guy with a bubbly, friendly personality and extremely competent at this job. Marshall was gay and in 1993 there was a great deal of homophobia around. Sadly, on 19 November 1993, Marshall was found murdered in his flat in the west end of Glasgow. He had been in a public house called The Tron in Glasgow with some work colleagues and left the pub around 11.30 p.m. It seems to be a bit unclear as to why Marshall was targeted. He was very intelligent and would have known what routes to avoid on the road to his house in the Kelvinside area of Glasgow. Tragically, Marshall was found strangled with a necktie and belt, his personal possessions had been stolen and the murderer(s) set fire to Marshall's flat with his body inside. In fact, his mortal remains were so charred that the body was almost unidentifiable. After investigation, a man called Steven Ryan (21) was charged with murdering Marshall. Ryan was assisted by his brother Dean (17). It would appear from researching articles on this that Steven Ryan was the main perpetrator and actually boasted to a crown prosecution witness that he had murdered a procurator fiscal. Marshall was in his early thirties when he was murdered. His killer Ryan was given a sentence of life imprisonment. However, shortly after his release from prison in 2015, Ryan murdered a 65-year-old man using scissor blades! He was given another life sentence. This time it is expected that he will die in prison and, after the horrific crimes he committed, he deserves his punishment.

Marshall's murder left us all reeling. No one could believe we would never see him again and, not too long after Marshall's death, a young, very competent fiscal by the name of Joan died from pancreatitis. Another young fiscal called Mike had a fatal heart attack and when my friend John Slowey went off sick for a couple of months, I just thought, *Mother of God, not another one!* John did come back to work, thank God, and although we may now only meet by chance, I still consider him a very dear friend. What a tumultuous time!

CHAPTER 75 –
CHARTER MARK

The next big responsibility I was given at work was something called Charter Mark which apparently was introduced in 1991. I had never heard of it, but Dan wanted East Kilbride District Court to submit an application. If I had known how much work would be involved, I would have run for dear life. But I agreed first and then started to look into what this involved. I was assigned a solicitor called Anne H. to help me out. I want to explain a little about Charter Mark. It is an award given for excellence in customer care, and we had to meet the ten criteria specified for consideration. It was agreed that we would have our application done in approximately six months.

Basically, and without boring you, we had to look at the workings of East Kilbride District Court and all that it entailed. Every item of work was scrutinised and improved upon resulting in committee groups being formed, pamphlets being printed and performance indicators for public transparency. Anne and I had meeting after meeting, and I stayed on late at work most nights just to meet the demanding criteria of Charter Mark. It was both exacting and exhausting and, obviously, we had to keep our Justices updated as to what was happening. We referenced and cross-referenced so much that I felt I was eating and sleeping Charter Mark and, after putting together a glossy brochure with my two children on the front and pictures of staff inside, we were ready to roll. As well as faxing the application, it was decided that I would go with one of the councillors to London and personally hand it to the powers that be.

I can't remember the name of the councillor I went to London with, but it was a really enjoyable day and we had photographs taken. Just after the London trip, a Charter Mark assessor arrived in person to verify everything that we had written. By this point, we had newspapers/magazines for witnesses to read, a vending machine, an induction loop system for those with hearing impairments and a mobility chair. I personally thought we just could not have done any more to improve the workings of the district court, but a few weeks later we received a 'Highly Commended' certificate which meant we had just fallen short of the award. Naturally, I was disappointed due to the work involved, but we had been told not to expect to win first time round by other organisations taking part. I put the whole thing to bed, thinking and thanking God that I wouldn't have to lead up the Charter Mark process a second time round, but I definitely got that one wrong!

CHAPTER 76 –
AN UNEXPECTED PHONE CALL

I haven't told you too much about my home life, but I remember Susan my colleague remarking that I never went out anywhere at the weekends. She and her friend were always going to a ceilidh or some other form of entertainment. I was just glad of a bottle of wine on a Friday night, and it never struck me as odd that Jack and I didn't go out as a couple. Ironically, I did remember the promise I made to Jack when I had been out with my shift and was locked out.

I loved spending the weekends with my children and going ice-skating with them on a Sunday morning. Mark loved cycling and my daughter was part of the Royal Scottish National Orchestra. I often reminisced that the little girl who seemed to be tone deaf suddenly woke up one morning with a lovely singing voice. Both my children were part of the Brownie/Guide and Cub/Scouts movements, and I tried where possible to ensure they had a good social life. By this point, my Diana doll had a makeover and, on a birthday occasion, Diana stood in the living room with outstretched arms holding gifts for my daughter. My beautiful doll from way back was part of the birthday surprise. It was a lovely moment for me to be able to pass it on and keep it in the family, although I would never part with my German teddy.

One night, just after work, I received a telephone call and the caller said to me, "Eunice?" I said, "Yes." She said, "It's Jean." It took me a few minutes to process that Jean Fitzpatrick my former English teacher was calling me. She told me that she was unwell. I knew this as my mum had attended the Royal Infirmary in Glasgow and was on the same bus as Jean but, although she didn't know her well enough to sit beside her, my mum saw her crying. I asked Jean what was wrong with her and she told me she had Parkinson's disease. She then informed me that I had been the only pupil to keep in touch with her and thanked me for all the postcards and Christmas cards I had sent to her over the years.

She said that she was a very hard taskmaster, but I was a very willing pupil. We spoke for a few more minutes and then ended the conversation. I felt both honoured by her call and perplexed at the same time. On 14 February the following year, Jean died with her rosary beads in her hands. If I had known about the funeral, I would certainly have gone to it. My mum told me when her first month's mind Mass was and I was glad to go. I spoke to Jean's friend Eileen Reilly and kept in touch with her until I no longer received a Christmas card. I am assuming she too is dead, because the last card I received she told me she was over 90 years of age. As a token of my love and gratitude to this fine teacher and her precious gift of the English language, every year, I ensured that there was a memorial entry in the *Scottish Catholic Observer* newspaper. In some way, it was all about Jean, but it also gave me time to reflect and remember someone who was not only a teacher to me but a very dear friend who had truly my best interests at heart and helped shape me into the person I have become.

CHAPTER 77 –
SIGN LANGUAGE

There was a British Sign Language course (BSL) being held at East Kilbride College and Dan asked June and I if we wanted to go. It was one night a week, and if anyone ever tells you that even Stage 1 of British Sign Language is easy, I would only say they were naturally gifted. The tutor was a lovely man called Brian who had a hearing impairment.

This number one numpty hadn't a clue what he was trying to teach us. He would stand in one position playing a character role and signing 'Are you deaf?'. He would then stand in the opposite direction and sign 'I can hear and speak'. I was totally bemused and kept wondering what on earth he was doing. But eventually the penny dropped and I understood.

At Tobago Street Police Office there was a centre just across the road for those with hearing impairments, and they would give out leaflets containing the sign language alphabet. I thought I was doing well when I learned the alphabet on my fingers after studying one of the leaflets, but this sign language course was on a whole new level and consisted of a six-month period with an exam at the end of it. I was in complete despair after that first night, because I thought I would never learn how to sign, let alone pass an exam. I think the course started in January and was due to end in July and, as the weeks went by, I was getting desperate. I grabbed as many easy books on sign language from the library as I could get my hands on.

I would practise for ages in front of the mirror and, somewhere along the line, I realised that if I watched Brian's lips I was able to understand what he was trying to sign. I taught my daughter the alphabet on her hands and, although it came in useful later on, I think I was just practising my skills (or lack of). The due date of the exam came. However, June had booked her summer holidays and wasn't available.

Our class consisted of seven or eight people, which is a small number but necessary for that type of course, and I was the second one up for the exam. When the first candidate came out of the room she whispered to me, "Eunice, the exam is about the Second World War." Honest to God I nearly dropped on the spot, but I knew I had to bite the bullet, no matter what the outcome. I can honestly say that it is an absolute miracle that I passed that exam and eventually received my Stage 1 BSL certificate.

I was glad that I had taught my daughter the sign language alphabet because, one night, I dropped her off at Guides whilst Mark was in the back seat of the car. It was a Girl Guide badge night and my daughter was excited. After the drop off, I went to put the car in the lock-up when I saw Jack coming out of another car. A former police colleague had offered him a lift home because Jack was staggering down St Leonards Road.

When I went to collect her, my daughter knew by the look on my face that something was wrong, so I quickly signed to her that her dad was drunk. I decided that when I got home I would phone my mum. I did so but burst into tears before I could explain how bad I felt and just asked my mum to take a taxi from Glasgow to East Kilbride and I would pay for the hire. Suffice to say it was one of the worst nights of my life. Mark recalls it as 'the night of darkness'. I should have left Jack the next day, but he apologised profusely for his behaviour and for the umpteenth time he told me he would stop drinking. As an incentive, he said to me that the mortgage on our house, which was in joint names, would be transferred over to me. The drinking stopped for a short period. It was clear that Jack needed help because alcoholism is an illness, but unfortunately he never saw what the rest of us did.

CHAPTER 78 –
SOCIAL LIFE

For the moment, I will concentrate on happier times, which at this juncture normally revolved one way or another around my working life.

We had some amazing Christmas dinner dances in the Ballerup Hall which was part of the civic centre where I worked. The hall looked amazing, and the highlight of our night was when the balloons hanging from the ceiling were burst because many of them contained £5 notes.

The Stuart Hotel in East Kilbride had some amazing Christmas party nights and the legal department, typists and general office staff really knew how to party. The last one I remember was December 1994/1995 where free drinks were the order of the day. The two memories I have of that night was Bill Dunn (solicitor) telling me that he had got engaged and I was the first to know, and then Dan taking my hand and inviting me up to dance. This was like a bolt out of the blue, and I suppose I remember that incident because he never danced with any other female (none that I can recall) and I was really flattered. I am so glad that night ended on a high, because there were some jungle drums that East Kilbride District Council was going to become part of South Lanarkshire Council. At the time, I never fully appreciated all that it entailed, but my friend Susan had been through something similar when she worked for a previous council and it had not been a smooth transition.

During office hours, Susan would frequently mention this new proposed amalgamation and if I had known what was in front of me, I would have seriously thought about tendering my resignation. I am an optimist and thought, *it surely can't be that bad*, but her words were prophetic, because in 1996 East Kilbride District Council was abolished and the new South Lanarkshire Council consisted of Hamilton, Rutherglen, Lanark and East Kilbride. Everyone was jumping ship, including Dan and the remaining solicitors, and Susan went to Hamilton. The new headquarters were and still are in Almada Street, Hamilton and, at that time, I never realised how much I would grow to hate the place.

Our new district court manager was a guy called Stephen. June and I had never received tapes from Dan where various forms of correspondence had to be typed up, but under the new regime we would get at least one per week. At first I was quite grudging about it, but we really had no choice but to comply. We suddenly found that licensing personnel were now sharing an office with us but, at this point, the district court department and the licensing department remained separate.

June and I got on quite well with our licensing colleagues which made the transition a bit smoother. Our new head of legal services was based in Hamilton and it was a woman by the name of Sandra. I had heard some formidable stories about Sandra and dreaded the thought of meeting her, but we immediately got on like a house on fire. I can honestly say that I never had a bad experience where Sandra was concerned, and June would ask me on several occasions, "What does it take for a woman like Sandra to respect you?" I didn't have an answer to that, but as the months went on and I had many more meetings with Sandra, I remember her saying to me that I could do anything I put my mind to.

Charter Mark reared its ugly head again and now, instead of just one district court to consider, there were three other courts in South Lanarkshire. The licensing manager wanted the district court and licensing to be amalgamated to one application, but Sandra wanted them to be separate. Thank God, because I don't know how I would have coped. It was pretty much the same as before only this one was multiplied by three which meant I had to work overtime. Sometimes I would go home, cook dinner for my children and bring them back to the district court with me, and they were as good as gold. I kept my children away from the licensing side of the office, and they were quite happy to have a drink of juice in the kitchen.

I was good at my job and remember the licensing manager commenting on my enthusiasm for court work. As soon as she came to visit her staff, I would offer her tea/coffee and, although she appeared to be quite hard on her staff, she seemed okay with me.

Stephen initially would be at the district court on a Tuesday and a Thursday whenever there was a Pleading Diet or trials, and one day there was an accused person in court who was hearing impaired. Since I had Stage 1 BSL, Stephen called me through to interpret which was easy enough because it was either a plea of guilty or not guilty. Thankfully, it was a not guilty plea because I would have been expected to sign the outcome had he pleaded guilty.

I remember a situation when a Justice was about to send an accused person to Barlinnie Prison. I have never seen someone look so scared in my life. His defence lawyer was trying everything to avoid his client going to prison. I was on the bench sitting next to the clerk of court (solicitor) and, as I was looking at the complaint, I noticed that the accused was under 21 years of age. I pointed this out to both the clerk of court and the justice, just prior to sentencing, and the young guy in the dock was given a fine instead of the alternative. His whole demeanour relaxed in front of me, and I remember thanking God I had spotted this major error in time.

One of my other court experiences was regarding a man charged with a breach of the peace. He pleaded not guilty and a trial date was set. The girlfriend of the accused, who was also a neighbour of mine, explained to me that her partner had not committed a breach of the peace but that she had a very jealous ex-husband who was telling a pack of lies. I just knew she was telling me the truth. Therefore, when the trial date duly came, I explained to the justice what I had been told. The fiscal and defence agent summarised the facts, but the accused had no previous convictions. The Justice was Patricia Pagan and whilst the court adjourned pending a decision, she came through to the court office and asked me to come into her office. It wasn't normal practice for me to sit through a trial because there was far too much administration work to be done in our office, but I left what I was doing and, after a discussion with the Justice and the presiding solicitor, I suggested that the accused receive an absolute discharge which meant that he kept his clean record of non-offending. This time I did go back into the court and sat on the bench when the Justice was administering her sentence. I wanted to know if she agreed with my advice and also I wanted to see the reaction of my neighbour who was sitting at the back of the court. The absolute discharge in this case was administered and, that night after work, I was handed a beautiful bouquet of flowers and some chocolates from my neighbour. She thanked me profusely, but I told her it was the ultimate decision of the Justice and in my opinion the right one.

As the months rolled on, June ended up bearing the brunt of the court workload because I was so busy with Charter Mark meetings and presentations. I was so wrapped up in work and making sure that we would win the Charter Mark award that my home and family life suffered. I would mention names of people involved and would catch my daughter saying, "I hate Malcolm M. because he's giving Mummy too much work." It wasn't a work-life balance but it was a holiday camp compared to what was to come.

My district court manager, Stephen, was a real gem of a man and, once things had settled after the transition from East Kilbride District Council to South Lanarkshire Council, Stephen would phone me on a Friday afternoon to tell me to have a nice weekend. He even sent a bouquet of flowers to the East Kilbride Office when I gave him a loan of my daughter's Communion dress for his own daughter. There was mutual respect between my boss and me, and Stephen really trusted me. There were rumblings about the merge of the district court and licensing manager with one of two people being chosen. Stephen kept me up to date at every opportunity, from letting me know what had been discussed at council meetings to the end result of who would take on the dual role. I was rooting for Stephen all the way. The man I had first resented for giving me typing tapes had now become more of a friend than a boss, and I don't think there was any doubt in my mind that the winner (for want of a better word) would be Stephen. The decision was made within a matter of weeks, and I don't think I've ever felt so gutted for anyone when in actual fact the licensing manager was now going to be the boss of both district court *and* licensing. This was a person, according to licensing employees, who hated inheriting staff, and unfortunately I was one of them.

The status quo remained for a short while until a staff member came to tell me that there would be radical changes. From here on in, I will be referring to anyone senior to myself as the hierarchy. The people know who they are and many staff members jumped ship because of the bullying that was going on. I am not including Sandra in this because, in my opinion, she was an absolute gem. However, bullying can take on many shapes and is not necessarily physical, as you well know, but mental torment is far worse, and my only regret is that I never did something about it years ago. We were controlled by emails and phone calls.

CHAPTER 79 –
RADICAL CHANGES

The radical changes did indeed take place. I lived in East Kilbride and was moved to Rutherglen – an office where the district court and licensing were separate with two people in each office. However, when I went to Rutherglen I had absolutely no clue about licensing and, to crown it all, I had been left with a massive district court backlog. It was inevitable that I would tackle what I knew, but I was acutely aware that the girl trying to manage licensing was, in my opinion, the equivalent of an administration assistant. What had been a four-manned office was now down to two people.

Despite living near the place they worked, senior court/licensing administrators found themselves in an office far from their own home town. It made no sense whatsoever to me. I remember telling June that my days in East Kilbride were numbered and, within the space of a fortnight, I ended up in Rutherglen. As well as doing two specialist jobs, I was still in charge of Charter Mark and Justices' training. At one point, a Justices' presentation was looming and one of the hierarchy sent me an email about it. I replied, and the next thing that happened was a phone call from a woman two grades higher than me telling me that she didn't like the tone of my email. At first I burst out laughing until I realised that the person concerned was deadly serious. I asked her what I had said to offend her, and she told me that I had said the word 'sure'. In the context, I meant that I was agreeable to having a pre-meeting with this woman prior to the presentation. It was decided by the licensing/district court manager that the individual I am talking about should do the presentation on her own and, according to other members of staff and Justices, the whole thing was a flop. I'm not vindictive but you know the old saying, 'what goes around comes around'.

One member of the hierarchy would come to the Rutherglen office on a regular basis, and she told me I was too nice and that I defied everything she ever thought of in a policewoman. I managed to clear up the district court backlog but, because I wasn't asking more about licensing work, and what it entailed, that was another fault.

One evening in Almada Street, Hamilton, there was an annual general meeting for the justices of the peace. Sandra was there as well as my district court/licensing manager and a few other members of staff. We were all sitting at the round table. After we had eaten from a buffet laid on by catering staff, Alan (the Justice that I had been asked to put a personal training plan together for due to him being the Lord Provost of East Kilbride) suddenly asked for silence. At this point, I had no idea what was coming next, but I can honestly say that I thought it was an announcement being made on behalf of the Justices. I couldn't believe it when he said he and his fellow Justices were there to honour a very special member of staff. The penny didn't drop for a few minutes and then I realised he was talking about me. He commended me on my Justices' training, my work ethic as a court administrator and also the fact that, no matter what, I always had a ready smile for everyone. I was then called up to the top table where a bouquet of flowers was handed to me, along with a large box of chocolates, a bottle of champagne and a beautiful gold bracelet. Jean Boyce had been instrumental in choosing these gifts, and I was completely overwhelmed. I got a massive round of applause followed by an impromptu speech. I am not shy when it comes to public speaking, but that night I had to keep my speech as short as possible because I felt like crying. I truly couldn't have expected anything like it and it is one night that I will never forget. When I returned to the table with my gifts, I felt so proud and humbled at the same time.

My Rutherglen days went from bad to worse. I was always being criticised one way or another, and I really felt I couldn't do right for doing wrong. The only way I could keep my head above water was to go into the office on a Sunday (I had the keys) and try to play catch-up. My flexi-hours accrued were far more than I could carry forward. During my working days, I was always glad when Pebbles (real name Susan) would do the court work whilst I tried to concentrate on licensing. Pebbles worked at the Hamilton office and never worked a minute over her time there but, when she was seconded to me, she would offer to stay on longer. One of the hierarchy, in a sarcastic voice said, "It must be a you thing." When Lindsay (the girl I thought was the equivalent of an admin assistant) was off on leave, my good friend Frances was sent to help me out. Frances is a very fast, efficient worker and she helped me clear up the licensing backlog. It was always in my mind that if I left the council, Frances would get my job. I was desperate to get away from licensing but just couldn't figure out what to do. I kept applying for other council jobs – even lower pay grades – but I was unsuccessful. One of my memories in the Rutherglen office was of a girl who was my assistant for the day. It was a Friday afternoon and we finished at 4.15 p.m. At approximately 4 p.m., Marion received a call from one of the hierarchy questioning her about her work and the mistakes she had made. Marion was visibly shaking, and I asked her what happened. She told me she forgot to do something and after a dressing down the caller finished the conversation by saying, "Have a nice weekend." I knew that was a deliberate tactic and Marion would have had anything *but* a nice weekend.

Our manager always attended licensing board meetings. Just before the board meeting, a pre-meeting was arranged in Almada Street just in case a member of the committee had something to raise prior to the relevant date of the meeting. Our manager was always really uptight before the meeting and visibly relaxed when the meeting was over. On that subject, it was decided that instead of Hamilton, meetings should be held in the relevant offices of South Lanarkshire because there was a district court in each area and on non-court days there was plenty of room for the councillors to look over applications and make a decision.

The first ever licensing board meeting held at Rutherglen meant that I had to put up directional signs for the councillors. I had bought dumpling and scones from the local shop for after. The first thing the manager said to me was, "Eunice, the council have been good to you. Can you not even put up signs for the licensing committee?" I pointed to the directional signs that clearly showed the way but, as far as I was concerned, that was the final straw.

At home, things were still bad with Jack. One night, Mark and Jack had a fight and the police were called. A male officer advised my son that, because he was over 16 years of age, he didn't need to be staying at home. Mark went from pillar to post after that. I felt guilty because it was a situation that could have been avoided if I hadn't been such a coward. Sometimes in life we regret our actions and, although we can't turn the clock back, we can try to improve for the future.

I don't know how I managed to fit everything in, but when the Charter Mark assessor came I had to drive him round the four offices of South Lanarkshire. Anne H. was with me and because she is so calm and collected, that seemed to rub off on me. I was glad that my anxiety levels were stable, because I had to answer a lot of questions from the assessor whilst driving. Shortly after that, we were informed that we had gained the Charter Mark award. By this point, I couldn't have cared less. You may well ask me why, but I was living to work instead of the other way round and to use a Scottish expression, I was totally scunnered.

I remember one afternoon whilst I was in the court office, Sandra came to visit. She called my name and then she said, "Is that Eunice?" I was so thin, I looked like a stick insect and Sandra had trouble recognising me. Not long after, I asked Sandra if I could take early retirement. Sandra asked if I was unhappy, but I did not have the heart to tell her how bad things had become. Sandra did allow me to retire early and she also gave me redundancy payment.

Shortly afterwards, I moved to the Hamilton office just to bide my time prior to retirement. Although Sandra had given me redundancy on top of my lump sum and pension, there was still the Rutherglen vacancy to be filled and my immediate thought was that Frances would be the best person for the job. On the day the applications had to be submitted, I phoned Frances to ask if she had applied. She told me that she didn't feel up to it. Because I now had a great deal of flexibility, I immediately drove to the Rutherglen office to help Frances with her application. The next day, I got an email from Frances telling me that she had got the job. There wasn't a more fitting candidate for that job and I was really pleased.

I could hardly wait to retire on my birthday, and I had discussed this with Pebbles. She too wanted to get out of council as fast as possible, so we came up with a secret plan to guide her along the way. She had asked me if she could trust me and I said I would not breathe a word about what we were plotting. It was the best-kept secret and everything went according to plan, because Pebbles left the council not long after me.

CHAPTER 80 –
MY 50TH BIRTHDAY PARTY

I planned a 50th birthday party for myself and hired a hall in one of the pubs in the village of East Kilbride. A catering company provided the food, and Jack took me to Lidl in Rutherglen so that I could put crisps, nuts and other small snacks on every table of the hall. En route to Rutherglen, I noticed that Jack's driving was really erratic and other drivers kept pumping their horns, but it was only when we stopped at the Lidl car park, I took one look at Jack and realised he was very drunk. I went to Lidl and bought some shopping, but there was no way I was going to allow Jack to drive back to East Kilbride. I didn't invite Jack to my party, and I know that's really sad, but I couldn't risk him showing me up. By this point, my mum now lived in East Kilbride and was the first resident in a building of cottage flats – the home I now live in. My mother loved her new home and became so friendly with one of the neighbours that she invited her to my party. Naturally, we were first to arrive at the hall and, for a brief moment, I thought no one would turn up, but there was a good turnout and the DJ did us proud.

I invited one of my Justices who served the Rutherglen court to my party. His name is Malcolm and I was on great terms with him. He had his own sandwich-making business and when I told one of my colleagues – a girl called Tracy – she said, "He truly is a Justice of the piece." I burst out laughing, but Tracy kept nonchalantly pondering over what she had just said. Anyway, at my 50th party, Malcolm asked my friend Frances out on a date and she accepted. I was pleased for her, because I thought Malcolm was a decent guy and he would look after her. At this point, he was divorced from his wife and everything was strictly above board. Sorry for the digression but, prior to applying for a job in the tax office, I asked Malcolm for a reference. He told me to write it myself and he would sign it. Not being too big-headed, I gave myself a glowing report!

CHAPTER 81 –
ONE OF THE BEST HOLDAYS EVER

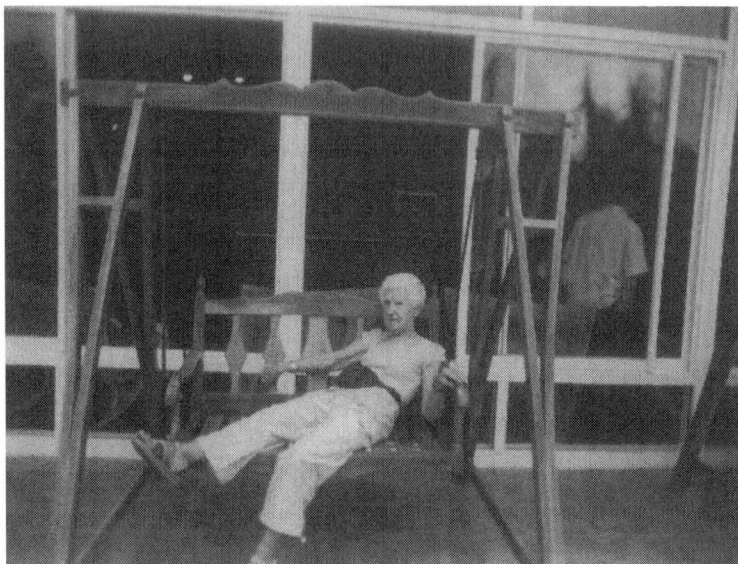

Having a swinging time in Cuba

Prior to leaving the council, I received quite a lot of gifts including a gorgeous watch, bikini and a sarong. I had booked a holiday for my mum and me to go to the Dominican Republic. However, about a month before the due date, I received a telephone call from the travel agency to say that all holidays to the Dominican Republic would be cancelled due to the worrying unrest in Haiti. I was then offered a holiday in Cuba for the same price and, at first, I thought I would prefer to go to Havana because I knew that Ernest Hemingway had lived on the outskirts there. I think I was meant to go to Cuba because, like Ernest Hemingway, I immediately fell in love with the place, and his words of "For a true writer, each book should be a new beginning" have become quite prophetic in my attempts to involve the reader of this autobiography of my life.

I informed my mum that we would be going to Cuba instead of the Dominican Republic and, for no extra cost, we could choose between a four-star hotel in Havana or an all-inclusive five-star hotel a bit further out but nearer the beach. Naturally, we chose the five-star hotel called the Barceló Solymar. I was paying for our holiday, but my mum insisted on having her own spending money so she cashed in her life insurance policy and left £2,000 in the bank to cover funeral costs. I didn't have the heart to tell her that the funeral costs would probably be more, as I wanted her to have the holiday of a lifetime.

Our holiday date arrived, and we flew with Zoom Airlines from Glasgow Airport with a stop-off in Toronto prior to boarding another plane to Cuba. Unfortunately, not long after our holiday, Zoom Airlines were in receivership but when we flew with them the service was outstanding.

On arrival at the Barceló Solymar, we were taken to our room by a bellboy and I couldn't believe how beautiful it was. The towels were on our beds in the shape of swans, the room itself was really spacious and we had our own gantry (drinks cabinet). My mum rarely expressed emotion, but her excitement was contagious. We had a look around the hotel, both inside and out, and there were several swimming pools as well as plenty of activities. I don't think I have ever enjoyed a holiday so much. We had our own beach, with an all-inclusive beach bar, and the sand was white. We met up with a younger couple who seemed happy enough to accompany us on our excursions which were really cheap. I loved snorkelling, swimming with the dolphins, horse riding, going on a jeep safari, visiting the ice caves and our trip to Havana. On the days when we weren't going on excursions, we would laze around the pool area until a staff member would call us up to dance or receive Spanish lessons.

As you will be aware, Cuba is a communist country, but we were able to attend Mass not too far from the hotel. Fidel Castro was the president at the time and, no matter what career path a person chose, they were all paid the same. In fact, the hotel staff were probably better off than doctors or dentists, because they had the perks of getting tips or little gifts. I asked a native of Cuba why you would spend time training (for example) to be a doctor when you got paid the same as a labourer, and I was informed that it was all about prestige.

We had 14 glorious days of sunshine, and all too soon the holiday was coming to an end. Naturally we took photographs, but the one that stands out for me was my mum lazing on a large swing with the biggest smile on her face that I had ever seen.

Me swimming with dolphins

CHAPTER 82 –
WORKING IN THE TAX OFFICE
CONTACT CENTRE

At the age of 50, I decided that I wasn't too old to get another job. I decided that I would work part time, and when an opportunity came up working in the contact centre of the tax office, I immediately applied. I put Anne H. down as one of my referees, and I remember her asking me if I was sure that I wanted to work in a contact centre. I don't know why, but at that point I didn't realise that it was a glorified name for a call centre. Nevertheless, I applied and received an interview date. The other thing I didn't realise was that, depending on the answers you gave to questions that you were asked, you were put on a grading scale. I later found out that I was the highest on the scale. I then received a letter telling me that I had been successful and was given a start date. I think there must have been about thirty of us starting on the same day, and I have to say, the training was second to none. It lasted about six weeks and, apart from learning, we also played lots of games and were taken out to dinner. On the day we started, we were all in a room where tea, coffee and biscuits were laid on and, since no one spoke, I decided to break the silence by asking who wanted tea/coffee. Before I knew it, we were introducing ourselves and I got particularly friendly with a woman called Mary Hilley. Mary and I were real soulmates and during our training course we became really close. The one thing that Mary said to me, and I will never forget it, was, "Eunice, I am fine whilst I am in the training room, but when we are work shadowing others, I actually hate the job that we are about to do." The thing is I felt exactly the same. The training was great but, when we were doing the real work, I was bored rigid. I then came up with the idea that if Mary and I were in the same team, it might make things more bearable. Mary had put herself down for full-time hours, and I asked her team leader – a beautiful woman called Marion Mehigan – if she would have me full time on her team and she agreed. Inwardly, I breathed a sigh of relief.

Eventually, our training finished and on Marion's team it was bearable. The main job we were doing was tax credits, but every day we would spend three hours on the dialler. This was mandatory and involved a mechanical system, dialling directors of companies that were in debt to the tax office. None of us had a clue what would come up on our computer screens because the dialler called random numbers, so we had to very quickly navigate the computer in order to know which firm we were speaking to. It might sound like quite a bit of pressure, but it was something we got used to very quickly and once our three hours' dialler time was finished, we took inbound calls instead of outbound ones. That gave us a bit of breathing space. With regard to tax credits, many people were in so much debt that a payment plan wasn't really an option, so we had an income and expenditure plan in place and if a person's outgoings were more than their income, we would go through a form with them that would last for at least half an hour. This gave us a rough idea whether or not to write off the debt or phone the defaulter at some later stage. We also did some self-assessment work and that too had an income and expenditure facility for those who were really struggling.

Marion was great with us. Even though she would record our calls, and individually take us to a private room to listen to them, her criticism was always constructive. We had an hour's team meeting on a Friday where we had general chit-chat and plenty of cakes and biscuits. We also had flexitime which was okay if you were in credit but murder if you owed time back. I never let myself get in that position because I knew I would have resented paying back the time I owed. I get bored really easily and, once I knew my job inside out, I started getting ants in my pants. By this time, we had another team leader who was lovely but she wasn't Marion, and the only things keeping me going were breaks and lunchtime with Mary. We also had days when we had time out for charities such as Red Nose Day. At one point, Mary said to me, "Eunice, I can see us getting split up because we are both good at our job and I don't think it will be too long before we are put in another team." I knew she was right because HMRC, as it is now called, had a tendency to move people into different teams, and I don't know if it was because we could get too comfy or because it was good to mix with other members of staff and team leaders. My heart sank at the thought of Mary and me getting split up. We kept each other buoyed up and would have a quick chat when we were wrapping up a call.

Mary lived in Lanark and had to be the breadwinner because her husband, who had owned his own business, had a heart attack. I met Robert once in Marks & Spencer and he mentioned trying to build up his own business again, but sadly that was just a pipe dream because, a few years later, Robert died and Mary moved to Glasgow with one of her sons. By this point, I was no longer in the contact centre, but I'll tell you more about that shortly.

I was in the contact centre for about a year and holiday time came round again. This time, my mum and I decided to go to Mexico. We went to Cancún, and I know lots of people love it and have their weddings there. Our hotel (can't remember the name) seemed particularly popular with weddings because almost every other time we went into the lift, there was a bride. I hated Mexico, and perhaps it was because we were in the middle of monsoon weather. I have never seen rain like it in my life. The roads were completely flooded and the rain came pouring down as my mum and I made our way to the nearest Catholic Church for Mass. This was a church without a roof so, naturally, we got soaked inside as well as out. I was wearing a little outfit that I had bought – a matching top and skirt – but because my skirt was slightly above my knee, just after I kneeled down beside my mum at the front of the church, a Mexican woman pointed to the rear and escorted me to the back seat. I very quickly realised that she thought that I was inappropriately dressed and, considering I was soaked to the skin, I was raging mad. I could not concentrate on the Mass because my temper was rising through the roof, and I decided that I would insist on getting a Mexican-to-English translator in order to give the woman a piece of my mind. I found a translator and I explained that I had made the effort to go to Mass despite the pouring rain. My outfit was certainly not inappropriate; I thought the woman was very ill-mannered. I said that I hoped God would forgive her, because I would find it hard, and if that's the attitude she had towards holidaymakers, it was time she had a long, hard look at herself and go to confession immediately. I don't think I have ever been so angry, and I am actually surprised that I didn't use profane language.

After my outrage, my mum and I got a taxi back to the hotel (thank God), and for the remainder of the holiday the weather was awful.

Whilst on holiday, I noticed that my mum was coughing a bit more than usual. I've said before that she was a smoker, but her cough didn't seem like the usual smoker's cough and that concerned me. I dismissed it in the hope that my mum was okay and we could enjoy what was left of the holiday. To be honest, although the hotel was really nice, it was not a patch on Cuba, and I couldn't wait to get home. The other thing that was nagging at me was going back to the contact centre, so I decided to resign.

The first person I told was Mary Hilley, and then my new team leader, a woman called Elaine, who arranged to meet me for a coffee in East Kilbride town centre. I thought it would be just a formality but, prior to meeting with Elaine, I was sent a bouquet of flowers from my team, a gift voucher and, when I finally caught up with Elaine, she informed me that my bosses did not want me to leave and I could work any hours I wanted to. I had well and truly made my mind up but felt terrible because everyone was being so nice. It was the year that the television programme, *I'm a Celebrity Get Me Out of Here* was first aired and I just kept saying inwardly, 'I'm NOT a celebrity get me out of the contact centre'. I was financially solvent because I had my occupational pension. However, I did miss my wages, but not enough to go back and do the same job

CHAPTER 83 –
MY MUM'S LUNG CANCER

I think it was October of 2005 that my mum phoned to tell me that she had had a dizzy turn at the supermarket across the road. She said a young couple had put her shopping in their car and drove her home. The supermarket is literally five minutes away, so I was concerned that my mum wasn't able to walk that distance back home. Because she was living in East Kilbride, and only five minutes away by car, I popped up to see her. She looked okay, but I asked her if she was taking care of herself and she said, "Not really." I said the usual platitudes about keeping herself healthy. After we'd had a cup of tea and I'd given her something to eat, I returned home. The cough that she had on holiday was really niggling me, so I decided to make an appointment with the doctor just to get my mum checked out. On entering the surgery, the doctor asked my mum how she was doing and she said, "Fine." I looked at the doctor and shook my head and, because of this, the doctor advised my mum that if I was worried about her, she was too and would do some blood tests. On leaving the surgery, my mum wasn't too happy because I didn't back her up, but I just felt something was completely off kilter.

Around November, Marie in Glenarm died and, naturally, my mum wanted to go to her funeral. My daughter decided to come as well, and we travelled by train and ship and stayed just outside Glenarm in Cushendall with people we regarded as relatives called Patrick and his wife Anne.

They drove us to the funeral Mass and, to my mother's embarrassment, she cried at Marie's funeral. I will never forget the look she gave me, because I don't think my mum could believe that she was in tears, and I know that's a natural thing to happen at funerals but it just seemed alien to my mum. I have to admit, I was a bit shocked, but I managed to calm her down and, afterwards, my mum got a lift to the cemetery because it was just too far for her to walk.

My daughter and I walked with the rest of the party and went back to Kathleen's house (remember Kathleen and Alec, whom I previously mentioned, and their son Michael?). Kathleen gave us some lunch and chatted for a while, but usually Kathleen would have talked for Ireland and the conversation was quite limited. Kathleen's house was very warm and, when I looked over, she and my mum had both fallen asleep. There was something about my mum that was decidedly off and, when I mentioned this to my daughter, she said it was probably because her gran was just tired. I had a really nagging doubt about my mum's health but chose to believe my daughter, because I couldn't bear the thought of it being something more sinister.

About an hour later, Patrick picked us up to take us to Larne in order to alight the boat. I had parked my car at Stranraer docking station and was not looking forward to the 84-mile drive back to East Kilbride. It was night-time and the road is bad enough in daylight, but I just had to suck it up. We were on the ship for about an hour when I got a phone call from my son Mark who by this point was living at home again. He had reacted badly to prescribed medication and was really panicking. I spoke to Jack and told him to take Mark to Hairmyres Hospital immediately, and once I got back to East Kilbride I would take over.

I think I broke the speed limit a few times on that journey to East Kilbride, because I was worried sick about my son. All three of us popped in to see Mark who was in Ward 2 by this point, and after talking to him, I told him that as soon as I had taken my daughter and my mum home, I would come back and sit with him all night if I had to. I duly did this and, after about three hours, Mark was completely zonked, so I took the opportunity to go home and get some shut-eye. I had been informed by the medical team that my son would probably get out of hospital the next day and they would phone me to collect him.

When the house phone rang, I thought it was the hospital arranging for me to collect Mark, but it was my mum and she was really panicky. She told me that she had received a letter from the hospital and had an appointment for the following week. After I picked up Mark, I phoned my local GP to find out what was wrong. When she established that I was my mum's daughter and was really concerned, she told me that she was 99% sure that the shadow showing up on my mother's lung was more than likely to be lung cancer. I thanked the doctor for being honest with me and sat down to process my thoughts. It was a Friday when I had phoned the GP and my mum and I normally went into the town centre on a Saturday. My mum repeatedly asked me what I thought was wrong with her and, although my heart was breaking inside, I managed to convince her that it was probably just routine procedure. One of the specifications for her hospital appointment was to have a full bladder in order for a scan, and other tests to be carried out. I was utterly dreading going with my mum to the hospital. Apart from giving birth to me and being in hospital when I was in the short-stay home, my mum never had any other admissions to hospital and this was something she loved to boast about. I felt that her world was about to come crashing down on her, and I truly believe that she thought she would live forever. Death was something that wasn't discussed and, at that point, I just kept hoping that her prognosis would not be too harsh.

After a long day full of tests and procedures, a lovely doctor called my mum through to her office. I managed to get in front of my mum and I asked the doctor that if the news was bad not to tell her my mum was dying. Fortunately, after looking at the test results, the doctor said she could offer my mum chemotherapy. My mum looked devastated, but I was nearly jumping up and down with excitement. At this point, I had been told that my mum would last a whole lot longer than six months and I was just delighted that I would have her in my life for quite some time.

I attended every chemotherapy session with my mum at Hairmyres and she reacted really well to it. It didn't cause her hair to fall out, but I'd been informed that when she received radiotherapy she would lose her hair and be totally fatigued. After the chemotherapy sessions had ended, I went with my mum to discuss her radiotherapy at a specialist cancer hospital in Glasgow called the Beatson. We were informed that, since the car parking situation was so bad, it would be better if a volunteer driver took my mum for her sessions and I am so glad he did. By this point, I had gradually moved some of my clothes to my mum's house in order to have a change whilst looking after her. Every week after she came home from the Beatson, my mum whined and whined. It was awful to watch and even worse to listen to and I just kept hoping and praying that the radiotherapy treatment would be over sooner rather than later. It was awful when I was washing my mum's hair to find chunks of it coming away in my hand and, in hindsight, I should have just shaved it all off because when eventually her hair came back in, one side was straight and the other side curly. My mum had been given a voucher for a wig, but she only wore it once and that was at my little cousin Adam's christening (Adam is now 17 years old).

CHAPTER 84 –
MY SEPARATION AND
SUBSEQUENT DIVORCE FROM JACK

I had been staying on and off with my mum for a few months by now and, eventually, I decided that I wasn't going back to the marital home. Jack's drinking was too much for me to deal with as well as caring for my mum, but my poor son had to put up with hell and I cannot apologise to him enough for allowing that to happen. Eventually, Mark moved into a private let to get away from Jack, and on the day I left, Moochie the cat decided to leave as well. He knew a family with a cat flap so Moochie, knowing he was on to a good thing, decided to stay with that family. Not only had the cat decided to leave Jack, I too was giving it serious consideration.

After living with my mum for months, I took everything I needed from Tarbolton and decided that I would live with my mother permanently. I then made the decision that I would divorce Jack. Jack signed the divorce papers without any problem but, oddly enough, I felt really upset about it. I knew I could not return to living with an alcoholic but decided I would keep things as amicable as possible

I don't think at any point my mum thought about my caring duties. It was just expected of me. Because I was sleeping on the settee in the living room, my mum decided I should have a fold-up bed, which we duly purchased, and I used for the duration she was with me. Because my mum was so ill, if I heard the least little noise coming from the bedroom, I would immediately jump out of my bed to find out what was going on. Inevitably, she would want a cup of tea with a cigarette to follow, but this pattern began to cause me many sleepless nights.

Eventually, I went to the doctor and he prescribed 2mg of sleeping tablets for me. It was such a low dosage that I was still able to hear my mum if she needed to go to the bathroom. Thankfully, I could sleep for a few hours. My mum was quite a private person; whether it was the great Macmillan nurses or any other organisation that could help me out, any offer of help was completely vetoed. My cousin Mary came a few times to give me a break which I felt was really decent of her. I was still friends with Susan, my colleague from the council, and she used to laugh when I would say, "Call me anything, just don't call me Eunice." It seemed as if every five minutes my mum would call me.

Every Saturday night, my third cousin Gerry (yes the one who tried to drown me way back then) phoned my mum to see how she was doing. He knew what it was like to lose his hair although his situation was due to stress. However, he was a great help in reassuring my mum that, after radiotherapy, her hair would grow back.

One Saturday night, Gerry phoned my mum and asked to speak to me. He told me that his son was getting married to a girl from the south of Ireland, and he invited my mum and me to the wedding. The soon-to-be newlyweds were building themselves a beautiful house in Sligo and were getting married in Ireland, but their main home, at that time, was in New York where they worked their socks off to achieve the house of their dreams.

My mum and I discussed the forthcoming wedding, which I think was around October/November, and we reached the conclusion that my mum at that point wasn't really fit to go. I phoned Gerry sooner rather than later, because I know how important it is when it comes to the number of guests, and I told him we wouldn't manage but to keep my mum and me updated as to how everything went. The celebrations were going to be lasting at least three days prior to the wedding and quite a crowd, including a celebrity singer Paddy Feeny, would be in attendance.

More about Gerry
A few weeks later, I got a phone call from Gerry, and the first question I asked was, "How did the wedding go?" He said it was great but that wasn't the reason he was calling. His wife normally went to bingo on a Wednesday night but had changed it to a Tuesday because her little grandchild had her second birthday that Wednesday and she wanted to be there for her.

I knew by the tone of Gerry's voice that something was wrong, and he informed me that whilst his wife was at bingo she collapsed. I think it was a brain aneurism, and she was immediately taken to the Mater Hospital where she died. Her organs were harvested for transplants but that was a real shocker. I felt sorry for Gerry, and indeed all his family, so I thought it would be nice if I invited him to Scotland in December just prior to Christmas. He accepted my invitation, and the arrangement was that I would pick him up at Glasgow Airport.

I duly arrived at the airport and I barely recognised Gerry. His wife's death had certainly taken its toll.

Gerry was only over for a few days. He brought a copy of the DVD of his son and daughter-in-law's wedding and gave it to my mum and me to give us a flavour of how the day had gone. Gerry's wife was as large as life, and it was really hard to process that someone could be so alive one minute and dead the next.

Gerry seemed to enjoy his stay in East Kilbride. There was a great toy shop in the town centre and he bought a large rocking horse for his granddaughter. The horse was called Buttercup and made all sorts of unusual noises. That night, I took Gerry to our local pub, The Bonnie Prince Charlie, because I thought he might like a pint or two. Gerry had been a bit of a drinker in his younger years and also a very heavy smoker but had given both up. Whilst Gerry and I were in the pub he said, "Do you mind if I put my arm around you?" I said it was okay but thought he must be really grieving for his wife.

The next day, I took Gerry to Glasgow Airport, and you can imagine people's faces when they saw a ruddy big great horse with a red ribbon attached to it whinnying and making all sorts of noises before checking it in through the baggage department. It was nice to see Gerry a lot happier, and I was glad because leading up to Christmas can be very difficult for those who have lost a loved one.

CHAPTER 85 –
A TRIP TO THE SKI RESORT
IN AVIEMORE

Shortly after that, my daughter came to see her gran and she wanted to know how Gerry's visit had gone. I distinctly remember telling her that everything had gone fine but hoped that Gerry would not fall in love with me. I don't know what made me say that because he was obviously still grieving.

It was the start of the weekend and, at this point, my mum was well enough to be on her own, so a promised trip to Aviemore was on the cards. I had booked a lovely hotel and, because it was the winter season, we could go skiing and sledging. It was a long drive but well worth it because the air was crisp and calm and the ski conditions were perfect. After checking into our hotel, we went to the nearest ski hire shop. My mum had given us £100 spending money which was truly appreciated. I hadn't skied since I was 16 or 17 years old and when I say I made a complete idiot of myself that is an understatement. I couldn't stand up on the skis, let alone ski down a slope. Every time I tried, I ended up falling down. My daughter was a lot better – she managed to ski so fast that she hit a shed! Thankfully, she was okay and no damage was done to the shed.

Tobogganing was much easier and we had great fun. We also went clay pigeon shooting and we both got quite high scores. We packed as much as we could into that weekend and had a couple of wee brandies after a delicious meal.

All too soon it was time to leave Aviemore but, as I have previously mentioned, although the drive is long it is so picturesque and as we sung along in the car to various CDs, the miles flew by. At one point, I put an Eva Cassidy CD on and it was the first time my daughter heard 'Fields of Gold'. I had to stop the car because we were both so emotional. For those of you who have never heard it, please listen. Eva died at a young age due to cancer and, whilst the song was playing, I knew my daughter like myself was thinking of her gran.

My mum's cancer was in remission but, in my heart and soul, I felt that it was just a stopgap and her time on earth would not be long from thereon in.

The following March I had arranged to go to a ceilidh with Bernadette, John and Elizabeth. I know that St Patrick's Day is a big thing in Ireland so, when I was speaking with Gerry, I invited him to join us. He was delighted to come and the ceilidh was a good laugh.

Gerry felt that I needed a wee holiday and spoke to Bernadette to get her opinion on the matter. Bernadette gave the go-ahead, and Gerry booked a week in the Costa del Sol. It was strictly Irish-themed and there was plenty to do both day and night.

There was a bit of an incident when we went into the outdoor swimming pool. It was in a shaded area, therefore the pool was freezing. I was swimming up and down when a panic-stricken Gerry called my name. He looked absolutely petrified and at first I thought he was joking with me, but his legs had cramped and I had to help him up the rungs of the swimming pool ladders to get him out. (God forgive me, but I thought it served him right after throwing me in the deep end of the pool in Belfast.)

While we were in Spain, my cousin Roddy and his wife June came to visit us at the hotel. At that time, Roddy and June had an apartment in Benalmádena which wasn't too far from our hotel. Gerry and June danced the night away whilst Roddy and I enjoyed the finest champagne.

It was a lovely holiday, great entertainment and weather and, when the holiday came to an end, we both went to Malaga Airport with Gerry heading to the terminal for the Belfast flight and me to Glasgow. I began to feel really unwell. I mean so unwell that I could hardly walk four steps to put some euros into the drinks machine. I was staggering about like a drunk but thought if I could get water into me I might feel a bit better. I phoned Gerry to let him know how unwell I was but, obviously, there was nothing he could do about it except try to stop me panicking about being too ill to get on the plane.

Eventually, the Glasgow flight was announced and, fortunately, I was next to a toilet. During the flight home, I was shaking like a jelly and I could only utter "water please" to the flight attendant.

When the plane landed and we were going down the mobile steps, I had to go sideways. I could hardly put one foot in front of the other and was desperate for the toilet so, whilst everyone was collecting their baggage from the carousel, I was in the toilet thinking the diarrhoea would never cease. When I finally got off the toilet, I noticed that my case was the only one on the carousel. I had no strength to get it off until, one point, I somehow mustered a little energy with all my willpower because another plane had landed and more passenger luggage was coming onto the carousel, as well as passengers eagerly waiting to claim their baggage.

CHAPTER 86 –
THE BOMBING OF
GLASGOW AIRPORT

My God-given fourth life

The next thing that happened can only be described as holy hell breaking loose. I could smell smoke and staff members were pushing us towards the exit doors. I was as weak as a kitten and just wanted to sit somewhere, but there was a real urgency to how members of staff were conducting themselves and I could see the serious looks on their faces. There were no customs checks and passengers were told to hurry as fast as they could. The date is ingrained in my memory because it was 30 June 2007 and terrorists tried to bomb Glasgow Airport. It was a Saturday and the first day of the school holidays. I just managed to get outside the terminal building when I saw a black jeep crashing into a concrete pillar. The next thing I saw was that the car was on fire but, for some reason, did not explode. Apparently, the two attackers were a Doctor Abdullah who worked at the Royal Alexandra Hospital in Paisley and an engineer by the name of Ahmed. When the jeep failed to explode, Abdullah threw petrol bombs from the passenger seat of the jeep and Ahmed completely doused himself in petrol prior to setting himself alight. As I have said, I felt really ill but all around me was utter chaos.

Glasgow had never seen the like and I saw holidaymakers running for their lives and even urinating with shock. If I had been well enough, I would have been a key witness to the attack, but I just stood against a wall until, like cattle being put into a pen, I was escorted to the Hertz Rent A Car department. Obviously, people were trying to figure out what had just happened and there was a lot of noisy conversation. By this point, I was too weak to stand and I sat on top of my suitcase. I don't know how long I was sitting, but I became aware of the silence in the room and, when I looked up, members of the public were staring at me. The next thing I was aware of was being guided by a staff member to one of the cars for rent and the man sat me down on the passenger seat. I think people must have thought I was in shock because of the incident, but I can only say that I was truly unwell. I tried to use my mobile phone but my hands and body were shaking so much that I couldn't dial a number. Naturally, because of the bombing, police cars, ambulances and the fire brigade were in full force. A police officer came to speak to me, and I asked him if he would take me to the toilet because I felt that I not only needed to vomit but knew I had diarrhoea. It was awful but thank God for that police officer, because not only did he take me to the toilet but he waited for me and escorted me back to the car. By this point I could hardly stand on my own two feet, and the police officer said he would get me an ambulance as soon as one became available. It seemed ages before the paramedics came, and I handed my phone to one of them to contact my daughter. Despite feeling so ill, I came to the conclusion that I was just about to use up my **fourth life**.

I was taken to the Southern General Hospital in Glasgow (now the Queen Elizabeth Hospital), by which point my temperature was through the roof, but my daughter managed to see me in a side room prior to my going for X-rays. I kept thinking I could hear Irish music and was seeing non-existent figures on walls. In the X-ray department, I was convinced that monsters were jumping out at me. Eventually, I was taken to a private room and a doctor explained that I had *Clostridium difficile* or C. diff as it is commonly referred to – the symptoms being persistent diarrhoea, stomach ache, loss of appetite, a high temperature and feeling sick. I was a physical wreck. As soon as my relatives heard of my plight, they came to visit me but had to wear protective clothing and masks whilst doing so.

I was put on a drip and constantly wanted to throw up. I remember seeing a creepy-crawly in my sick bowl, and I asked a nurse if I was imagining it because of the hallucinations I'd been having. I felt so relieved when she told me it was real. It was only natural that the doctors and nurses wanted to know what had happened at Glasgow Airport, but I just gave snippets here and there because it took me all my time to speak and I wanted to wallow in my own misery.

After some time, my appetite came back slowly but surely and I was moved to another ward with a single room. Gerry had sent me a bouquet of flowers and that really cheered me up. I was worried about my mum because she was only meant to be in respite for one week when I was on holiday but, because of my illness, she had to change her respite accommodation for another week.

My cousin Bernadette told me that my mum was really angry and refused to go but after Bernadette explained the situation my mum knew she had to. In fact, when I finally got out of hospital, my mum was transferred to a home in East Kilbride in order to give me some extra respite, and when I went to visit her I got the lecture of the year because I hadn't phoned her. I tried to explain how ill I was, but she didn't look convinced. Unfortunately, my mum came home with a urine infection but was quickly given antibiotics to clear it up and life as I now knew it was back to normal.

Mum's last holiday abroad

Roddy and June invited us to their apartment in Benalmádena so that my mum could get a wee holiday. Due to her lung cancer, the insurance for that holiday was astronomical. I had to hire a wheelchair for my mother and it was a ton weight. When we finally got to the apartment, I had to wheel her down a ramp – it was a terrible moment as I couldn't hold on to the wheelchair. I was shouting "Mum, mum!", but thankfully the wheelchair came to a stop between a couple of iron bars.

Benalmádena is a lovely resort but extremely hilly depending on where you are staying and we were staying in Arroyo which is notoriously hilly. The fact that Elizabeth was going to be joining us a few days later kept me going because, although my mum was as thin as a rake, pushing the wheelchair in hot weather was not the most desirable way of getting from A to B, particularly pushing uphill. Thankfully, my mum realised this and decided that rather than go out anywhere she would sunbathe on the balcony.

When Elizabeth left, Roddy and June hired an apartment upstairs from us and came to see us. It was great company for my mum, and she and Roddy would talk about the good old days in Glenarm. The holiday soon came to an end and I got the impression that my mum was glad to be back home.

CHAPTER 87 –
ELIZABETH'S 40TH BIRTHDAY
AND A TRIP TO DUBLIN

On 6 December 2007, it was Elizabeth's 40th birthday. I wanted to make it special for her so, with Gerry's help, I made a collage of photographs, invited all my relatives who know that Elizabeth is like a sister to me and we had party games, loads to eat and a very competitive game of *Family Fortunes.*

Sadly, the day before the party, my mum was taken into Hairmyres Hospital. She had been struggling with her bowels and intestines.

At one point, I called an ambulance because she seemed to be as stiff as a board and I had no idea what was wrong with her. Gerry was over from Ireland, and he thought my mum was having a stroke but she wasn't presenting with stroke symptoms. Anyway, the root cause of the problem was her intestinal/bowel problems.

I visited her in hospital the next day, and she told me how much she was looking forward to Elizabeth's party. I felt terrible having to tell her that the festivities were the previous evening and she had missed it. I can still see the disappointed look on her face and, to this day, I still feel dreadful about it. The following day my mum was discharged from hospital, but I realised that she wasn't her usual self. She was coming out with random rubbish like, "I feel sorry for you, Eunice. Mark didn't give you a roll and sausage." And then she became really quiet.

As we approached the house, my mum was showing no emotion. I put her to bed and, as it transpires, she left the hospital with a urine infection. It was cured with a dose of antibiotics, but I felt the hospital had really let her down. Thankfully, once the antibiotics kicked in she was her usual, chatty self.

As well as arranging a family gathering for Elizabeth, I booked a hotel and flight to Dublin, but I knew that the only way I could go was by getting someone to look after my mum. I phoned Bernadette and her and John came from Dumbarton to stay for the weekend with my mum. I was so grateful.

Elizabeth and I were like two excited children when we embarked on the plane. When we arrived in Dublin, I felt at home straight away. The centrally located hotel also facilitated a nightclub which could be a bit noisy, but thankfully there were earplugs in the bathroom which we definitely needed.

The hotel was gorgeous and the weather was crisp. Elizabeth loves to have a 'nana nap', but I was desperate to get out and about in the crisp, sunny weather so I had a wee wander to myself and when I got back to the hotel Elizabeth had woken up. We went shopping, had dinner and, for the first time in our lives, we tasted the famous Guinness. It was so creamy and went down a treat.

We stayed in Dublin for two nights and Gerry came to visit on the Saturday. We sneaked him into our hotel, went sightseeing, had dinner and hit the Temple Bar in Dublin which had live, traditional Irish music as well as Guinness, of course.

The next day, I headed for the nearest Catholic Church for Sunday Mass. Like everywhere, Dublin wasn't short of beggars and I normally give euros or whatever the currency dictates, but when I saw a beggar outside the church talking to someone on her state-of-the-art mobile phone I decided to keep my money. Whilst on that subject, something that still annoys me is that when I was in Dublin I bought a new handbag. That's quite unusual for me because I'm not a handbag person, but I thought I would treat myself and just leave my other handbag in the bedroom. The problem is that I not only left the handbag but left £70 inside one of the zipped pockets. Taught me a lesson – always check your bag.

Gerry went back to Belfast and Elizabeth and I flew back to Glasgow. There was a man sleeping on a bench and Elizabeth went up to him, gave him a shake and shouted, "Wakey-wakey!" The poor bleary-eyed man hadn't a clue what was happening, because he woke up to two people gutting themselves laughing. All in all, that weekend in Dublin is definitely in my top ten mini breaks. It was amazing.

When I got home, Bernadette looked really shattered. I was grateful to her and John for the break, and Bernadette had done some of my washing, but I'm sure she was really glad to go back to her own house.

CHAPTER 88 –
MY MUM'S
DETERIORATING HEALTH

By this point, my mum was a bit of a handful and needed careful supervision. I was so glad that I had arranged for her to be looked after, as truth is when you're living with someone on a daily basis you don't realise the deterioration. My mum was skeletal and her appetite appalling.

I went into the bedroom one day and mum was dancing in front of the mirror. My mum had always loved dancing, but regrettably I said, "Mum, you're acting really daft." She said, "You're right, Eunice." She immediately stopped and never danced again. I will regret my comments until the day I die and, as I type this, I feel real sadness in my heart. Words are so powerful and when you say them you cannot take them back.

Apart from the frailty and loss of appetite, I thought if I got a carer to look after my mum for a couple of nights, I could get myself a part-time job. An advert had come up for fixed-term appointment staff at HMRC, and I decided to apply. It was flexible and you could work anything up to 25 hours in the twilight shift. At the interview, I explained that I could only do ten hours a week because I was looking after my mum. The interviewer agreed with that and, the next day, I received a telephone call with a starting date of the following week.

I started working with HMRC at the beginning of December 2007. The first night, we all assembled in a large hall where the social club was and, as we were gathered into our various groups, I chatted to someone who used to work in the video shop in the village of East Kilbride. Unfortunately, it had closed down and Irene was out of a job, hence the HMRC application. There was a woman standing in the middle of the hall who told us to keep quiet because she wanted to share some information.

She seemed really formidable to me and I *nearly* said to Irene, "I really don't like the look of that woman." Thank God I didn't because, as it turned out, the woman, whose name was Christine and a higher officer, was actually Irene's sister! Later on, I got to know Christine and she was as lovely as Irene. After the prep talk, a young-looking man sat down in our group and I thought he was a latecomer. He said his name was Allan and, to my great surprise, he was our team leader. Once again, I nearly put my foot in it because I was about to say, "If you are our team leader then I'm the Queen of Sheba!" He was so young-looking that, when I realised he was actually being serious, I found it difficult to believe he would be my boss.

The training was given by a woman called Dot and she was great, but I quickly realised that figures were concerned and the work that was expected of us simply baffled me. It was an administration assistant job and you couldn't get a lower band, but I have to confess that not only was I out of my depth, but I was glad that I was only working two nights per week.

On the other hand, I quite looked forward to Tuesdays, because the social hall had a line-dancing class and where our offices were we could hear the music. I just thought to myself, I might be crap at this job but at least I can sing along to the music.

There were actually two teams in the offices we occupied. Mine was run by Allan and the other team by Bev. One night, I came into the office with a very large birthday cake. I'd been to the bakery across the road from my mum's house, and the owner told me that the person who bought it hadn't collected it so he gave it to me. It was music to my ears because handing out cake allowed for delaying tactics where the work awaiting me was concerned. All I could think was, if the work is so hard at admin assistant level, what on earth would it be like at admin officer level!

However, my two nights flew by, and I was home shortly after 10 p.m. to allow the carer to leave. Since she arrived around 6 p.m., my mum was on her own for just over an hour. She had an alert button around her neck, and I always made sure that she wore it just in case of an accident.

A key safe had also been installed outside the front door with a pass code known to my mum's carer. One night, I completely forgot to put the alert lanyard around my mum's neck and, lo and behold, that's the night the carer found my mum lying on her bedroom floor. You can imagine my anguish. I felt sick to the stomach and vowed that it would never happen again. My mum was okay when I got home. She hadn't hurt herself, but it didn't make my guilt go away. Obviously, I cooked meals and desserts that just required heating in the microwave to ensure my mum got enough nourishment.

I had only worked a few weeks in my team at work when I got moved to another one in the main part of the building. It wasn't because my work was rubbish, believe it or not, but it was due to the number of hours I worked per week.

I found my new team great, some of whom I am still friends with on Facebook. The team consisted mainly of young people and they would make you laugh at every opportunity. You never knew when an elastic band would be fired at you or someone would try to saw the leg off a chair with a ruler. It was crazy to say the least, but I was much happier. There was an older guy in our team called Robbie, and I used to give him a run home at night after our shift was finished. He was a really wacky type of person and, in work, he would randomly sing, "She was always on the wine" to the tune of 'Always on my Mind'. I have to say, he did have an amazing voice. Robbie was a pal of Tam Campbell who was similar in age to Robbie, and I ended up getting to know Tam really well because he stayed just a short distance from Robbie. I would ask Tam what it was like being an admin officer and he used to say to me, "If you think it's bad at the minute, you'll find it a hundred times worse if you're an admin officer working on P92s" (which is a form sent out to people from HMRC to get information about a specific tax year). The trouble was that many people hopped from one job to another and it could be murder trying to fill in the gaps. I didn't pay too much attention to that when he told me but, by God, further down the line, I realised exactly why it was (if you'll pardon the pun) so very taxing!

My mum had now reached the stage that she could hardly stand on her own two feet, and by this point, I was on 10mg of Zolpidem just to get some sleep. I realised my stress levels were rising.

Apart from the nights I wasn't working, I looked forward to drinking a bottle of Cava at night. I don't have an addictive personality so it never entered my head that I'd end up with an alcohol problem, and thank God I have not – but during the night it was relentless. I was either making tea or running like crazy into the bedroom when I thought my mum was getting out of bed. She liked to have her tea and a cigarette in the kitchen and that could not go unsupervised. She wasn't just unsteady on her feet, but by this point she could hardly walk. Gerry had bought me a computer chair and I would use that as a wheelchair for her, but she still insisted on sitting on her favourite stool in the kitchen which had no back support. That in itself was another problem.

My mum was strange in that she was able to convince herself that if something bad happened it didn't really, and in this situation her lung cancer was no different. She kept saying to me that she thought the hospital had made a mistake and I just went along with it to keep her happy, but her appetite and weight loss told me otherwise.

I was a Eucharistic minister and attended Our Lady of Lourdes Church in East Kilbride. This church served hospital patients in Hairmyres. I was a Eucharistic Minister for approximately seven years prior to my mum being diagnosed with lung cancer, so I was able to give her the Sacrament every week. Sometimes I took things slowly and other times I'd be rushing the prayers. I don't know why, because I had time, but I was getting a bit resentful at having to wait on my mum hand and foot.

On looking back, I truly regret that, but I think my stress levels were at breaking point. I began to wonder how many more years I would be my mum's carer. I suppose I could have got some help from Macmillan nurses, but as previously mentioned my mum just wanted me and no one else to look after her.

What really started to worry me was that my mum was falling a lot. I had already put a baby gate at the top of the stairs to prevent her tumbling down them, and I'd organised for two banisters either side of the stairs just in case she had to get outside.

My doctor kindly organised for my mum to go weekly to one of the facilities in East Kilbride where she could mix with people her own age and, at the same time, give me a break. My mum was averse to it at first but, after speaking to a staff member, she said that she would be willing to try it and, as it was coming up to Christmas, lots of arts and crafts as well as quizzes kept her attention.

Just after Christmas, I was seriously worried about how many times my mum was falling and, when I called the doctor, I asked if she could be referred to the Falls Clinic. My great doctor, Ian Chisholm, said, "Eunice, I think you really need a rest. I'm going to try and get your mum into hospital." I was so relieved the majority of the burden was about to be taken off me that I booked a bed and breakfast for Hogmanay where Gerry, my daughter and her friend and I stayed after the New Year celebrations on the River Boat at the Clydeside in Glasgow. It was a good enough celebration with plenty of dancing, but the seating arrangement was terrible and we just had to sit on the floor in our best gear drinking out of plastic cups. Gerry was certainly not impressed, but it was great to get back to our little bed and breakfast to get some shut-eye.

When I went to visit my mum on the first of January 2011, she was in a mainstream ward and looked better than I had seen her in a long time. She asked me why I hadn't been up to see her on Hogmanay, and I gently reminded her that I'd told her I had other plans. She then proceeded to tell me all about the cooked breakfast she had that morning. She seemed as bright as a button. When visiting time was over, I felt that a weight had been lifted off my shoulders.

My mum was subsequently moved to Ward 16 in Hairmyres which is one of the geriatric wards, and I went up to see her every afternoon before starting my evening shift in HMRC at 5 p.m. One of the nurses asked me how I was coping with my mum, and I truthfully replied that I really needed a break. The next day, my mum said that the staff felt she should go into a home because it wasn't fair on me and she said, "Eunice, what do you think?" She looked really frightened and I knew there and then that there was no way I could put her in a nursing home, so I replied, "Mum, I just want what you want. Does that answer your question?" The relief that washed over her was tangible.

I visited her every day and began to feel far more relaxed and rested than I had felt in a long time. She was still in a ward with other patients and, you'll know what it's like when you visit someone, it is inevitable that you get to know the other patients, particularly when they don't have a visitor. I went over to speak to the woman in the opposite bed, and she told me that my mum had fallen out of her own bed during the night. I immediately went to the nurses' station and demanded an explanation, as they had not recorded it. I was really livid and stated that if my mum fell again and there was no record of it, I would go to the ombudsman. I then said I would be up the following day to cut my mum's hair and shower her. There were no objections!

CHAPTER 89 – PREPARING FOR DEATH AND THE LOSS OF MY BEST FRIEND

It was still the month of January and my mum's appetite was terrible. She was being spoon-fed soup but couldn't keep it down. My mum liked a McDonald's, so I drove there and back to the hospital to try and tempt her with something she liked, but she could only take a small bite. She had that skeletal look about her and my two nights at work were the only things that distracted me from worrying.

The next afternoon, I was at my mum's bedside and I could see the nurse was struggling to get blood from her. The thought that went through my mind was there couldn't be that much blood left because she was skin and bone. A short while after, a female doctor asked me to accompany her to her office. As we were walking along the corridor, the doctor told me that she had found 'coffee granules' in my mum's sickness which I now know is coagulated blood in the vomit.

I was talking ten to the dozen to the doctor before we reached her office. I knew something was seriously wrong and the doctor wasn't giving me any answers except for, "Well, you know your mother has had cancer?" I felt like saying, 'Of course I know. I've been looking after her for two years.'

The doctor asked me to take a seat and told me that my mum's cancer had come back and she would not be resuscitated. I asked if the cancer was in her stomach, but I think I was too shocked to hear the answer to my question. The doctor told me she would be moving my mum to a side ward later on that evening.

I asked the doctor not to tell my mum she hadn't long to live because my mum was terrified of death. The doctor said she would have to be honest with my mother if she asked, but I told the doctor my mum wouldn't be having that conversation with her. With everything I had in me, I tried to keep it together before going back to see my mum. I was dreading her asking me why the doctor wanted to see me but, fortunately, she was sleeping. I went to the patient in the bed opposite and told her my mum was dying. I still don't know if it was the right or wrong thing to do, but I really needed to speak to someone. At the end of visiting time, I kissed my mum on her forehead and went into my car where I sobbed my heart out. I left the hospital at 4.30 p.m. but when I looked at the clock on my car it was 5.10 p.m. I was already ten minutes late for work, and to be honest, I think I was on autopilot on that drive. When I finally arrived at work, my team leader was having a night off so I spoke to a lovely person called Lynne Murie, apologised for being late and explained why. She looked up at me and told me to take my time before doing any work (a far cry from when I worked in Rutherglen). As soon as I told my team members what had happened, they got into action by getting me hot chocolate from the vending machine and offering me biscuits. Their kindness was quite overwhelming, and I had to take a few 'toilet breaks' that night in order to compose myself.

What struck me about that night was how concerned everyone was and how much they buoyed me up just to get me through the shift. I was worried about the drive home because, by this time, Robbie had left HMRC and I knew there would be nothing to distract me from what was going on in my personal life. As soon as I arrived at the house, my downstairs neighbour Betty (RIP) was standing outside and when she asked how my mum was I burst into tears. She put her arms around me and told me she understood what I was going through. I miss Betty very much because she was a great neighbour.

Once my mum had been moved into a side ward and I had notified my relatives and neighbours about her condition, she had a plethora of visitors. Whenever I went to see her, she never asked me why so many people were visiting her. I honestly believe that she thought it was a rite of passage, and I'm glad, for her sake and mine, that it didn't seem as if the penny had dropped. My son and daughter were both really supportive, and my son's 21st birthday was spent at his gran's bedside. I had bought some presents and wrapped them up for my mum to give to Mark, because she was really anxious about not getting to Debenhams in time for his birthday.

God help her, at that point she never realised how ill she really was. She didn't appear to be in any pain and seemed lucid enough except when she said, "Eunice, how did the gathering go?" I hadn't a clue what my mum was talking about, so I told her I was getting a wee bit forgetful and asked her to remind me. My mum told me it was the gathering of the Robinson clan (my mum's maiden name) and there had been a newspaper article about it because it was such a success. At that point, the only living Robinson relative was my Aunt Lena (RIP), so I knew my mum must have been thinking or dreaming about her deceased relatives, but I humoured her and said that everything had gone really well. The next thing she said really took me by surprise. "Eunice, I know the gathering went really well but I didn't want to read about it in the newspaper because I felt if I read all about it I would be dead." I was quite perturbed and I am still unclear if at that point, my mum knew she was about to join the dearly departed, so I changed the topic and told her all about my work.

On 28 January 2011, I came home from work around 10.12 p.m. and the landline number rang. The staff nurse at Hairmyres was on the phone and all she said was that my mum's breathing was laboured. At that time, my daughter was staying over and, as soon as I got off the phone, I told her we needed to get to the hospital urgently. My son Mark had his own flat just down the road from me, but I think the news of his grandmother's imminent death was too much for him. I had to give him the chance to see her but perhaps I could have handled it better.

As we were driving to the hospital, I asked my daughter to let our parish priest know what was happening. As soon as I saw my mum, I was relieved because she was still alive, but I could see how laboured her breathing was. Not long after, Father MacNamee (RIP) came into the side room. He allowed me to administer the Sacrament of the Sick and my mum was actually able to receive Holy Communion. This gave me much peace.

My daughter and I sat for a while and spoke with my mum intermittently. Although I had already bought a little white nightdress, pants and socks for my mum and contacted the graveyard to see about a lair, nothing prepares you for the death of a loved one. My cousins Mary and Bernadette arrived, accompanied by Bernadette's husband

John. We were all gathered around my mum. I asked my beautiful daughter to hold my mum's hand because I could not have faced that feeling of her life slipping away, so she willingly obliged.

Dying can have humorous moments and my mum's case was no different. She kept smoking an imaginary cigarette, and I suggested that she could hold an unlit real one instead, but she handed it back with a distasteful look and kept on smoking the imaginary one whilst using the sick bowl as an ash tray. When she was finished, she said to me, "Eunice, am I dying?" I knew that I couldn't tell my mum the truth, but I didn't want to lie to her either, so I just said, "You're not very well, Mum."

The nurse then administered morphine. My mum didn't appear to be in pain but at least she was relaxed. A few hours later, my mum was unconscious but if you have never heard a death rattle before, it's horrible. It was like my mum was drowning in her own fluids, and I ran to the nursing station and asked if she could be aspirated. At that point, she was given her second dose of morphine. My cousin Bernadette heard the nurse saying "That should do it" and wondered if perhaps my mum was being helped along the way, but I guess I will never know. We were all told to go and rest in the lounge area because my mum's heart was so strong and, by this time, we were well into the early hours of the morning. I knew I wouldn't be able to sleep, but no sooner had we settled down when the nurse came running through to tell us that my mum was about to die. As promised, my daughter held her hand whilst the rest of us prayed and, at 7.40 a.m. on 29 January 2008, I not only lost my mother but my best friend. I took strength from my faith – a strength I really needed in the knowledge that my mother was now with God.

The minute my mum died, I ran to the toilet and was violently sick. When I stopped vomiting, the cramps in my stomach were terrible and I think the shock of what had just happened gave me gastroenteritis.

Bernadette's husband John told me to go home, take a sleeping tablet and then do what was necessary to plan the funeral. I took this advice, and my daughter and I went to bed and fell asleep until 3.40 p.m. We quickly got dressed and went across the road to the supermarket. I thought it would be a good idea if I phoned one of my mum's neighbours to let her know what had happened.

To my great surprise, she became very upset with me after I told her what time my mum had died. Her exact words to me were, "I might only be a neighbour but I was also a friend of your mother." I proceeded to tell her that I hadn't even spoken to my son, but nothing would appease her.

I understood that she might be grieving so, when I finally made all the necessary arrangements for my mum's funeral, I told the neighbours that her casket would be open at the Heritage Funeral Parlour in the village of East Kilbride. When I saw the lady in question, I opened my arms as wide as I could to give her a massive hug but she refused. However, I was glad she came to the funeral parlour.

Once my relatives said their final goodbyes, the undertaker and I put the lid on my mum's coffin. Her casket would be at the altar of St Leonard's Church the following week where a short service was said to welcome her into the church. Her body remained overnight prior to the Requiem Mass and this gave me the comfort I needed knowing that Jesus himself would be watching over her.

That night we had a wake for my mum and the house was crowded. My cousins had come from England and Ireland and it was a very fitting send-off. The only time my mum had spoken about death was that when she died she wanted it to be a celebration and if I had her cremated she would come back and haunt me!

The wake night was indeed very celebratory and lots of stories were shared about my mum as well as people eating the spread that was laid on. We had a right good sing-song accompanied by the guitar. We had some great laughs that night, and I think it was some light relief preceding the Requiem Mass.

CHAPTER 90 –
MY MUM'S FUNERAL

In the morning, my cousin Roddy played the bagpipes outside the church, and I could not have been more proud of my son for turning up on time to carry his grandmother's coffin. I knew that was probably one of the biggest ordeals of his life but he did well.

Just towards the end of Mass, my daughter sang her own rendition of 'Bring Him Home' from *Les Misérables* only she substituted 'Bring her home'. I don't know how she managed to pull that one off, but she sang like an angel and the words were really fitting.

Father MacNamee accompanied us to the graveyard at Phillipshill Cemetery in East Kilbride, where I held the cord at the top of her casket. My daughter held the one at the bottom and my son and a couple of other relatives took a cord to lower my beloved mum into her final resting spot, while Father MacNamee said the relevant prayers. We all then went back to the Bruce Hotel in East Kilbride where there was plenty to eat, and I had also arranged a meal at a place called The Crooked Lum, which was conveniently attached to a Premier Inn for those wishing to stay overnight.

On another note, I think the most embarrassing moment of my life was assuming that, having had their fill of food at the Bruce Hotel, this would last until we went to The Crooked Lum for a two-course meal, but it didn't. I had to run across the road to get bread and fillers for everyone. Gerry, on the other hand, was raging because, in Ireland when anyone passes away, people come to houses armed with sandwiches and cakes. The patter was good, but I found myself clock-watching until the two-course dinner was ready. I would have to pay the bill for The Crooked Lum. Unfortunately for me and my finances, some people opted for three courses and the bill was really steep.

I will be eternally grateful that Roddy and Gerry decided they would split the bill because otherwise my credit card would have been hammered. The £2,000 my mum thought would cover her funeral was not enough – it was double that amount, and I knew it would be a while before I would be able to put up a headstone.

It was a difficult time for me and, for the first time in my life, I was plagued with sleep paralysis or demons as I like to call them. That was the worst night of my life. It was so terrifying that I thought a couple of people were sitting on my chest and I was too paralysed to move. I found that although I tried to scream, nothing was coming from my voice. It seemed to go on for hours and, although I was exhausted, there was no way I could sleep. I must have drifted for a couple of hours because around 8 a.m. Gerry and Mary awoke, and when I asked them if they had managed to sleep, they both assured me that the beds were really comfortable and that they'd had a great sleep. I never uttered a word about the 'demonic' experience I had been subjected to.

We all went over to The Crooked Lum for breakfast and soon it was time to say goodbye to everyone and thank them for attending my mum's funeral. We all went our separate ways, but I remained really bothered about not having enough money to put a headstone on my mum's grave. I decided to go into the town centre and bought a wooden cross which I had engraved. I then went to the cemetery and put it on my mother's grave to commemorate her life on this earth. I promised myself that I would have a stone erected as soon as I could afford it.

I decided I could now increase my working hours from 10 to 25 and there was no problem with that. A temporary, fixed-term appointment normally worked for six months and then was laid off for a wee while, so I knew that I wouldn't have much problem upping my hours and, besides, it kept me from thinking about my mum.

Her funeral was a true celebration of her life, and I could hardly believe the amount of thank-you cards I received from those who attended her funeral. I still have those cards because I was both honoured and touched that my relatives and friends had taken the time to share their sentiments with me.

Back at HMRC, I was friendly with a Japanese girl called OT and a Chinese girl called Jia. It never ceases to amaze me that when English is a person's second language, they seem to grasp the context. A quality I really admire.

Although my first team leader was Allan, when I was put into another team, my team leader was a girl called Sam Leslie who in fact ended up going out with and marrying a guy from my team called John Alexander. John and Sam are a lovely couple and eventually, a number of years later, John became a higher officer which is a higher promotion than being a Band O team leader. However, getting to the present, Sam went on to manage another team and I had Lynne Murie for a while, and I promised her that if I helped her when she was doing her self-appraisal, she could perhaps help me with some of the interview questions when I came back to HMRC after being laid off for a couple of months. That said, I went in early one evening, looked over Lynne's appraisal, changed a few things (not much because she was a great team leader) and then she let me have a wee look at some of the harder questions I would be asked in a few months' time when I applied to be an administrative officer.

The months flew by and, before I knew it, the time had come for my interview which I totally skated. I could answer most of the questions but the one question I knew I would be asked was the date Inland Revenue and Customs became HMRC. I am glad Lynne gave me that prompt, since I didn't really remember the exact date. A few days later, I was notified that I had been successful in my application and, if I am being truly honest, life as an administrative officer, albeit a higher grade, was easier than an admin assistant.

I loved going to work because I had an excellent team leader called Gary Whyte who would have a team meeting every night just to see how we were all getting on. Gary is an absolute gentleman and my team members were amazing. Although tax wasn't one of my best subjects, I volunteered for any admin work that needed to be done towards the end of the night and, when I hadn't a clue about tax, I always had someone on hand to help me out. On a Friday night, most of the staff went to the social club for their favourite tipple, and I remember Jia being totally shocked because I drank a pint of beer. Needless to say, I didn't have the car that night because I would never drink and drive. I remember that team with great fondness, particularly when Verda joined us. It was like manna from heaven for me because Verda was a tax wizard but needed to brush up on her English skills, so any time letters had to be written to customers, I was at Verda's side.

CHAPTER 91 –
A TRIP TO NEW YORK

By this point, Gerry and me were partners and had planned a trip to New York where his son and daughter-in-law lived. They stayed in the Queens area of New York where most of Gerry's daughter-in-law's family lived and, admittedly, although Gerry's son and daughter worked really hard, the benefits outweighed the hard graft that was required to earn some really good money.

The night before we were due to go to New York, I phoned Gerry to tell him that I had misplaced my passport. I always keep my passport in my suitcase but, for some reason, I had taken it out and I had absolutely no clue what I had done with it. I immediately went to the toilet because, believe it or not, that's where my thinking cap seems to allow me to recall where I've lost things, and after a considerable time, I suddenly remembered putting it on top of the shelf in my computer room. I have no idea why I put it there, but I phoned Gerry and told him where the passport was. Sure enough, it was beside my files and a very relieved Gerry was able to confirm that he'd found it. To be honest, I don't know who was more relieved. I used to get excited about going on holiday and a trip to New York would have been wonderful but, as far as I was concerned, it was just another holiday and I couldn't figure out my lack of excitement. I had told my team that I couldn't find my passport and they seemed more upset than me when I thought it was lost and equally jubilant when I told them I had found it. I really am an oddball at times!

The flight to New York went really smoothly and the airline staff really paid attention to detail. Gerry and I watched some Christmas films and, although it was a long flight, it was over before we knew it. After we had gone through customs, Gerry's son and daughter were waiting for us to take us to their apartment. The time difference between Glasgow and America is about seven hours, so we arrived in time for breakfast at a place just around the corner from the apartment.

We went back to the apartment afterwards and watched television for a while. It was the presidential election and Barack Obama seemed to be the clear favourite. Needless to say, he won the election but, around 9 p.m. New York time, Gerry and I were totally jet-lagged and went to sleep. A few days later it was Thanksgiving and we were all invited to celebrate at a relative's house.

That Thanksgiving is embedded in my mind because the house was packed to the gunnels and the amount of food was insane. We were served about 13 courses in total and when I say I was full up, I mean that I could not have put another thing in my mouth. Although I was made truly welcome, I excused myself a bit earlier than the rest of the crowd because I had to walk and digest the amount of food I had eaten. I had a good excuse – the dog needed a walk and I was able to keep walking until I felt better. I didn't go back to the Thanksgiving celebrations. I just wanted to spend some time on my own in the peaceful apartment.

Since Gerry and I were a couple, his son and daughter-in-law kindly allowed us to reside with them during that vacation. The only regret about New York was that Gerry and I didn't seem to get enough time on our own to take in the sightseeing. I enjoy going to restaurants and there were plenty on offer in New York. One evening, Gerry proposed to me right there and then on the famous Fifth Avenue. We went into a jewellers and I picked a white gold solitaire ring. We then went for a walk as the staff wanted to give it a clean and polish.

I remember thinking it was a rather odd request, but I assumed it was customary, so Gerry and I went to an Irish bar for a pint of Guinness and then back for the ring.

That night, we ate at the apartment but we were all tired. The next day was Black Friday and we were going to one of the outlets miles away from Queens. I fell asleep in the car for a while before we began some serious Christmas present shopping and, after many hours of seeing what was on offer, I knew there were some things I couldn't afford. Gerry came to my rescue and, on more than one occasion, had to subsidise me because at that time the dollar and the pound were equal. I bought all my Christmas presents in New York because everything was so unique and different.

We were all shattered by the time we got home so, once again, an early night was in order. At that point, I was still getting sleeping tablets from the doctor which came in handy for Gerry because he was in agony with some internal pain and needed some kind of relief.

Gerry and I announced that we were engaged and the news didn't seem to come as a surprise. However, that evening, Gerry's son told his dad that he and his wife were finding themselves in a compromising position because Gerry's daughter had been asking questions about the relationship and they found themselves covering it up. It was a very tense and awkward moment, and I offered to go for a walk whilst this discussion was taking place. Gerry and I were like soulmates and not in a proper relationship, but we both knew that marriage would be inevitable at some point. Gerry's son told me to stay where I was and then he and his wife stated it was unfair that Gerry's daughter was being kept out of the loop. It totally made sense, but the conversation seemed endless and I hate confrontation, so I don't know how Gerry must have felt, but he did agree to tell his daughter as soon as he got back home.

Eventually, our time in New York came to an end. Before we left, I cleaned up the apartment and I think I left the keys with one of the relatives.

CHAPTER 92 –
MY PART-TIME BAKERY JOB

There was a brand-new baker's shop opened just across the road from me, and the owner asked me if I would like to work for him. Most of his staff were mature. The baker's shop was always busy, never more so than when the teenagers from the local high school came in for their lunchtime deals. I was opposed to the idea at first because I felt that working 25 hours in the evening was enough, but eventually, after being persuaded to try out the job, I thoroughly enjoyed it. My hours were 9 a.m. until 1 p.m., Monday through to Wednesday, which gave me enough relaxation time before driving to HMRC. The staff were pleasant and we were never idle. At lunchtime, when the schoolkids came into the shop, the place was bedlam, but we always pre-empted the numbers and had everything ready for their £2 meal deal. On some occasions it wasn't possible for me to work a Monday because I had been over to see Gerry for the weekend, but my boss never seemed to have a problem with that because I had been told prior to commencing work that my working hours weren't a big problem. We worked the occasional Saturday, and I distinctly remember one Saturday when I was washing large trays and attending to customer needs at the same time, the owner told the other staff to "take a leaf out of my book".

That in mind, the following week my daughter was going abroad to do her Erasmus and I offered to go with her. I am so glad I did because the accommodation she had arranged prior to going had no record of it. It was boiling hot and my daughter is very fair-skinned so our first port of call was to buy sunblock. We stayed in a hotel overnight and another the following night until my daughter's lecturer could arrange alternative accommodation. I was with her Sunday, Monday and Tuesday before flying back to Glasgow.

Obviously, I had told my boss about my arrangements and it was agreed that I would work Wednesday, Thursday and Friday of that same week. What I was unprepared for was, at the end of my shift on the Wednesday, my boss's wife came up to me and said they would have to let me go. She proceeded to tell me that, since opening a second shop in Rutherglen, they could only employ full-time members of staff. My boss had been full of praise regarding my work ethic but went to the back of the shop whilst his wife was doing the hatchet job. I hung up my tabard and, as I was leaving, another member of staff said, "You are the seventh person he has done that to." I couldn't quite believe what had happened and when I told Gerry he was livid. In some ways, I was one of the lucky ones because, after a few weeks of threatening them with an employment tribunal, I managed to get my wages. I often wonder if other staff members who were let go received what they were entitled to. Somehow I doubt it. Eventually, the shop closed and the former owner was selling Christmas items from a stand in East Kilbride town centre.

CHAPTER 93 –
GOOD OLD HMRC

All in all, HMRC wasn't the worst place to work. Nobody seemed to like e-learning, but I didn't mind it too much. It made up for some of the skills I obviously lacked. In general, my work colleagues were really nice and there was always someone bringing in home baking or sweets. I was in several teams throughout my time at HMRC and we all shared so that everyone could have something nice during our break.

We could drink endless amounts of coffee from the vending machine, and we were sent on loads of courses which mainly happened during the day or earlier in the evening. This was great because not only was it time away from the computer, but it meant an early finish. I remember one night my team and the other teams were going to the meeting room, but my team leader asked if I would stay and sit beside a girl called Laura. Gary (my team leader) said to me that it would be a short meeting and because I would talk to anyone, he felt that Laura would be at ease with having some company beside her. I readily agreed, but the thing is that Laura is blind and her work was in Braille. I had no sooner powered up my computer and got my work together when I introduced myself to Laura and then put my foot in it after a remark about needing glasses. What a faux pas! I was glad Laura couldn't see the colour of my crimson face. Eventually my team came back from the meeting, I was debriefed about what was happening and felt very thankful to be back at my own desk. It reminded me of the time I worked in HMRC Contact Centre and, just as my shift was about to finish, I was next in turn to take an incoming call. I was so afraid it would be a lengthy income and expenditure call that I pretended to be an answer phone! Whilst working in Queensway House (the original tax office), I phoned a woman one night about underpaid tax and her attitude was terrible. Most people that I managed to contact were quite friendly once they had established that it was genuine and not a scam call, but that woman was something else. I sat next to my team leader Chris and, as I put the phone on silent, I told Chris that I had a right "cheeky bitch" on the phone. Well, you've probably guessed it, the silent button hadn't been pressed hard enough and the woman heard every word that I had said. When I found that out, I started to back-pedal like crazy, but how do you manage to sweeten up a 'cheeky bitch' that was frosty to start with? She said to me that she used to work in a call centre and whenever she was talking about someone she made sure the phone was on silent. I just didn't stand a chance but, believe it or not, after a lengthy conversation and a lot of divertive tactics on my part, the woman agreed to pay back her underpayment in monthly instalments.

HMRC is a very inclusive organisation and staff would dress whatever way they wanted. We had many young team leaders as well as senior officers, but I have to say that my two favourite senior officers were Nazia Hanif and Scott Durbin. The teams themselves were a healthy mix of young and mature, but the younger members beat us hands down when it came to whatever workload we had to get through. They were so computer literate, and I must have driven them mad by the amount of questions I asked. I rarely became angry but one night, after being on annual leave, I came back to a change in the phone systems. We had become more and more like a call centre and knowledge of the phone system is imperative. The night I returned after my holidays, I spent at least 30 minutes trying to use my phone. I got snippets of information about what was required, but I truly lost the plot when I shouted as loud as I could, "Would someone show me how to operate this f*****g phone!" Before I knew it, members of my own team and others were around me like bees around honey, and yes, I did eventually understand it, but I'll never forget the anxious looks on the faces of my colleagues.

My two particular friends were Tam Campbell and Nicola Morton-Smith. I would drive Tam home after work and we would be choking with laughter on the journey. I missed Tam when he was offered day shift hours, but he always told me that if a chance of a dayshift job came up he would definitely go for it. Nicola is one of the wackiest people you could ever meet. She would cycle to work but, one night at a roundabout quite near Queensway House, she was knocked over by a car. If that wasn't enough, the driver reversed over Nicola's foot in an attempt to see if she was injured. Despite that, Nicola came into work with a 'moon boot'. Nicola and I have kept in touch regularly since I left HMRC, and Tam and I just never seem to get round to meeting up for that coffee we always promise ourselves.

CHAPTER 94 –
MY UNIVERSITY DAYS

Around 2009, I requested to work 20 hours in HMRC instead of the usual 25 hours. This request was granted and I decided that I would take a Tuesday night off. By this point, we could work a 3 p.m. until 8 p.m. on a Friday instead of staying until 10 p.m. The reason I wanted less hours was to facilitate university studies. This notion of going to university came about when one day I dropped my cousin off at Sauchiehall Street in Glasgow. I think my cousin needed emergency treatment, but I can't remember. I parked my car round the corner in Hill Street, and I watched as school pupils from St Aloysius' private school came walking down the street. I remember thinking that these children would go on to university because St Aloysius' is a selective, fee-paying school and their reputation is nothing short of excellent. As I watched these young people, I suddenly thought to myself I am going to phone one of the lecturers at the University of the West of Scotland in Hamilton. I wanted to do my degree in criminal justice and, fortunately, I was put through to Geraldine O'Donnell, the course leader. I explained that I had the entrance qualifications for university and told her my work background. Geraldine was brilliant with me and she said to me, "Eunice, how would it be if you skipped first year and went straight into second year? I would be more than happy to have you." I could hardly believe it. She told me to turn up at the university when the course started in September 2009. When I came off the phone, I was delighted and couldn't wait to share my news with my family and work colleagues.

Around September 2009, HMRC took on some more fixed-term appointments. It was a mix of mature and younger people. That is when I was introduced to Nicola and a woman I will call Beebee, who made the most amazing cakes. When I told them I was only working 20 hours to facilitate university, they bought me a pencil case and pens and wished me luck. I remember thinking there was no turning back. I had boasted to too many people and I couldn't renege, but probably it was the kick up the backside that I needed. I began to look forward to the studying and going into second year, but God has a wicked sense of humour because I ended up with 'flu and couldn't start at the same time as everyone else. I had to wait until mid October 2009 and the class was well under way. I went to see Geraldine who gave me a ticking off for missing coursework, but after talking to her for a while she understood that I wasn't well. It's a wonder Geraldine never caught my bug, but eventually I felt better and attended my first lecture which was about serial killing and, in particular, Ted Bundy the infamous serial killer.

On the day I walked into the lecture hall, the first thing that struck me was that the mature students sat right at the back of the tiered seating arrangement. I think there was one seat available, but I got the impression they all knew each other from the first year and had become friends. I remember thinking that not only had I arrived later than everyone else, but cliques had been formed and I certainly wasn't part of that. I sat beside some younger people and was well equipped for taking notes. At lunchtime, the food in the canteen was amazing and none of my lectures went beyond 4 p.m. which meant I could get to work at 5 p.m.

There was a student by the name of Caroline whom I greatly admired. I found out that she had seven children and worked part time at night. Caroline is a lovely person and I really warmed to her. She was desperate to get a degree in psychology even though it meant her having to do an extra year. It was Caroline I sat next to most of the time and, when Geraldine handed out our essay marks, Caroline said to me that Geraldine had given me a really good mark. I honestly hadn't noticed what mark I was given but, when I looked at the bottom of the page, I saw that I had been given 70% which merited an A grade.

During university life in second year, there were a variety of subjects. Obviously I loved law and, as class work progressed, a presentation on 'murder' was required. Naturally, I was nervous because I didn't even know what a memory stick was, but I was determined and my sole presentation seemed to go well. My lecturer asked me if I was used to public speaking, and I admitted that it was required when I was working with the council. The feedback I got was that I had put my own twist on the presentation which apparently never really worked but, on this occasion, my lecturer told me that I had explained all aspects of the presentation with clarity and I managed to get another A mark.

Criminal justice involved every topic that I loved except politics. Every time I had a lecture on politics, I fell asleep in class. It wasn't just sleeping normally, I found myself drifting into my previous class which involved criminology. My lecturer was great and I really made a concerted effort to concentrate on what he was saying but, no matter how hard I tried, I drifted off. Because of my ignorant behaviour I made a special effort on my essay, and I was absolutely astounded to get the top mark of 80%.

Before I knew it, exams were upon us and my second-year results were two As and four B1s. I loved being at university and, despite the pressure to meet deadlines and the exams, I knew that I had made the right decision. Don't get me wrong, it wasn't a breeze, and it was a long time before I was accepted by the mature students, but I always had Caroline by my side. It saddened me that she wouldn't be going into third year with me because of her chosen career path, but we phoned each other on a regular basis.

Third year at university was great. I had an amazing lecturer called Isabella Boyce and I couldn't get enough of criminology or penology. I wasn't so keen on research, but I took a keen interest in it because I wanted good grades. At one point, we had group essay working and it was based on questions from the Woolf Report. Lord Woolf, inter alia, headed the inquiries into prison riots, in particular one of the most serious riots that occurred in Strangeways Prison in April 1990. There were 12 aspects to that report, and Isabella split us up into teams of four to investigate and report back in the form of an essay. However, our team only had three people, a girl called Corina McCann and another who shall remain nameless. By this point, I knew what was needed to get a good essay mark, but when in a team, you gave your peers a mark out of ten. I remember Isabella asking me why I had taken the four hardest categories and replied that I knew my categories would be done as efficiently as possible. The overall outcome, after submitting the essay, was Corina and I got 87% (the highest mark in the class) and the other member of our team got 82%. We gave her five out of ten when we were peer marking, not to be malicious but she simply did not pull her weight as much as Corina and me. That is one of the hardest things I've ever done but it was fair and it was just. However, the third party member went mental at me and spread the word to her friends which resulted in me getting the silent treatment in the second half of third year. Oddly enough, Corina was let off the academic hook, but I was totally ignored. I'm not going to say it didn't bother me because it did, but I just knuckled down and concentrated on submitting my six essays prior to the exam.

Geraldine called me into her office one day and informed me that I was on course for distinction. Third year was nearly over and my essay marks were four As and two B1s. All I needed to do was study for my exams and make sure I maintained the A grades, so I took a couple of weeks annual leave from HMRC, studied like crazy, sat the exam and found out that I had passed with distinction. Geraldine was raging with me for not going on to do honours, but I knew that there was a marriage taking place and I'm so competitive that my studies would have been put before Gerry. As things turned out, I really made one of the wisest decisions of my life.

CHAPTER 95 –
WEDDING BELLS AGAIN!

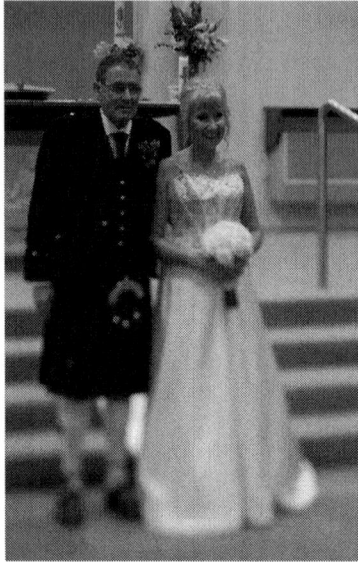

Gerry and me and Roddy the piper

In 2010, Gerry and I set a date for our wedding but, due to the fact that he was in Ireland and me in Scotland, I was the one who made all the arrangements. My wedding dress was bought in Ireland, a long, stunningly beautiful cream gown with maroon through the bodice of the dress. I had decided that I would have my hair in an up-do and I bought a tiara which wasn't too ostentatious. Every weekend off I had was spent trying to arrange everything and, to be fair to myself, Gerry was only involved in the venue which was the Alona Hotel near Strathclyde Country Park, roughly a 15-minute drive from St Leonard's Roman Catholic Church. Everything else was left to me. I would phone Gerry on a Saturday or Sunday to get his opinion on everything that a wedding entails and, it is safe to say, I was far more enthusiastic about the forthcoming nuptials than he was. Please don't get me wrong, Gerry did all the running in our relationship and the wedding date was set five years after his wife had died. The date was 1 October 2011. I chose this particular date because it is the Feast Day of St Thérèse of Lisieux. I have previously mentioned this little saint, but I firmly believe in her intercession. Sometimes, when a rose pops up in an obscure place, it's her way of telling you that your prayer has been answered. Not everyone will believe this and that's fine by me, but this little saint said that she would spend her time in Heaven doing good upon earth. She is also known as the 'Little Flower', hence the roses. In 2011, the University of the West of Scotland decided to allow students to vote for their best lecturer. I was determined that Isabella Boyce would get some form of recognition and I submitted the reasons why I thought she would be a worthy winner. When I got confirmation by email that Isabella was being considered, I immediately phoned her office. I was so excited that I could hardly contain myself.

The STARS Award day duly arrived and guests, as well as nominees, were provided with the most delicious three-course meal prior to the ceremony. Isabella didn't win the award outright, but she did get a substantial crystal paperweight which had her name engraved on it. What a great day. We had our photographs taken, and Isabella and I were so happy that we hugged each other.

Gerry was due to turn 65 years of age, and whenever I was over in Belfast, we always went to a club that he was a member of. I got to know lots of people who frequented that establishment but, if we went too early, inevitably I would end up reading whatever was available to me. To be honest, I didn't really mind. I knew Gerry loved going to the club and it seemed to me to be the best place for him to have a surprise party.

His 65th birthday was on 27 July 2011, and my first cousin Christina (one of the Bennett family) and I flew over to Belfast on the Friday night prior to the party which was the following night. I had let his son in on the secret and he told his sister. Gerry knew nothing about this but some of my other relatives had come from Scotland.

I remember as clear as day, Christina sitting in Gerry's back garden doing a French manicure on her nails whilst basking in the sun. Gerry's friend 'Paddywack' (nicknamed that because he had been a member of the IRA and kneecapped troublemakers) got all the bunting, I paid for the hire of the hall and a few other things, and Gerry's son and daughter supplied the buffet and birthday cake. I also hired a duet that I'd heard previously and they were amazing.

I'll never forget walking up the stairs to that hall. Christina was in front of me and Gerry behind. As Christina went to open the function room door, I thought Gerry was just about to have kittens. He told me to say to Christina that there was a private function going on, but I just said to Gerry to tell Christina himself. By this point, she had opened the door and when Gerry popped his head round the door he saw banners and pictures of himself all over the walls. It was just at that moment that I told Gerry that the private function was for him. I have to say that there was an amazing turnout and Gerry was completely overwhelmed.

The fifth of my nine lives

On 15 August 2011, when my son Mark was staying in the Greenhills area of East Kilbride, I drove to his flat to deliver medication. He said that I didn't look all that well and made me sit down with a cup of tea. After the tea, I stopped feeling dizzy and was quite sure I was fit to drive and get on with the rest of the day. I got into my car – a Suzuki Liana GLX which I had bought from my neighbours Bill and Hannah. The car was really sturdy but, just after I left Mark's flat, I can only remember driving to the junction and turning right into Stroud Road which could be very busy with schoolchildren. It was lunchtime and the schools were still closed for the holidays. Thankfully the children were not going back to school until 16 August.

I was truly not prepared for what was about to happen. I passed out at the wheel of the car which began to roll down the hill and wrapped itself around a lamp post at the grassy embankment. Apparently, the car turned upside down and then rolled the right way up. I was completely oblivious to it all, but when I became conscious, I discovered that the airbag in the car had inflated and there was a smell of burning. There was a very kind gentleman further up the hill and he helped me out of the car. I'm not sure if he was the one who called the police and ambulance service, but I think he must have been. When he got me out of the car, he too thought the car was about to go on fire. The smell of burning was awful. However, after about five minutes, the burning smell stopped and the man asked me if there was anything I needed from the car. I asked him to get my handbag. By this point, the police and ambulance crew were on the scene and, after a negative breath test, I was helped into the ambulance. I remember one of the paramedics saying to me, "I don't believe in anything, but if anyone has a guardian angel, you definitely have." My car was a complete write-off. When the lady said this to me, I realised that, once again, I had used up another one of my **nine lives**.

I went to the hospital to get checked out, and the doctor informed me that I had managed to escape with a cracked sternum which was as a result of the airbag in my car being ejected towards me. That did not bother me, but when he said it would be at least six months before I was able to drive again, I burst into tears. However, I knew it was for the best and I was lucky to be alive. For some reason, 15 August was ringing bells with me and then I remembered *that was the date Gerry married his first wife.*

A few weeks later, I was in my local pharmacy and one of the assistants at the counter asked me how I was doing. I told her I was fine, but I had been in an accident on Stroud Road. Before I knew it, the pharmacist came over to me and said that the man who had helped me from the car was her husband. Now, here is the incredible part of the story. The pharmacist told me that her husband had come home from his lunch and, as he was walking down Stroud Road on his way to work, something made him turn back and that's when he witnessed the entire accident. He went home after I went into the ambulance and, obviously, his wife was curious as to why her husband had arrived home instead of heading for work. He told her that he had just seen the most horrific accident and couldn't believe that I had escaped unscathed.

It was now time for me to concentrate on the forthcoming nuptials. I believe that a marriage where this is no chance of procreation can still be as happy as people who are in love and need the sexual attraction. We were just two happy people who enjoyed each other's company.

The 1 October duly arrived, and the service itself took place in St Leonard's Roman Catholic Church officiated by Father MacNamee.

It was a lovely service and I was so proud of my daughter who was my maid of honour, Elizabeth my second bridesmaid and last, but certainly not least, my son Mark who gave me away. The colours they wore all tied in with the maroon on my dress.

Roddy the piper – a man of many talents and the best big 'brother' ever.

Apart from the photographer getting lost on his way to the hotel, everything went really well. My team leader Chris had said to me, "Eunice, are you sure you want us all to come to the night-time celebrations because people *will* come to your wedding." It was a real compliment, and I reassured Chris that I could have as many night-time guests as I wanted to. I had invited most of my neighbours for the day event, amongst who were my fiscal friend John Slowey and his wife. In total there were around 70 people for the meal and perhaps 60 or 70 night-time guests.

CHAPTER 96 –
A MEDITERRANEAN
HONEYMOON CRUISE

My team and other members of HMRC were brilliant and the money collected, as well as money gifts from relatives, covered the cost of the Mediterranean cruise we were about to embark on. I think, at this juncture, it is important to mention that we had been on a cruise before with Bernadette and John, whereby we met Gerry in Belfast prior to flying to our cruise ship destination. I clearly remember thinking that John's driving was somewhat erratic and his responses were slow, particularly when it came to traffic lights. I have never been a nervous passenger, but I honestly thought we were all about to meet our Maker. We boarded the ferry from Stranraer to Belfast and, as soon as we got off the ship, I ran to Gerry's car. I explained that something wasn't quite right with John. John did not touch a drop of alcohol so there had to be some explanation. As it turned out, John had been suffering a series of mini strokes (which he tried to keep private) after which, a major stroke rendered him almost speechless until the day he died. Perhaps, if the signs of his stroke had been identified sooner it would have made a difference to his quality of life. There again, perhaps not.

Getting back to the honeymoon, Gerry didn't seem his usual self. I know that he was a bit mad at me for making him wear a kilt and, in hindsight, I shouldn't have insisted on it, but I had covered all the other wedding arrangements and I thought having a groom with a kilt would be no problem. Gerry seemed content to spend a lot of time in his cabin until I managed to coax him to enjoy the sun. Even to this day, I am unsure as to why Gerry, who was always a barrel of laughs, didn't seem the least bit excited about our honeymoon. However, after a few days, Gerry was back to his usual self and we had a great vacation.

It was agreed that Gerry would stay in Ireland to work off his notice with his employer and I would remain in Scotland during the interim period. There was never any question that I would move to Belfast. I am far too proud of my Scottish heritage and Gerry knew that, so he agreed to come and live with me in East Kilbride.

CHAPTER 97 –
MY GRADUATION

A very proud graduation moment with a degree in criminal justice (distinction)

The next exciting thing on my horizon was my graduation due to take place in early November. Gerry, my daughter and my cousin Mary all attended the ceremony. I remember queuing outside Hamilton Town Hall and it seemed to me as if there were at least one hundred students waiting to graduate in their respective degrees. As we were waiting outside, there was a man selling *The Herald* newspaper and our names were listed there. We picked up our gowns and were allowed to wear them but not the scapular that went over our heads. We carried this in our arms until our degree was conferred upon us and we were handed our diplomas. I was the only person in the field of criminal justice to be graduating with distinction in my third year, and it was a really proud moment because I was put to the front of the row and the remainder of my peers followed. I just hoped to God that when I stepped onto that stage I wouldn't slip, but Isabella and Pete my lecturers were there to cheer me on, as well as the family members I brought with me. Afterwards, I had my photograph taken and it was worth the long waiting period. Just as our little group were about to go and get some food and drink, I met Isabella and Pete who had apparently been looking for me in the dining hall. I am so glad that I didn't miss seeing them and, after exchanging some banter, I went to get some food and drink which was simply delicious. Family photographs were taken and, because I had hired my gown for 24 hours, each of my family members took it in turn to put on my gown.

I had booked a restaurant called Cooks that wasn't far from where I lived and I had invited most of my friends and neighbours for a meal which Gerry and I were paying for. We all had a great time, and I look back at 2011 with memories that were not only fond but filled me with confidence in my achievement. Everyone enjoyed their dinner and some of us went to a nightclub across the street from where I live for a karaoke session. I was absolutely buzzing and belted out as many songs as I could. But like everything, good things come to an end and the following day it was time for me to return my gown.

CHAPTER 98 –
DREAM THEMES

I was still working with HMRC and Gerry was working in Bedford House in Belfast. It was agreed that Gerry would come over to Scotland in March 2012 and then we could begin our married life together. It was purely platonic, but Gerry and I rubbed along nicely. It was a real gift.

Just after my mum died, I kept dreaming she was alive again and I had to explain to her that I had buried her and no one ever gets two funerals in their lives. Boy was I wrong! I kept hoping that when I fell asleep that particular dream would not rear its ugly head because I found that when I woke up I was lost and confused, but it got more and more vivid.

When Gerry came over to Scotland, I booked a mystery coach tour for both of us and, just a few days prior to going on holiday, I was told the destination, which was Southport. There were a mix of middle-aged and elderly people on the coach, and we were bound for the Britannia Hotel in Southport. The first mishap occurred when the driver got lost.

Me being my usual, shy self, went to the front of the coach and used the driver's equipment to contact the hotel for directions. This occurred only after the driver had driven around the block at least three times. Anyway, I introduced myself to everyone on the coach prior to getting directions and kept the passengers informed as to what was happening until we safely reached our destination. By this point, every passenger knew who I was. Everything after that went smoothly. We checked into the hotel, had our dinner and after an evening's entertainment we retired for the night. I vaguely remember getting up to go to the toilet and knocking on a door but thought I must have been dreaming. The next morning, I told Gerry that the soles of my feet were sore and, with a bemused look, he asked me if I had remembered going outside in the middle of the night. I truly hadn't a clue what he was on about but, apparently, I had got up to go to the toilet and when Gerry realised I was gone from the room for quite some time, he went to reception and asked them to look at the security cameras that covered outside the hotel. On closer inspection, Gerry saw me wandering around aimlessly with my hands across my chest and nothing on my feet. The ground was covered in gravel (hence the sore feet) and I was escorted back to bed.

The next day, I overheard people talking about some demented woman knocking on doors shouting, "Jenny or Gerry can you let me in please!" The residents ignored the knocking, but the upshot was that they had come on a coach trip with a demented passenger. As far as I was concerned, I felt I had to put the record straight.

Later that evening, the entertainment was karaoke but, before I began singing, I announced to all and sundry that the 'demented' passenger knocking on doors was me and that I had been wandering outside half-naked but hardly remembered a thing about it. The coach party were laughing like crazy, and I assured them I didn't have dementia. That night, I didn't have to pay for a single drink. The other passengers told me that I'd given them the best laugh in years.

Whilst talking about having a laugh, Gerry would regale me with stories about whenever he was out at lunchtime. On one such occasion, he went to the cafeteria part in Marks & Spencer, Belfast. As he added tomato sauce to his bacon roll, he opened it in such a way that it splattered onto the ceiling just before it landed. Not only had it landed on a customer but the poor man was completely bald. He kept wiping his head to find out if there was blood on it whilst his wife kept staring up at the ceiling in case there was another downpour of ketchup. Gerry made good his escape as quickly as possible! He could hardly make sense of his phone call to me for laughing.

CHAPTER 99 –
MY SPOOKY VISITOR

One time, Gerry and I were staying in a bed and breakfast in the north of England because we were visiting relatives. The landlady checked us in and showed us to our room. We were going to meet with my cousins the next day. What I am about to tell you is totally unrealistic, but it still feels very real to me. Not long after we had booked in, Gerry said that he couldn't pinpoint it but something in that room was making him feel uneasy. I dismissed it and went to bed early, because we were due to rise early the next day. As soon as I woke up I said to Gerry, "Do you think that should be allowed?" At this point, I'm sure Gerry thought I had lost my marbles but he humoured me by saying, "What should be allowed, Eunice?" I proceeded to tell him that during the night the bedroom door was unlocked and a man holding a tray with water in it came over to me and told me to have a drink. Gerry said that he didn't like the feeling in that room but drew the line at people opening doors in the middle of the night and then walking through the same door to exit. I chalked it up to my imagination, but I still sit on the fence on deciding whether or not it was true. It was unbelievably realistic and do you know what? When we went for breakfast the next morning, the man I saw come into my room during the night was the landlady's husband!

After having a lovely family meal with my cousin Margaret, her husband George and family, we left England and went back to Scotland. Gerry went to Ireland the next day and, naturally, we communicated by telephone every day until it was time for him to take up residency with me in East Kilbride. Gerry worked his notice, and during the month of March he formally handed it in. He then flew over to Scotland where I met him at Glasgow Airport. He didn't have a lot of stuff with him which makes me reflect on how much stuff any of us really need in life. Gerry was able to put things in his side of the wardrobe and drawers and the remainder went into the shed.

Gerry loved going to our local pub, The Bonnie Prince Charlie, after he picked me up from work. He would drop me off, I would get the pints in and he would park the car and walk over. This arrangement was a long-lasting one but wasn't doing my waistline any good, and I was feeling fat as a pig in a relatively short period. The other thing that Gerry loved was the karaoke sessions on a Friday and Saturday night. All of this was fine by me, but my brain was craving something other than going to the pub. University had set me up for that, and I realised that my happiness lay in challenges and furthering my education.

We had a nice circle of friends in the pub and a couple who frequented it were Beth and Kenny. I felt at home in their company and one night, when Kenny went outside for a cigarette, Beth asked me to go with her to the toilet. She then pulled a bit of cardboard from underneath her sleeve and it said on it, "Will you marry me?" I don't know who was crying with happiness the most, but it was to be kept a secret for a short while and I was glad that I had the privilege to be one of the first to know.

Naomi, a friend of Beth and Kenny's, asked me to join them when picking out a venue. We were going to do everything in our power to make this happen, and we paid the deposit for the wedding in a beautiful hotel called The Torrance. We had done this whilst the wedding planner was showing everyone what was on offer. Needless to say, Beth and Kenny were delighted and Gerry and I were a big part of their wedding day. This is something I will touch on later in the book.

More cruises

Gerry and I went on quite a few cruises. Sometimes we would go on our own and sometimes with friends and family. There was a friend of Gerry's called Cyril who suffered from depression but decided the cruise might do him good. Cyril is Irish and had spent a lot of time with Gerry when he lived in Wolverhampton, but he hardly said a word that whole cruise and I thought his depression was more serious than I first thought.

The Caribbean cruises were great fun, and one of the times when my first cousin Christina came we had a ball. Another cruise involved

Gerry having shingles and me with a very large bump on my head after slipping in the shower. The ship docked in France and the captain ordered that we get medical treatment. If you can picture a couple of people in a foreign country sitting side by side in wheelchairs, you are spot on, because that's exactly what happened to Gerry and me. Honestly, you just could not make it up! As well as cruising, Gerry would go to Benidorm with a few people who frequented The Bonnie Prince Charlie. The duration was always only for one week and the first time Gerry went, he told me that he would have been happier if I had been at his side but, for some reason, I thought it would be a nice change for Gerry to go on holiday with friends.

Gerry's health began to deteriorate. He always said to me, "Your health is your wealth" and he was spot on. When I was 59 years of age, he organised a party for me in The Bonnie Prince Charlie. I think Beth did most of the arrangements but it was so unexpected, I can only say that I was completely blown away. It was an amazing night and one that I will treasure until I die.

CHAPTER 100 –
HOSPITAL APPOINTMENTS

This topic is somewhat disgusting, but I had a prolapsed womb which had festered and was really sore. Because Gerry wasn't his usual self, I prompted him to go to the doctor where he was subsequently referred to Hairmyres Hospital for tests. A letter popped through my letter box and it was for Gerry. He told me that he had an 'irregularity of the gullet'. I had never heard this terminology and, of course, I had to find out via Google what was wrong. I almost collapsed when every link I clicked on was screaming cancer of the oesophagus. Once again, I found myself in a position whether or not to tell him before he went for his follow-up hospital appointment. I knew Gerry was feeling really unwell when he didn't want to go to the pub on a Friday or Saturday night. This was approximately a fortnight later after I had been on Google. Gerry's exact words to me were, "Once you get that prolapsed fixed and I get my polyp seen to, we'll be swinging." At that point, I burst into tears and was inconsolable. Gerry hadn't a clue why I was sobbing, so I had to let him see what I had been reading. My daughter was in Russia at the time and Gerry asked her to put my mind at rest. She said it could be any number of things and not to worry until Gerry's next hospital appointment. I visibly cheered up and so did Gerry.

As things happened, Gerry kept his appointment with the hospital. After the examination of his gullet, Gerry asked the nurse if I should go ahead and get my prolapse repaired or a hysterectomy. All along I wanted a hysterectomy, because I had already been the subject of two botched repair jobs. However, the nurse said to Gerry that it would be unwise for me to get my operation due to the recovery period. When he heard that, he asked the nurse if he had cancer and she told him she was 99% sure. In some ways, I was glad that I had prepared Gerry for what was in front of him, but there will always be that part of me that is sorry for giving him the shock of his life.

It was almost as if Gerry had given up the ghost. I went to see him every day in hospital, and I have my daughter to thank for that admission because, originally, Gerry was going to be treated as an outpatient. It was my daughter's persistence that swayed the medical staff to admit Gerry to a ward where mainly amputees were inpatients.

As well as going to see Gerry every day, I also phoned him on his mobile, but on one occasion I dropped the phone when I heard that our beloved Canon MacNamee had died with his breviary in his hand just before the morning 10 a.m. Mass at St Leonards RC Church. Facebook was buzzing with the news and, believe me, he was known up and down the various countries. My son and I viewed his body and, after a three-hour wait, we managed to get to the funeral Mass. The church was absolutely mobbed. It was a fitting tribute to such a wonderful priest.

A few weeks earlier, Canon Mac said to me that he had spoken with the headmaster of St Leonard's Primary School and told Des that he felt God was calling him. No one could have predicted that a few short weeks later Canon Mac would be dead.

The next time I visited Gerry, I explained why I had dropped my mobile and, even whilst doing so, I couldn't quite believe that I was imparting such terrible news. I got to know the patients in the ward and we all had a good banter. Because he had cancer of the oesophagus, Gerry couldn't swallow anything but liquids. It was decided by the medical staff that Gerry needed to be hooked up to a feeding tube which involved priming it prior to insertion. It was a very tricky procedure because, if the tube went into his lungs instead of his stomach, death would be the likely result.

I think Gerry was in hospital for about five weeks, during which time I was getting all sorts of threatening letters from HMRC due to my absence. Thank God for Marion Forbes, because she approached a higher officer who insisted that my team leader should not send me any more generic letters and common sense had to prevail. I knew that wild horses wouldn't bring me back to work until Gerry was more stabilised and the higher officers in HMRC accepted that. Unfortunately, I had a young and very inexperienced team leader who took a black-and-white approach when it came to sensitive situations. Eventually that team leader went back to being an administration assistant.

Naturally, the oncology team at Hairmyres had regular meetings about Gerry's cancer, at which point I found out that his condition had metastasised causing secondary tumours to spread. Gerry had been a very heavy smoker when younger and previously had chest surgery. His condition was so bad that I was informed that if the staff performed surgery, he would most certainly die. His body was riddled with cancer, and I was informed that palliation was the only alternative. At one point he was considered for chemotherapy, but even that was put on the back burner.

I remember one day sitting in the car park and phoning Gerry's daughter. I got the impression that Gerry was hiding things from her. I had to impart the news that Gerry's cancer had spread. It was one of the worst conversations of my life, because she thought her dad would be treated and everything would be as semi-normal as it could be.

CHAPTER 101 –
WHAT HAPPENED AFTER
DISCHARGE FROM HOSPITAL

Eventually, Gerry was discharged from hospital but he had the feeding tube with him, and I had to prime it and pray every time it would fill his stomach rather than his lungs. Gerry seemed a bit brighter within himself and he asked me if I would buy his granddaughter a trampoline and take him over to Belfast.

We set out, trampoline in the boot of the car, loads of oral morphine in various containers and energy drinks, but the thing that bothered me most was that the brakes in the car didn't feel right. My cousin Roddy and Gerry took the car for a spin round the block and told me there was nothing wrong with the brakes. This of course eased my mind, and we duly set off to Troon in Ayrshire to catch the ferry to Belfast. Of course, with me, nothing ever goes smoothly and there were road works and diversions everywhere. I had never sailed from Troon to Belfast, but it was easier to get to than going by Stranraer to Larne. At this point, I really began to panic just in case we missed the ferry, but eventually a Good Samaritan came to my aid and I think we got on that ship by the skin of our teeth.

We had an unremarkable journey, and I had plenty of build-up liquids for Gerry as well as coffee by the gallon full. We eventually docked, were allowed entry into our cars and, with Gerry navigating, we arrived at Gerry's daughter's house. She showed us to our room which was up in the attic but had a bathroom just down the stairs. Her house is beautiful and she made me feel most welcome. Whenever Gerry was in pain, he would point to his mouth for me to inject morphine into it. The trampoline was a huge success and we all took a turn on it (except Gerry, of course).

Gerry's son lives with his wife and family in the south of Ireland near Sligo, but a new, wee baby had joined their family and Gerry

357

was desperate to see his little granddaughter, who was the spitting image of her older brother. The next day we decided to set off. I could see Gerry deteriorating rapidly, and I did whatever I could to make him comfortable, but the thought of driving almost 250 miles to the south of Ireland filled me with dread. I was convinced that the brakes on the car needed brake pads but, since both Gerry and Roddy assured me I had nothing to worry about, I carried on regardless. I packed everything into the car and we set off. It was the month of July and the hottest one on record, so it wasn't the most comfortable drive I have ever made.

Eventually, a couple of hours later, we arrived at Gerry's son and daughter-in-law's house and the whole family were out on the driveway to meet us. I knew that Gerry looked awful, but I didn't realise I looked just as bad. My weight had completely plummeted, and I was constantly living on my nerves. When Gerry's son and daughter-in-law saw us both, they remarked on how tired we looked. After the usual greetings, we were taken upstairs. The bed was American in size with a very high up mattress. Fortunately, I could lift Gerry onto the bed but nearly needed a stepladder for myself!

The next day, I played with the children (apart from a wee cuddle from the baby), but whenever Gerry's son raised his voice (which didn't seem too loud to me), Gerry would give his son trouble. Gerry was obviously in a lot of pain and the oral morphine was getting tanked whenever he pointed to his mouth, but everything just seemed to annoy him and that certainly was not the Gerry that I knew.

A few days later, we set off on our journey back to Belfast but, approximately 45 minutes into the journey, I must have run over broken glass or something because one of the tyres was cut to shreds. The weather was so hot it was excruciating. All windows were down in the car, but the flat tyre put the tin lid on it. I don't have a clue how to change a tyre, so I found myself in the middle of the road waving down lorries. Eventually, a man parked just in front of us and, after explaining the circumstances, he said he would change the tyre. He informed me that he and his wife had only stopped by chance on that road because the shop that they were going to, just around the corner, was closed for lunch. I honestly could have kissed the driver of that car, but instead I gave him loads of packets of wipes for him and his wife to freshen up.

On the road again, with a 50 mph speed limit due to the spare wheel being used, Gerry asked me if we could stop for a coffee. I duly pulled into a restaurant and ordered a couple of coffees but, when I looked into the zipped bag containing build-up drinks and morphine, they had spilled and all I could do was wash the bag out. Gerry fell asleep whilst drinking his coffee and I immediately made a plea bargain with God that he would let Gerry sleep the remainder of the journey without needing morphine.

When we arrived at his daughter's house, a mechanic across the road said that he would have the puncture repaired, but he also said that we were very lucky to have got home alive because the brake pads were completely worn out.

It was around 12/13 July when Marie took us to see a Bell Doc. Please bear in mind that we were in the Shankill Road area which is predominately Protestant and where Catholics are still not welcomed. In Ireland, they offer a Bell Doc service if someone cannot get a GP appointment. At this point I was going crazy, because Gerry was in real pain and needed morphine. It was a buzzer system and when the man at the other end of the intercom asked me why I didn't use the Bell Doc in Mayfair (where Gerry's daughter lived), I remember shouting that I was from Scotland and I needed a bloody doctor right away. I think the urgency in my voice was enough, because we were seen within minutes and a doctor gave me a prescription to last Gerry until we got back to Scotland.

CHAPTER 102 –
BACK TO BONNIE SCOTLAND
AND BEYOND

On the ferry back, Gerry wanted coffee but wouldn't drink it. Instead, he kept standing up to go to the vehicle car parking area, and if I said it once, I said it at least half a dozen times that it was not permissible to make our way to the car prior to docking.

We eventually alighted at Troon, and I was praying away the minutes to get home. Although there were no build-up drinks left, Gerry still had morphine from the Bell Doc. At this point, apart from getting Gerry into bed and in the most comfortable position, I really wasn't sure what to do next. I had a chat with my daughter, and she said it might be worth giving the nutritionist a call. I duly did so, but the dietician told me she was going to phone a doctor just to check up on Gerry. I could not have been more grateful. The upshot was that a locum came out to check Gerry over and give him more pain relief. As soon as we got Gerry back into bed, out of earshot, I asked the doctor how long Gerry had left. I needed to know the answer because I wasn't sure when his family should come over to Scotland. The doctor responded, "Double chest infection? He'll be dead within a week." Almost as though he was trying to convince himself, he reiterated that remark. I thanked him for his honesty but hadn't a clue what to do next. However, the matter was taken out of my hands when the Marie Curie nurses were allocated a time slot. I was so glad I had someone in my corner.

The first Marie Curie nurse was a woman called Mary who was a relative of Archbishop Leo Cushley. I asked her honest opinion about bringing Gerry's family over and she told me that, in her notes, Gerry had only days to live and those days would quickly become hours. She advised me that it would be better to call the family sooner rather than later, because she had witnessed instances when relatives never got the chance to say goodbye to their loved ones and, inevitably, the wife got the brunt of it.

The next morning, I phoned Gerry's daughter and asked her to make arrangements for her and her brother to come over. Cyril (the man who had been on a cruise with us) came over just prior to Gerry's 67th birthday on 27 July 2012. He slept on my settee whilst awaiting the arrival of a mutual friend called Brendan. At this point due to Gerry's impending death, I was panicking like crazy inside, but my demeanour gave nothing away. The deacon from St Bride's Church, East Kilbride stayed in the bedroom with me until I had read out a birthday card I had picked for Gerry. I also put a crucifix and a Miraculous Medal around Gerry's neck. I can only thank God that I kept composure throughout. Cyril was awaiting a phone call from Brendan but had buried his cell phone so far inside his bag he couldn't take the call. Brendan also knew my house number, and the one thing I said to Cyril was to please answer the house phone when it rang. Cyril didn't take any notice, by which point I was so angry that I was shouting and bawling at Cyril, telling him he had only one thing to do and he couldn't even do that!

CHAPTER 103 –
GERRY'S FAMILY

Before I knew it, Gerry's daughter, son and his wife arrived and immediately went to see their dad. If he was sleeping, I was at peace. From the minute he awoke until the drugs kicked in, Gerry was in mortal agony, and I am only sorry I never alerted his daughter, son and daughter-in-law sooner to this so that he could get some pain-free rest.

My house was nothing short of a circus, with people coming and going, but I was really grateful for my neighbours Hannah and Bill Dykes, because they travelled almost the whole distance of East Kilbride to get morphine and there was only one chemist that would supply it. Some of Gerry's friends came to see him on his birthday, but he felt so ill they had to leave.

I think Gerry's son brought his wife for some moral support, safe in the knowledge that their children would be cared for by his mother-in-law. Gerry's daughter did not bring her husband because he was looking after their little girl.

My home became more like a circus every day, and I hardly had any time on my own with Gerry. Precious time that I realised later I had been robbed of in those last moments. However, I will never forget Gerry's words to me on his birthday when he said to me, "I wish I could hate you but I can't, and I also know that you're probably feeling the same way but you can't do that either." I knew he meant that it would have been easier if we weren't soulmates. Those few short words took everything out of Gerry. By this point, I was like a nodding donkey. The only thing I could say was that I would take Gerry back through to the bedroom. Once I had managed to make him comfortable, he said, "I love you, Eunice. I wish you were coming with me and I am really scared."

The Marie Curie nurses were nothing short of amazing and, as a result, I donate to them on a monthly basis. I cannot describe how I was feeling. I think numbness had taken over and all I can say is that if someone close to you is dying hold their hand, speak when you can and try not to keep your emotions under wraps. I'm not saying wailing and gnashing of teeth, but I think you get the picture.

In hindsight, I can hardly believe that my house turned into a conveyor belt overnight when there are plenty of Premier Inns close by. That would have been the most sensible and practical thing to do. Maybe in all trials in life, we need to feel close, we need to feel there are others in our family, friends who understand the pain and want to be together. At that level, my crowded house made sense.

Gerry did not speak at all on Sunday 28 July 2013. He was getting weaker and weaker and more support nurses were coming into the house. They decided that instead of being on a morphine driver, it should be switched to a heroin driver, and the only word I could hear from Gerry's mouth was "STOP!". He must have been in mortal agony. God knows how many visitors were in my house, but after a short spell in the kitchen, I heard a nurse call out, "Eunice!" I knew that was it and, within a few minutes in the afternoon of 29 July 2013, I once again lost my best friend.

CHAPTER 104 –
FUNERAL ARRANGEMENTS
AND REQUIEM MASS

Gerry's daughter had pre-booked a holiday to Portugal, and prior to leaving she asked me to put Mass cards in Gerry's coffin. I willingly complied with this request. Gerry's son had previously remarked that he was glad I was the one dealing with cancer because his own mother could not have coped. Anyway, I told Gerry's daughter to go on her holiday with her husband and child, and I would speak to the Heritage Funeral Parlour to try and keep Gerry's coffin open until she got home.

The due date for her flight home was within a week and as well as all the Requiem Mass arrangements, the Heritage Funeral Parlour carried out my wishes to leave the coffin open, but this is where things get a bit mixed up. Yes, Gerry's daughter was due to arrive home timeously and yes, Gerry's son and I thought that she would come to the funeral parlour, but by this point Gerry's mouth was turning blue and one of the Heritage staff said that they couldn't keep the coffin open any longer. Gerry's son and I put the lid on the coffin just exactly the same as I had done for my mum.

I wanted the Requiem Mass to be a celebration of Gerry's life. Canon Mac was dead, so I had no idea who would officiate. Just a few days prior to the funeral, I was told that the deacon from St Bride's would not be officiating as St Leonard's now had a resident priest called Father Tata. I think he was from Cambodia.

When we were in the church, Bernadette sat behind me and told me not to cry. The strange thing with me is that a Requiem Mass for a complete stranger really makes me cry, but I seem to remain peaceful when it is a relative. I believe God gives you the strength in that moment when you truly need it.

Gerry was cremated in South Lanarkshire Crematorium and, rather than flowers, I asked for a donation to be made to the Marie

Curie organisation. At that time and perhaps it has changed now, the Marie Curie organisation depended solely on public funding. I can't remember how much money was raised, but it was a few hundred pounds. I was glad to do this for them.

It seemed only fitting that the function room of The Bonnie Prince Charlie would do the catering. In a very short time, Gerry had become really popular because he was always up for a laugh. There was a good turnout at The Bonnie Prince Charlie (perhaps the thought of a free drink was an incentive) and after the reception, we all went our different ways. We knew that Gerry was free from all his suffering and it gave us some peace in our hearts.

The second requiem Mass and fulfilment of a prophetic dream

Exactly one month later – August 2013 – there was a funeral Mass for Gerry in the church where he had married his first wife. I could hardly believe that having had that recurring dream about my mum, now having a **second funeral** was exactly what I was about to go through with Gerry.

When Gerry's family had attended his funeral in Scotland, I made sure that everyone got their place. I wasn't in the least bit bothered about myself, but I knew that I would have done Gerry proud by making sure his family were included. In fact, one of my neighbours said to me that she thought the priest would have referred to me a bit more often than he did. I told her it was a celebration of Gerry's life and not about me.

Whilst in Ireland, Roddy's wife June and I stayed with her daughter-in-law's aunt and we had the place to ourselves. I was dreading the second funeral, but I knew it was something I had to attend.

I thought that I should be in the front bench but Gerry's daughter told me that, unlike Scotland, I could sit anywhere. His daughter-in-law however, told me just to sit at the front and June, who is a non-Catholic, said she would sit behind me knowing that I would keep her right whenever we had to stand up or sit down.

The chapel was packed and it was agreed, prior to the service, that Gerry's granddaughter and June would do a reading. The priest duly said the Mass. Gerry's son and daughter had taken some of Gerry's ashes but had put them in a much sturdier container, and those ashes remained on the altar throughout the Mass. At no point did I hear the priest mention me, and I felt quite hurt by that. I don't think I was the only one who noticed because, at the Sign of Peace, Gerry's daughter's mother-in-law held my hand for a long time. It was as if she just knew how I was feeling.

As soon as the Mass finished, the priest shook hands with the immediate family. I knew a lot of the congregation, because they went to the club that Gerry and I went to, and I had been told that there was going to be a massive buffet laid on as a good turnout was expected.

The priest accompanied us to the graveyard, and I remember just staring at the hole where the ashes were to be interned. I remember thinking that in a four-week period, not only had the grave been dug up, but the headstone which was either buffed up or new had the inscription, 'A father and mother like no other'. I introduced myself to the priest as Gerry's wife, and he gave me a massive hug. The double whammy came when a friend of Gerry's called Paddy Mulholland heard me speak. Up until then, he had spoken to June and thought she was Gerry's second wife. He said, "Another Scottish voice? Who are you?" I replied that I was Gerry's wife and the poor man became really flustered. He genuinely thought June was Gerry's wife and I was there to give her moral support. He then said, "Gerry can certainly pick the good-looking ones."

What got me through the burial was Gerry's granddaughter who was holding a rose in her hand and wanted me to smell it. It was a very welcome gesture and then she threw it, as is customary, onto the dug-up grave.

There was a lot of food at the reception hall, but the only people apart from family and friends of Gerry's daughter that went to the venue were Paddy Mulholland and I think his granddaughter. June and I were told where to sit, which was in a corner of the hall.

Perhaps I'm old-fashioned, but entertainment at a funeral is not on my priority list. However, a singer and guitarist had been hired, and it turned out to be one half of the duo I had hired for Gerry's 65th birthday. I know that Gerry would have wanted me to stay in touch with his family, and in my mind, it was something I agreed to do.

Moreover, the one thing that I am glad of is that I stood my ground about moving to Ireland and a potential granny flat being built on his son's land. I can only thank God for that inspiration because, although life isn't a bed of roses, I am proud to live in Scotland and, at some point, I would have had to return to my native homeland.

Elizabeth offered to go to Belfast with me in December 2013 in order to give out Christmas presents to Gerry's family.

CHAPTER 105 –
PHYSICAL AND
MENTAL BREAKDOWN

This is a raw topic for me, but I'm writing an autobiography and I feel you deserve to know what happened next.

Elizabeth and I booked into a hotel and the entertainment was great. I hadn't a drop of alcohol to drink but felt euphoric for some reason. Elizabeth dropped me off at Belfast for my flight home but, although I still had that euphoric feeling, I was also very tired. I think my mind and my body had decided to give up on me, and I remember just sitting in the terminal building looking at the flights on the screens. I have no idea who got in contact with Elizabeth and, to be honest, I really don't want to know, but I took my eyes off the screens for a moment and there was Elizabeth standing beside me. She told me that I had missed my flight, and quite nonchalantly I said, "I can always get the next one." Elizabeth told me to come with her to the car park and began to drive to the Mater Hospital in Belfast. When we arrived, she got me a wheelchair, which I tried to escape from, but when I saw Elizabeth crying and telling me that "I was scaring her", it was the only thing that stopped me from running away.

After a physical and psyche assessment, it was decided that I would go into Ward 10. Years ago, there was a programme on television called *Emergency Ward 10* and in some ways that felt quite apt. As soon as I got into the ward, I was put opposite the nurses' station and was accompanied to the toilet every time I felt sick. I couldn't even keep water down, but eventually that stopped and I can't remember what type of tablets I was given but I had the appetite of a horse. The food in the hospital was amazing, and I wolfed it down as fast as it went on my plate.

Occupational therapy was great, and we would take various trips as well as make loads of cakes. I nearly stole one from the fridge but they were so neatly placed, I didn't succumb to my hunger pangs. The patients were really lovely, although there was one woman who got so drunk every day that she ended up being barred.

I went to Mass every day. This was something I insisted on and, thankfully, near to the ward there was a corridor leading to the chapel. On the first few occasions, I was accompanied by a nurse or doctor, but eventually I was left to my own devices, and I would go to the Catholic Church where Gerry and his first wife were married, after which I went for a cheeky wee sunbed!

The other patients in the hospital were lovely. They would put my hair in a French pleat and, likewise, I would dye or cut hair. Some of the patients had been admitted because their medication was making them too fat, and I was akin to that feeling because whatever drug I was on made me feel thirsty all night and ravenous throughout the day. Eventually, I was given my own room with a very large wardrobe that some of student nurses would hide in when the staff nurse was about. Those girls were lovely and really made me laugh.

I was called a wee 'dote' – something I had never heard of but apparently means sweet and adorable. I also received gifts from the patients such as a radio, perfume and toiletries, but the best gift for me was a pair of tartan slippers. There was an old lady in the ward and, when I went passed her bed, I used to do a wee dance. Usually, I had a terrible attempt at dancing the Highland fling but, none the less, it kept old Cissie amused. In fact, it was Cissie's daughter who bought me the slippers.

Gerry's daughter came up to see me on several occasions, and for the first time ever, I really felt a special connection with her. Gerry would have been delighted at how well we were getting on and, somewhere in my heart; she will always have a special place.

I have been in hospital more times than I care to remember, but the Mater Hospital was second to none. I spent five weeks in total in the hospital and would gladly have spent another five weeks; however, the tablets I was on would have made me ridiculously fat.

Before I go on to the next chapter, I have to admit that if it wasn't for the care and attention of all the staff at the Mater Hospital, I could have remained unhinged for the rest of my life. I thought it was perfectly acceptable to wear a red, patterned tea cosy on my head as a hat. My daughter had been informed not to expect miracles because I was so far gone when I arrived, the staff genuinely thought I might never get my sanity back. If that had been the case, it would have not only affected the quality of my life but that of my family. **God gave me my sixth life back.**

Homeward bound

When I arrived home, accompanied by my daughter, I was a lot more mentally and physically healthy. My daughter had been in England, Ireland and Scotland all in the same day, and I am truly grateful for her support. My son Mark was desperate to see me but had no formal identification and couldn't travel.

I did go back to HMRC but I knew that by this point I had nothing left to give and I retired on ill health.

CHAPTER 106 –
VOLUNTARY WORK

Christmas came and went, but I was starting to feel restless and I knew that I needed some kind of purpose but wasn't sure what that was. However, one day when I was in the coffee shop in Waterstones, I recognised a former colleague who was in my team in the HMRC contact centre. He was sitting at a table with a couple and, when he saw me, he said that he knew me from somewhere. My immediate response was, "David, of course you know me. We used to be in the same team." The upshot was that I began talking to the strangers at his table, a woman called Anne and her husband Ron.

Anne told me that she was a volunteer with Agape in the town centre of East Kilbride where nearly new children's clothes were sold, hand and body massages given and even a little prayer offered. I had the light-bulb moment of knowing which direction I was going in and, as soon as I had my coffee, I decided I was going to do voluntary work. Bold as brass, I walked into the shop, told all and sundry that I was going to volunteer and started by giving a lady a hand massage. I never thought twice about formally applying or supplying the appropriate references.

I eventually got a reference from my parish priest and Marion Forbes and became an official volunteer with Agape. My hours were Wednesday through until Friday, and I looked forward to spending my time in the shop, but like everything, all good things come to an end, because the lease on the shop was about to expire and Agape wasn't making anything like the money needed for the lease renewal.

We were instead given a large space in the Plaza Tower, but we were so out of the way and high up we weren't getting customers. A lady called Gail and I decided to update the computerised records, and we *literally* had our heads together whilst inputting data. Gail and I worked really hard in the Plaza Tower and then, just as things were peachy, we were told that the Ramada Hotel chain would be taking over that part of the building. Not long after that, Gail decided to leave, and I really don't blame her because she wanted to utilise her nursing qualifications to get ahead in life. She also needed the money.

The person who ran the organisation was a lady called Heather, and she asked if I would check over three funding applications – one of them being The Big Lottery funding. I spent the whole day with her, and we did get financial support that facilitated a shop and community centre at East Kilbride bus station. Most of the staff in Agape went to East Mains Baptist Church, and at one point Gail enrolled me on an Alpha Course where we had a brilliant meal prior to religious discussion. It was a six-week course and I loved it.

Gail was no longer in my life and I missed her, not just because she was funny and great to be around, but because she had an amazing work ethic. But when one door closes another one opens, and I became really friendly with Amanda Bishop who volunteered on a Friday. The laughs we had in that shop were something else. Amanda is as crazy as I am, and we would make the dummy dolls wave to people who passed by the shop, but more on that later.

CHAPTER 107 –
60TH BIRTHDAY AND AN
UNOFFICIAL 61st PITY PARTY

On my 60th birthday, Elizabeth brought me tea and my presents to her spare room. I was delighted with the gifts and, after opening my goody bags, I got ready for the drive home. By this point, I was starting to feel really unwell. Elizabeth lives in Blantyre, which is ten minutes from East Kilbride, but I was so disorientated that I was an accident waiting to happen.

It was a Friday, and I had already invited friends and neighbours to my 60th birthday party in The Bonnie Prince Charlie the following evening. I received lots of flowers and one of my neighbours helped me put them in vases as well as putting up my cards, but my anxiety about how I was feeling started to spiral out of control. I think the upcoming party worsened my coping mechanisms, and I knew that I would be too ashamed and embarrassed to cancel it. I decided to call the doctor who came to the house and gave me an injection in the bottom. It was sore and I was convinced the doctor had left the needle in my posterior, but she hadn't. I was just feeling the sensation of it. Thank God it worked wonders and I started feeling better.

The 60th birthday party went well and everyone seemed to have a good time. It was bittersweet because Gerry had organised that surprise party for me when I was 59, in the knowledge that by the time I reached 60 he would no longer be with me.

The following year, on 1 and 2 May, I felt as though I was coming down with the flu or something. However, because I felt better on 3 May, I decided I would have a little' 'pity party' to myself. Biggest mistake of my life! I had the remainder of a bottle of vodka and then took my prescribed sleeping tablets. The last thing I remember was going to the toilet and nothing else.

My seventh life

My son had a feeling that something was wrong because I wouldn't open the door to him, and he contacted my daughter who then got in contact with Elizabeth. I will always give my heartfelt thanks to Mark for raising the alarm. I had locked my front door, left my keys in it and the police burst open the door. An ambulance had been called because I wasn't responsive and blood was trickling out of my mouth. I am relating what I was told because I was oblivious to what actually happened. If my son hadn't been so concerned and persistent that something was wrong, I would have definitely died.

My vital organs began to shut down, and my daughter was sent for because the staff in the intensive care unit thought I wouldn't last the night. I am thoroughly ashamed that I put my family through that particularly when (at that time) my daughter wasn't a driver and had to get a taxi from England. I was in an induced coma with tubes popping out everywhere, but the one thing I remember was briefly thinking, *Please God don't let me die.* It must have been around the time the hospital staff tried to get me out of the coma but, apparently, I was pulling like crazy on the tubes in my throat and the decision was taken to keep me in the coma until I was a bit more stable.

At this point, the medical staff felt that my life was no longer in danger because my vital signs were improving.

I was in intensive care for a week or so, and it was the most horrific experience of my life. I wish I had the words to describe how crazy things were but I don't. I was hallucinating, constantly thirsty, completely confused and thought I was in some other country rather than Scotland. I then thought I was in Glasgow Royal Infirmary, but a nurse assured me that I was in my local hospital in Hairmyres.

Eventually, I was taken to a mainstream ward but was still really confused. I believed my crazy thoughts until the confusion left me and I was back to my cheeky self.

I had loads of visitors and the patients were lovely. My Agape colleagues came to see me, which was a nice surprise, and brought me toiletries and practical gifts you need for hospital. The hospital staff were truly amazing and eventually, after five weeks, I was allowed home. At this juncture, I thanked God for keeping me alive. I did not deserve it, but He must have spared me for some other purpose and perhaps writing this book was one of them. Hopefully, my experience and faith and trust in God will be of some help to you. When all is lost please do not give up hope.

My eighth life

In August 2016, just like the previous accident, I was driving up Stroud Road when I began feeling quite dizzy. I fainted at the wheel of the car and crashed right through a roundabout. The directional poles at the roundabout were very badly damaged and my car was a write-off, but I was fine and, after a negative breath test, the police allowed me to go home. However, they did notify DVLA that there could be an underlying medical condition so, for my sake and the sake of others, I decided to stop driving. I pondered over what had just happened. Had the road been busier, I might have either injured someone or been the victim of another near fatal accident. Only by the Grace of God was I spared to tell the tale, because life number eight was nearly used up.

For a long time, I was a 'priority customer' with Kelvin Kabs until I decided that, at some point, I would reapply for my driving licence.

CHAPTER 108 –
AMANDA BISHOP

Amanda with a shark

After a short rest, I decided it was time to go back to Agape. The best day of the week was Friday and, as I've said before, Amanda and I had some great laughs with the dummies. Donations of clothing, books, toys, prams and loads of other items were handed into the shop, but the one thing that sticks in my memory was a red shark. Every time I looked at it, I kept hoping someone would buy it because I hated the thing. One day, Amanda pulled out a knitted baby hat from one of the boxes, stuck it on her head and started riding around the shop on the shark. My ribs were aching with laughter, and I decided I needed to capture that image so I took a photograph of Amanda whilst she was hopping about. A short time later, a man came in and bought the shark. I don't know if he had seen the antics we were up to, but I was glad to get rid of the thing. What I did do was have the picture transferred to a canvas print so that I could I give it to Amanda for Christmas.

One Friday, I took a taxi to Agape in order to get there in time. Everything was hunky-dory in the taxi but, as soon as I got out, I knew something was wrong. I was wearing a dress without tights and my underwear elastic burst. The underwear was slowly creeping down my legs and, as soon as I got into the shop, Amanda, who was there before me, began to say, "Hi Mrs how are you doing?" The only thing I could say was, "Amanda, Amanda, have a look at my legs!" By this time, the underwear was down to my ankles and I nonchalantly stuffed it into my handbag. To say Amanda was gutting herself is an understatement.

There were many Friday afternoons when two ladies from Kilmarnock in Ayrshire got the bus to East Kilbride town centre. They were both quite elderly and the first time they came into the shop, Amanda and I said in unison, "Hi-de-hi." The two ladies immediately responded in unison, "Ho-de-ho." From thereon in, they were known as the 'Hi-de-hi' ladies.

In the main, I enjoyed my time at Agape but, after four years and the loss of long-term volunteers including Amanda, the place wasn't the same and, in my heart, I knew that my own time there was ending. I normally think things through before making a decision, but I just walked into Agape one day and said that I was leaving. It was exactly the right thing for me to do. I had given everything I could and, just prior to moving to the shop and community centre, I spent many long hours helping Heather get things ready. I spoke to Amanda and we were both of the opinion that we had done our bit. We had many laughs and became excellent friends, but it was time for another chapter in our lives.

CHAPTER 109 –
JACK THE JOKER

My life is quite mental, to be honest. Jack (ex-husband) was certainly king of the one-liners. When he was mobile, he would go into a supermarket in the town centre, get his shopping but more importantly his booze. One day on the bus home, there was an elderly woman who was using her mobile phone and kept shouting, "Whit are ye sayin', could you speak up I can hardly hear you" to which Jack loudly retorted, "We can all f*****g hear ye, Mrs." I don't know how Jack managed to get away with some of the things he did because, not long after that, he was walking Carrie the dog up the street when one of two young guys in a white van shouted, "Can you no keep that thing on a leash?" Jack's response was, "Is that yer wife yer talking about!"

However, I did manage to get my own back on Jack when he told me that he had got first prize when he got me. I immediately retorted, "Yeah, and I got the bloody booby prize." Jack and the carers who were attending him at the time just burst out laughing.

Jack was in hospital more times that I care to remember, mainly due to falling, but one time he had a urine infection and he believed that he was Australian. He'd never been to Australia in his life but, according to him, he presented his own television programme, had a ranch with horses on it and, although he gave shelter to an Indian chief (or so he thought), Jack said he was the 'Big Chief'. I had to go with him in the ambulance because nobody else could calm him down. Jack was waiting for his own private plane to take him back to Australia. He ended up in a bed in Accident and Emergency and told one of the nurses that she looked like a tart and belonged in a brothel! When the doctor went to assess him, I had to call him out of the room to tell him that Jack didn't live in Australia and that he must be suffering from some kind of infection. He was so convincing that the doctor believed him until I told him otherwise. Eventually, it was discovered that he had a urine infection and was going quite loopy with it.

On another occasion after a fall, Jack ended up in the geriatric ward. A couple of rooms down the corridor, Bishop Devine who confirmed my two children happened to be there at the same time. I would pop in and see the Bishop whenever I could. Bishop Devine was a what-you-see-is-what-you-get type of person and the two of us got on like a house on fire. Whenever I didn't visit him, I would get into trouble (in a nice way). Eventually, Jack got moved and was in the bed opposite the bishop so that made things easier all round. It was probably March or April 2019 when he was in hospital and we were due to get a new parish priest. We had been extremely lucky with Canon MacNamee and Father Chromy but, by this point, Joe Devine and I were on first-name terms and, being my usual, inquisitive self, I asked what Father Dominic Quinn (the new parish priest) was like. His answer to me was, "Wee Dominic? He's a great wee guy." Not long after that, Bishop Devine was being discharged and he said to me in Latin, "*ut custodiant te in se orations*" which means, 'We will keep each other in our prayers'. I am so privileged to have had that time with Bishop Devine and remember him with fondness. He died on 23 May 2019 but not before I had told my new parish priest that Bishop Devine was right about him, he *is* a great wee guy.

On the subject of Jack, what can I say now about his twilight years? He was a terrible role model as a father and, unfortunately, my son bore the brunt of his dad's drunken abuse. On broaching this with Jack, he did not remember what he was like and how he endangered the lives of my children when he was drinking and then driving. At this point in my autobiography, Jack was no longer driving and had become very frail and infirm and completely immobile. I can't help but reminisce about the younger Jack who took me up Ben Nevis when I started hill-climbing with him. I don't believe in bearing grudges and it takes everything in my power to shut certain people out of my life. I give chance after chance, but there comes a time with me when enough is enough and I just refuse to speak to them. I can count these occasions on one hand, and it's a trait that I don't particularly like in myself, but there is that side of my character which is certainly not in keeping with my Christian ethos.

Jack lived alone in a nice block of flats in East Kilbride, and I regularly visited him to ensure that he had enough food etc. He had carers who came to his house three times a day and, if I'm honest, he should probably have been in residential care but that's not a route he wanted to go down. Many people asked me why I still maintained contact with my ex-husband, but divorces can be amicable and grudges can be put aside.

Moreover, who am I to judge? God alone has that power and will judge each one of us when our time comes. Jack, being the father of my two children, merited respect and it was mutual.

CHAPTER 110 –
HOSPITAL ADMISSION AND MY
DAUGHTER'S WEDDING

I've mentioned hospital admissions that I have had and, to be honest, there are far too many to count, but like a cat with nine lives, I always seem to come out the other end relatively unscathed. One of those admissions was in late October 2019. My son had been staying overnight with me and was shouting in his sleep because his antidepressants had run out. I awoke with terrible back pain and I knew that I needed to be hospitalised. The pain was agony. When I spoke to Jack, he said he would come with me to Hairmyres. It was a Saturday and normally the Accident and Emergency Department would be jumping, but I was seen within five minutes. I was immediately put into the high dependency ward because I had a severe case of pneumonia and pleurisy. You would think by now I would be careful about my health, but I was acting as if nothing had happened whilst in hospital. My lung was so black that my consultant thought it was a mass. I was told that I did not realise how ill I really was. I can only thank God once again that, after testing for cancer, I was given the all-clear.

During that four-week stay in hospital, Jack had a fall and became delirious. One of the doctors drew my bed curtains round me to tell me that Jack was dying. I immediately contacted my parish priest to ensure that Jack got the Sacrament of Sick. Mark came to visit, as did my sister-in-law and her husband, and we all decided to grab a coffee. When we went back to Jack's ward, he was sitting up right as rain.

My daughter was due to be married in early November of 2019, and I worried that I might not get to the wedding. However, Elizabeth's fiancé John spoke to my medical team and it was agreed that I would get out on a day pass for the wedding. My daughter looked beautiful and I felt really proud, albeit having some happy tears in my eyes. I didn't look too bad either by the time my hair and make-up was applied. I had a lovely outfit and the guests at the wedding could hardly believe that I had pneumonia and technically was still in hospital. Shortly after the meal, I felt really tired and John ran me back to Hairmyres. I got into my nightdress but not before I gave the medical staff and patients a twirl. (Talk about full of myself?)

My ninth life

I have mentioned that I was in hospital for four weeks during which time my lung was drained (really painful), I had 13 scans (one of which was for cancer) and my son, whose mental health had gone down the tubes, was also admitted to Hairmyres Hospital. To be honest, you couldn't make this up if you tried!

Eventually, I was discharged and at my outpatient appointment the doctor, who had very kindly let me go to my daughter's wedding, showed me how bad my lung had been. (I recently found out that the clot in my lung had burst.) As previously stated, it was completely black, hence all the scans, but by this point both my lungs looked the same and, prior to leaving the doctor's office, I gave her a massive hug.

On the journey back home, I realised I had indeed been very unwell. If the tumour had been malignant, with everything else that was going on in my body, I would have used up my **ninth life.**

CHAPTER 111 –
THE PANDEMIC AND MY FUTURE

I think living through this pandemic has given us all time to reflect, particularly when we were in lockdown. My own reflections have been how different my life would have turned out if I remained in the convent. I know that as a religious person, I would always have worn my veil. It is not mandatory now, but I was proud to wear it when I was 18 and I think, at the age of 69, I would still be proud. Sometimes, when life is really difficult, I wish I had stayed in the convent, but I know God had other plans. I always wanted to be a teacher, but my career path has mainly been in law.

I also understand why my mum was angry with me for deciding to become a nun. She had sacrificed everything for my education and I was giving nothing in return.

On the Our Lady and St Francis Facebook forum, people have asked me why I chose convent life. I can only reply by saying that my vocation was far stronger than any jobs I was offered.

That forum has also allowed me to reconnect with some old school friends and perhaps one day we will have a reunion. I was friendly with a girl called Rita Brophy who tells me that, when we occasionally walked home together, I was so enthusiastic about becoming a nun, she nearly joined me! However, I have to give Yvonne Burke a special mention for founding the forum. There are now over 1,000 members and Yvonne deserves a medal.

My late husband Gerry was nine years dead on 29 July 2022 and I do miss him. It's always great to be able to bounce ideas off people and when it's your best friend you know that you will get an honest opinion.

I would dearly love to say that I kept in touch with Gerry's family, but a few months after the second funeral his daughter-in-law texted me to see how I was getting on. I could give no other answer than, "I think Gerry's death is really just hitting me now and I just need some space." I never heard from Gerry's family again. I am not bearing grudges. For Gerry's sake, I wish I could have maintained some form of contact, but I think I was just a small chapter in a book which was of interest for a short time and then forgotten.

CHAPTER 112 –
DEARLY DEPARTED

This chapter is important to me because, towards the end of lockdown, Jack's health was rapidly deteriorating. He ended up in hospital five times in a two-month period and it was one chest infection after another. Professional people were in his house and could not see what I was seeing. On one such occasion, he had a bout of pneumonia. I called an ambulance and that was his first admission. After coming home, Jack completely lost his appetite and told me that he was having difficulty swallowing. He went 12 days without eating any food.

During the following hospital admissions, I went to see him almost every day, but the man lying in the bed was skeletal. I knew it was a matter of time, but Jack had always wanted to live until his 85th birthday on 27 December 2021. He then contracted Covid and moved wards. Because his death was imminent, I called my parish priest to administer the Sacrament of the Sick which he duly did.

On 25 January 2022, I received a call from the staff nurse at Hairmyres to attend there as a matter of urgency. I phoned Mark and told him to make his own way to the hospital because time was of the essence. I was praying like crazy whilst driving but, on arrival, I was taken to the ward office. I knew then that I was too late to see Jack alive. I arrived at 10.05 p.m. and Jack had died at 10 p.m. I was absolutely gutted and *his* death has affected our immediate family more than any other. Jack wanted to be cremated without too much fuss. On 14 February 2022, Father Dominic offered up the 10 a.m. Mass for Jack and then officiated at his cremation at 3 p.m. that afternoon. I cannot thank Father Dominic enough for the way he handled things. It was such a comfort.

These days, I mainly concentrate on this biography which has taken years to write. I have only recently discovered that when you finish a draft of a book, that is only the beginning. There is so much more to be done: the editing, copy-editing, design, proofreading and final preparation for the publisher.

One can ask, is this truly all worth the enormous effort of digging back into one's life with the joys, mistakes, failure and not even knowing how it will go? Will it be a success or failure? I can only answer that with a resounding YES, because any author of any genre leaves a legacy behind.

Having had a great English teacher has helped me immensely, and I think if she was still alive today she would have been really proud.

Since Gerry died, I am not the 'party animal' I used to be but every week I go to the hairdresser's, sometimes out of laziness and other times for the banter. Tracy is my own little hairdresser and is almost like a daughter to me. Her partner in crime is a woman called Teresa and she is an unconscious comedian. She told me about the time a customer went into the shop and, whilst she was cutting the customer's hair, she accidentally nicked her ear with a pair of scissors. Poor Teresa was just about passing out when she saw the blood but finally, when everything was done and dusted, the parting remark from the customer was, "You come in here for a laugh and go out in stitches!"

As I end this book, I sincerely hope you have enjoyed journeying through my life with me. I have tried to remain truthful throughout, and if anyone is offended by my comments I apologise unreservedly.

Although God saved me from death on at least **nine** occasions, I know that He has been present throughout my entire life especially when times were so bleak that I felt I couldn't carry on. Somehow I have always been given the strength and courage that I have needed just to get me through another day.

Without hesitation, I am so grateful to God for my Catholic faith and the many blessings which He has bestowed upon me. I want to thank my mother Mary as well as all the saints I pray to when I am storming Heaven asking for miracles. We are all special in our own way and I hope the story of my life will give you hope when you feel discouraged. There are far too many people to individually give thanks to, but those who know me will also know that they are in my prayers and that I more than appreciate their friendship. Life is short and I wish to make use of the time that remains. Everything else, the past, present and future are in God's hands.

At some point in the future I hope to be fluent in German. I have now grown to love the German language. The other thing on my bucket list is to play the piano and, unlike when I used to go to piano lessons, I will be more focused and hopefully successful. However, when you have had a *STORM* named after you, what more could a girl want!

Thank you for keeping me company and just like the picture above, I hope this book goes down a STORM.

God bless each and every one of you

Eunice.

Just to recap my God-given nine lives

- **Being knocked down by a car whilst at primary school.**
- **Almost being raped and murdered.**
- **The power of the Miraculous Medal after the car jack knifed.**
- **The terrorist attack at Glasgow Airport.**

- Being involved in a near fatal accident in Stroud Road, East Kilbride.
- Having another near fatal accident at a roundabout in Stroud Road.
- Being in the Mater Hospital in Belfast when I had lost the plot.
- Being taken to intensive care due to my son Mark raising the alarm.
- Being in hospital with life-threatening pneumonia, pleurisy and suspected cancer.

ACKNOWLEDGEMENTS

Firstly I would like to thank the Creator of Life, His Blessed Mother, the Angels and the Saints who have protected me from harm.

A massive thank you to my mother for ensuring my education was second to none. She would have been really proud of my achievement.

The late Jean Fitzpatrick my brilliant English teacher.

A thank you to my son Mark who constantly encouraged me to keep writing until my autobiography was finished. Also I thank Mark for his research into publishing companies and pointing me in the direction of "Spiffing Covers".

To my daughter for helping me understand that when you think your manuscript is finished, the real work has just begun *(Thanks for that!!)*

I have to thank my friend Maria Dalgarno, Editor and Writer, for her editing skills, patience and advice not forgetting the wonderful charisma that comes so naturally to her.

SPIFFING COVERS
To all the team who have been so professional and patient with me. I highly recommend this company to anyone seeking to have their work published.

I would like to give Stefan a special thank you for a cover design that completely 'blew me away'.

RT HON ANN WIDDECOMBE
My heartfelt thanks to Ann Widdecombe who despite being so busy, still took the time to read my Manuscript and endorse it. May God bless you Ann.

OUR LADY AND ST FRANCIS FACEBOOK FORUM

Thank you to Yvonne Burke for setting this forum up. I think we all agree that many happy memories have been shared and I for one am so glad that Yvonne had the foresight to do this. Not only do I thank Yvonne but I want to take the opportunity to thank each and every single one of you who have kept me buoyed up throughout my writing stages. I did not expect the amount of positivity I have experienced even from those who do not know me. I wish you all nothing but the best and I give you my heartfelt thanks.

BERNADETTE

These acknowledgments would not be complete without mentioning my cousin Bernadette who was more like a sister to me. Tragically, she died on the 29th of January 2023. I will miss her so very much but I am glad that her memory will live on in my autobiography.

Printed in Great Britain
by Amazon